RsF

A

D0344154

Review for Newman

Celibacy, Ministry, Church

By the same author

*

A SKETCHBOOK OF BIBLICAL THEOLOGY

CELIBACY, MINISTRY, CHURCH

by
JOSEPH BLENKINSOPP

LONDON · BURNS & OATES

BURNS & OATES LIMITED
25 Ashley Place, London S.W.1

First publication in Great Britain, 1969

© 1968 by Herder and Herder, Inc.

SBN: 223 78291 2

Reproduced and printed in Great Britain by
Redwood Press Limited, Trowbridge & London

Contents

For all troubled Christians
who stay in the church without despairing

And no one puts new wine into old wineskins; if he does, the wine
will burst the skins, and the wine is lost, and so are the skins;
but new wine is for fresh skins.

Mark 2, 22

The new wine of ecclesiological concepts springing from a serious
confrontation of the biblical message with the entirely novel conditions of present-day society cannot be put into the old bottles of an
institutional framework which developed with the needs of men
in ages past.

Paul Kraemer in *Concept*, September 1963

Foreword

In view of the expectations which the title of this book is likely to raise the reader is advised that it does not belong to the confessional and autobiographical genre. As the subtitle indicates, it purports to be an examination of the self-understanding of the Roman Catholic church as it stands in the post-conciliar era between disappointed hopes and an uncertain future.

Mandatory clerical celibacy has been taken as a starting point in the belief that it is an important symptom of sickness, and, to pursue the metaphor, symptoms are not cured but diagnosed in hope of finding the basic cause of the trouble. The conviction behind this attempt at theological diagnosis is that the church's present self-understanding is to a great extent determined by the understanding of ministry or priesthood which are, in practice if not in theory, taken to be synonymous. The order: celibacy, ministry, church is dictated by the belief that until the present discipline on clerical celibacy is changed there cannot take place a reform in the understanding and practice of Christian ministry which will enable the church to be a church for the world. Yet the order could have been reversed: until the church comes to terms with its own self-understanding, and therefore with its past, we will be unable to think creatively of ministry or conceive of it as anything but "sacred ministry," and celibacy will continue to be a running sore.

This book speaks, obviously enough, to a situation (that of mandatory clerical celibacy) which is peculiar to the Roman Catholic church. In a world in which so many exciting and ominous things are happening, in which for many people, among them Christian theologians, God is missing and presumed dead, it might be thought we could find something better to talk about. I can only answer that, when all is said and done, the Roman church is still a mainstream Christian body which influences the lives of a great number of people. For those who still have faith in the ecumenical movement it can be added that until the problem dealt with in this book is satisfactorily solved there can be no real progress from the Roman Catholic side. I would think that the solution of this problem can hardly be a matter of indifference to Christians not of the Roman communion who still believe that the church has a future.

Though the theme pursued in this book involves speaking for a good part of the time about the past, the emphasis is meant to be on the future throughout. But the future is not going to open its doors miraculously to us. Biblical faith implies that we are being beckoned continually into the future, but the only criterion we have for the direction we take into the future is our understanding of our own past and present. To attempt to unmask false understandings of our historical reality and point to facts and processes which are too easily and conveniently forgotten seems to me, therefore, to give body to the Christian hope.

One of the most recurrent and archetypal motifs in the literature of both the ancient and modern worlds is that of a man setting out on a journey. The journey of Gilgamesh in search of the plant which gives eternal youth ends in death. After much travelling Ulysses returns to the point from which he began. The journey to which Abraham was summoned was into an unpredictable future away from the security of a settled way of life and a world of sacred meanings. Biblical tradition represents the undertaking of this perilous journey as the paradigmatic act of faith. It may not be too late for the Catholic church to make the same act of faith today.

Vanderbilt University   JOSEPH BLENKINSOPP

Celibacy, Ministry, Church

1. Clerical Celibacy:
The Roots of the Problem

I

Characteristic of all our Christian life today, nowhere more in evidence than in Roman Catholicism, is the asking new questions of the Scriptures and early Christian tradition common to all the churches. This process was rather hazardous for Roman Catholics before Vatican II since the official assumption was that the church had already extracted from the Scriptures all that was essential for doctrine and morals and packaged it in a form suited to the average church-going consumer. Rudolph Adolfs put it forcibly in an article in *New Christian*:

> Also, there was little left over to believe in. We did not have to believe in God any more; neither in man. All we had to do was to believe in the Church-institution with the pope at its head; the rest we knew.[1]

Vatican II's *Constitution on Divine Revelation,* though not without its difficulties of interpretation and even inconsistencies, has at least made it clear that we as the church must question the Scriptures in the painful process of growth in self-understanding in which, after two thousand years, we are still engaged.

In the post-conciliar epoch the main problem for Roman Catholics has been loss of confidence in the church-institution.

1. August 10, 1967.

In the English-speaking world this has been highlighted by the connected cases of Davis and McCabe, and the grounds for loss of confidence have been cogently and thoroughly set out in the former's *A Question of Conscience*. People are asking themselves whether this system we have with us, with its authoritative organs, legalized morality and comprehensive penal system, is really what Christ wished to represent him on earth; whether the Vatican power-structure, with its enormous untaxed wealth and its own brand of subterranean politics, is really serving God's purposes in the world; whether papal infallibility, with the complex process of rationalization and explaining away it entails, is really at all credible; whether the large, anonymous "eucharists" in city-churches really represent what Christ commanded us to do before he died. There is a general feeling about that we have had too much certainty and have been too prone to absolutize our current ecclesiastical structures. This loss of confidence will be apparent in most conversations among educated Catholics today. It is also reflected in the growing disregard for directives or pronouncements emanating from the Vatican of which many recent examples could be given. It goes with a re-awakening of the local church in some parts of the world and the springing up of "underground churches" especially in the United States. In every case the target is the institution.

I want to examine this question of institution and institutionalization at a later stage. For the moment we should recall that all the great charismatic movements in the history of the church have been directed against the absolutization of the institution. This would include the Protestant reform of the sixteenth century even though it resulted in a further break-up of unity. Many aspects of reform in modern Roman Catholicism are really nothing more than a belated acceptance of the charismatic insights of one or other of the Protestant reformers—emphasis on vernacular liturgy, the one priesthood of Christ shared by the entire People of God, the importance of the local church, the insistence on

Christian freedom. The fundamental question facing the Roman Catholic church now is whether it is prepared to make the renunciation required for further progress towards the one church of the future willed by Christ. The situation is basically very simple. If we accept the premiss of one united church, with whatever variations of practice and belief we may wish to postulate, as the embodiment of God's will expressed in Christ, it is inevitable that the Roman Catholic church modify its present self-understanding since otherwise this end will never be achieved. This means first of all that it must be prepared to restate the position and function of the papacy within the church more in keeping with the relevant scriptural data and early Christian tradition. This means in its turn that Roman Catholics must bring themselves to abandon ecclesiastical fundamentalism as they have already, by and large, abandoned biblical fundamentalism. Progress has already been made insofar as Roman Catholic theologians no longer identify the kingdom of God with the Roman Catholic church as they used to and have admitted that the totality of the *ekklesia* is not confined to the Roman Catholic communion. But the decisive step concerns the papal position and this still has to be taken.

Beyond this and other intra-confessional crises the basic problem today seems to be that of reconciling *any* current form of ecclesiastical institutionalism with the eschatological message which stands at the heart of the early Christian tradition. Did Jesus intend to found any kind of institution? Are the words of Jesus usually relied on to establish this thesis authentic Jesus-sayings or a reflection of the *de facto* Christian community coming to terms with and authenticating its own continuing existence? Standard pre-conciliar Roman Catholic ecclesiology was, it is safe to say, more a *rationale* of the existing Roman Catholic institution than a serious coming to grips with the relevant New Testament texts. Roman Catholic reaction to Schweizer's thorough-going eschatological interpretation of the intentions of Jesus

15

lasted longer than elsewhere and led to many exegetically unsound readings of key texts like Mark 9, 1 and 13, 30. In the last few years Roman scholars have shown a greater readiness to admit a decisively eschatological dimension to the thinking of Jesus, as recent writings of Rigaux and Vögtle testify. This is an important development since without it a truly biblical formulation of the nature of the church is bound to be incomplete if not downright false.

An objective study of the earliest synoptic tradition reveals that it contains very little indeed about the setting-up, constitution and organization of a new society. The earliest society of the disciples of Jesus, and the early churches which came into existence after his death, have to be seen within an eschatological context, living out a tension between the *already* and the *not yet*. There was, of course, as all admit, a development within these early churches in the way they thought of the eschatological reality, and this can to some extent be traced in sayings attributed to Jesus in the tradition. When Christians of the first generation began to die off with their hope of seeing the coming of the Lord unfulfilled there was bound to be some wavering in faith and a need to adjust and reappraise. The Thessalonians, for example, were worried about how their dear departed could share in the *parousia* (1 Thess. 4, 13–18) and Paul told the Corinthians that deaths would not have occurred in their community if they had celebrated the eucharist with decorum (1 Cor. 11, 30). The need for reappraisal can be heard in the sharp words which the author of Second Peter addresses to those "scoffers" who were hinting broadly that there was not going to be a Second Coming (2 Pet. 3, 3–4). Different reasons begin to appear to explain the delay: that for the Lord a thousand years is but as a day, that he was giving them time for repentance, that first the universal mission had to be carried out, that the Jews had to return to God and enter the eschatological community. But no matter how reinterpreted, the basic premiss remained that

16

salvation or the completion of all that Christ came to offer men does not come on this side of the *eschaton.*

Christian history, right from the second generation after Christ, has witnessed to the difficulty of maintaining this eschatological tension. The first persecutions which were visited on the Palestinian communities and some of those founded by Paul were interpreted as harbingers of the imminent end of the age. This was also true, though to a gradually decreasing extent, of the Roman persecutions beginning with that of Nero. In keeping with this way of thinking, forms of church government and organization would have been understood as provisional. Yet imperceptibly we find the emphasis changing, no doubt due in part to the gradual preponderance of Greek ways of thinking and the consequent erosion of the primitive framework of Jewish apocalyptic eschatology. In the earliest period of enthusiasm, organization of the communities and of the eucharistic gatherings was minimal, yet as early as the second century we find the monarchic episcopate emerging clearly, and not long after that the beginnings of a process by which the whole cultic apparatus of Judaism was reintroduced. We shall look more closely at some aspects of this in later chapters. The problem of coming to terms with the eschatological element in the teaching of Jesus and the early Christian understanding of Jesus is, at any rate, still with us. We have rightly reacted against the individualized and conceptualized eschatology which has been standard teaching for so long (death, judgment, hell and heaven) but still have difficulty in formulating an alternative doctrine. Many theologians pay lip-service to the Christian metahistorical goal while transposing it into evolutionary (transformist) or existentialistic terms which are not always clearly reconcilable with primitive Christian tradition. Others simply capitulate before the problem and ask us to address ourselves to the here-and-now tasks. All in all, the tense eschatological drama in which Jesus and his first disciples

17

understood themselves to be engaged remains at the center of our perplexity.

II

This rather long introduction was necessary if we are not to isolate the celibacy question and take it out of its context. Within this context clerical celibacy is seen as part of the wider question of the relation between eschatology and institution. There is no clerical celibacy in the New Testament for the simple and banal reason that there are no clerics. Both Jesus and Paul speak of the capacity for dedicated celibacy as a gift and refrain from any imperative. On this basis we can consider it as a unique and highly individual way of witnessing to the eschatological reality of the kingdom. It falls wholly under the dispensation of the Spirit (as do the other gifts), that Spirit which brings into existence and fecundates the life and witness of Christian communities. It is one of those "variety of gifts" distributed among the individual Christian of a community for the common good (1 Cor. 12, 4–7). In being attached mandatorily as a necessary precondition to the ministerial priesthood it has been institutionalized, a fate which has befallen other gifts referred to in the well-known New Testament passages which speak of them. My purpose in what follows is not to trace in detail how this came about—though necessarily something will have to be said about it—but to suggest some approaches to a realistic understanding of what it meant in the original New Testament context and that of the early centuries of Christianity. Though it cannot by itself solve the critical problem facing us today, this kind of investigation must surely be a necessary prerequisite for an eventual solution. After all, theologians are doing the same in every other area.

In general, three aspects of the practice of dedicated celibacy have to be considered: the ascetical, the ritual and the eschatological. It may be useful to examine the problem under these headings.

Long before Christ the disciples of Buddha and Pythagoras practiced voluntary celibacy for ascetical reasons. Despite some sporadic attempts in recent years to explore possible points of contact between Western monasticism and that of Buddhism—to which we can add the Hindu ideal of "sannyasi," or total abnegation which included celibacy—the former has had little or no influence on the Christian practice. The situation was quite different with ascetical practice based on the Platonist and Neo-Platonist concept of the body-soul relationship. This provided a religious and anthropological framework within which voluntary abstention from marriage could be seen as part of the purification, *katharsis* which led to *elampsis* and eventual *henosis,* union with the One. This way of thinking can be found among Gnostic Christians at a very early stage. Before the middle of the second century Marcion had established groups of celibates, and the practice was found also in the Encratist sect.

This kind of celibacy, based on a pessimistic assessment of the body and sexual relations, was never accepted by the church as a whole, and its philosophical and anthropological presuppositions are combatted in the New Testament itself. But it exerted a powerful influence on some important Christian thinkers, and a good dossier of texts could be assembled from writers such as Origen and Augustine to show how finely the line was drawn between orthodoxy and heterodoxy. The communal practice of celibacy entered Christianity from monasticism, and it is difficult to decide what reason for its adoption predominated at any given time. From one point of view, the monk saw his struggle against sexual temptation as involvement in the eschatological battle engaged by Jesus, though the kingdom is no longer the future that lies open but a world different from this where one is happy for ever with God. This is particularly clear in the *Life of Saint Anthony* which had such an influence on the later development of monastic spirituality. There was no room at all for women in this kind of perspective. The fact that monasticism reached its peak in the period after the persecutions suggests that it was part of a reaction against the general laxity of moral life, especially in the sexual field, which resulted from great numbers of people mostly uninstructed, pouring into the church which up till then had been something of a spiritual élite. In this new situation the monk represented the true Christian ideal of life as opposed to its many caricatures. The monastery contained the élite. In this scheme it was easy to think of celibacy as somehow integral with a genuine Christian life.

The first attempts to impose celibacy on the secular clergy can be traced back to the practice of instituting common life among the city clergy on a more or less monastic pattern. The first recorded case occurs in the Council of Elvira in Spain at the beginning of the fourth century. A motion to impose celibacy on bishops was tabled at the ecumenical Council of Nicaea (325 A.D.), and it is interesting to note that the monk Paphnutius, himself a celibate, spoke out strongly against it on the ground that it would be the occasion for sexual temptation and irregularity.

The *fact* of monastic influence on the development of a celibate secular clergy has always been noticed but the *reason* for it has not always been explored. While the chief reason for monastic celibacy was asceticism, often in the form of a dangerously pessimistic (and therefore unchristian) dualism, the main historical reason for the development of a specifically clerical celibacy is to be sought in the gradual sacralization of the Christian cult and the ministers responsible for it. Interaction between a monastic community-ideal and a gradually emerging sacred clerical order was inevitable and resulted in the latter being drawn into the category of the Christian élite, which made the adoption of celibacy more or less inevitable at least in those cases where the clergy could practice some form of common life. But this would hardly have taken place had not the clergy already begun to appear as a sacred order similar to the Jewish priesthood in the Old Testament.

The great influence of figures like Augustine, Jerome and Benedict resulted in the widespread practice of communal celibacy, but for individual clerics marriage and the full use of marriage was still the rule. We have to remember that a married man (Hadrian II) was made pope as late as the ninth century.

There is, perhaps, little likelihood today of celibacy being practiced purely for ascetical reasons. Life in the body is life in the world, a being visible and present to and in communication with others. In this context of understanding celibacy can be a communicating sign, a style of life adopted to witness to the transcending significance of Christ and his act. To have any meaning at all it has to be a sign, and to be a sign it must be allied with genuine not just nominal poverty, witnessing that the church is the community of the *anawim,* the poor of the beatitudes, who await everything from God and identify themselves with the poor and dispossessed of the world. It is hard to believe that this has been facilitated by the present juridical dispensation in the church.

III

The requirement of periodic or total sexual abstention for cultic persons—priests, shamans and the like—is often found in ancient religions. In some ancient Semitic cultures the word "eunuch" is synonymous with "priest." The culture and religion of the Hebrews had, as we now know, much in common with the culture and religion of their neighbors. In particular, they took over from the Canaanites much besides their language—including the religious calendar with many of the festivals, different forms of sacrifice, the temple plan, ecstatic propheticism and several cultic offices. It is therefore not surprising to find in Hebrew literature a whole range of sexual taboos which can be paralleled among their Semitic neighbors. The candidate for the priesthood had to abstain sexually for seven days previous to ordination in order to be ritually pure. We learn this from Leviticus 8, 33, a text referred to with approval by Pius XI in his encyclical *Ad Catholici Sacerdotii* where he compares it with a similar practice in ancient Rome noted by Cicero in his treatise on the laws. The high priest also had to abstain for the seven days before *Yom Kippur,* the great Day of Expiation, and in one case the priestly requirement is extended to the whole people, for the three days, that is, during which they awaited the giving of the law on Sinai (Ex. 19, 6). As we shall see more in detail in a later chapter, one of the main confluent forces at work in the process which we have called sacralization was the application of these and similar Old Testament texts to the Christian ministry. By the time of Cyprian of Carthage (about the middle of the third century) this was quite common practice. There can be little doubt that this idea of a sacred reality ministered to by a sacred person which repels any form of sexuality was the decisive factor in changing what was originally a form of free eschatological witness to a ritual precept; and the justification for the change was found in a kind of biblical typology much in vogue down to the end of the Middle Ages but rarely practiced today.

Little if anything of this cultic deterrence of the sexual survives into the New Testament. It has been pointed out that "at no point does Jesus seem to have wanted to integrate his activities into the sacral apparatus of the Palestinian Judaism of his age"[2]; and we may even suggest that the sayings about what is pure and impure suggest a rejection of the ritual criterion of such overriding importance for Judaism at that time. Beyond this, the conviction of New Testament writers is that the escha-

2. Jean-Paul Audet, *Structures of Christian Priesthood,* London and New York, 1967, p. 23.

tological reality is now present and that therefore the old order with its cultic institutions and cultic personnel had been superseded. In Hebrews we find a very early and very acute case of the tension between eschatology and institution which was referred to earlier. The author argues that Jesus is the one priest and his self-offering in death in perfect obedience to the Father the one all-sufficing cultic act which superseded the endless round of cultic acts of the old order. He is evidently presenting his arguments to a group of Christians who had accepted the revolutionary, eschatological message but were beginning to be deeply disillusioned. They wanted to go back to the old institution with its concrete and visible system of reassurances; and this must have been the situation for many converts from Judaism in the early days.

With the inevitable decline of early Christian eschatological enthusiasm the need for some form of institutionalization reasserted itself and, predictably, the forms this process took were to a great extent dictated by the Scriptures (the Old Testament) which provided *the* terms of reference for the early church. In a later chapter we will look more closely at how this affected the ministerial priesthood. Without prejudicing the question of what Jesus really did in the Upper Room, a question still at the center of ecumenical debate, we can say that with the increasing emphasis on the eucharist as a sacral and sacrificial cult-action the president or celebrant was increasingly thought of as a specifically sacred person. In other words, the eucharist, as *the* Christian act of cult, was increasingly drawn into a pre-established pattern of the sacred. At an early stage we begin to hear of the greater purity required of the person who approaches most closely to the Mystery, a purity which was at the same time moral and cultic. Of early writers, perhaps Tertullian stresses this most,[3] no doubt due to those tendencies in his thinking which eventually led him to break with the church. It receives lapidary expression

3. E.g., *In Cast.* vii, ix; *Ad Uxor.* ii.

23

in St. Jerome: "in the presence of the purity of Christ's body, all sexual union is impure"[4]; but much earlier the question of the use of or abstention from sexual relations by the minister of the eucharist had already become acute. So, as we saw, the first legal enactment we know of prohibited sexual relations on the part of the married minister of the sacraments. Much later we shall find scholastics like Anselm and Thomas Aquinas using the Old Testament texts about ritual abstention as proof-texts in favor of *total* clerical celibacy.

The gradual change of emphasis in favor of the sacred which began in the second century gained great impetus in the third, and was rounded off in the Middle Ages, merits a closer study than it has so far received. We have come so much to take for granted that Christianity has to do with sacred things, places and persons that we find it difficult even to see, much less be disturbed, by what the New Testament says. It is not just a question of noting that in the earliest period, that is, until Christianity became a recognized *religio,* the eucharist was held wherever the *ekklesia* could conveniently gather, generally in a private house; or that the terms for ministry are taken from ordinary secular speech; or that the old cultic vocabulary was desacralized and applied to the mission. What is at stake is the newness of the Christian message. In the New Testament, especially in Paul, the Christian message brings liberation from forces which had dominated life up till then. Above all, it was a liberation from fear. By revealing the true face of God, by showing him not in power (which evokes the feeling for the sacred) but in love and forgiveness, Jesus gave the capacity to overcome fear. If we study those passages of the Old Testament which are more obviously dominated by the concept of the sacred, especially those from the hand of the so-called Priestly Writer, we cannot fail to detect the strong undercurrent of fear. While making all due allowance for the genuine and deep insights which they con-

4. *Adversus Iovinianum* I, 20.

tain, it will be obvious that the God of whom they speak is distant, removed, hidden and unpredictable. Hence the need for a comprehensive protection of ritual law and an elaborate penal code, illustrating the fact that the sacred tends to the fixity of a rule of law. My contention here is that the same tendency emerged in Western Christianity once Christianity itself began to be re-interpreted as a religion and therefore within the sphere of the sacred. This, it seems to me, is the context in which we must study this process by which what was originally thought of as a useful though not indispensable condition for the ministry and mission gradually achieved the fixity of law.

We should add that appeal to certain Old Testament texts, especially the ritual laws of purity, is no longer made with the same confidence either in official documents or by apologists for the ecclesiastical law imposing clerical celibacy. This is, of course, due to a sounder hermeneutical approach to the Old Testament. Some progress can therefore be recorded at least here. Whereas the encyclical of Pius XI on the priesthood still refers to these texts, *Sacerdotalis Caelibatus* of Paul VI passes over them in silence and puts the emphasis on the celibate life as a following of Christ the celibate priest of the new order. But there is still an underlying *outlook* prevalent in the decision-making sector of the Roman Catholic church—which is exclusively celibate— that sexuality as such is incompatible with sacramental ministry. This attitude is today being increasingly scrutinized and questioned. To quote once again from Père Audet:

> There are many of us, both clergy and laity, whose outlook on life is no longer such that we perceive any inherent "impurity" in the expression of sexuality. And for the future, one needs no special prophetic insight to foresee that mankind as a whole is gradually moving, slowly but inevitably, towards a complete elimination of this spiritual archaism.[5]

5. *Op. cit.,* p. 174.

An indication may be that recent constructive contributions to the debate about dedicated celibacy have centered on this life-style as a witness and in doing so have had to return to the eschatological dimension of life in the early church. And with this we come to the third and final aspect of the question.

IV

The only kind of voluntary celibacy inculcated or practiced in the New Testament is "for the sake of the kingdom of heaven." There are two questions here: what this kind of celibacy meant for Jesus; what it can mean for us today.

One possible approach to what Jesus meant by "eunuchs for the kingdom of heaven" (Mt. 19, 12) would start from the celibacy of Jeremiah imposed on him by God as a sign of coming judgment on Jerusalem (Jer. 16, 1–4).[6] For a Jew to remain unwed was in itself extraordinary enough to be a highly visible sign, and could hardly be a good sign as the sequence of the chapter in Jeremiah shows. It is not impossible that somewhere back of the eunuch-saying in Matthew 19, 12 there lies a tradition that Jesus defended the celibate life which he himself, and possibly some of his disciples, led, with reference to the coming kingdom of God which would be inaugurated by a catastrophic divine visitation on Jerusalem and the Jewish theocratic state. Several exegetes have defended the view that the eschatological discourse in the same gospel refers, at one level of meaning, to this coming event. Significantly, Josephus tells us of a prophet with the same name as Jesus who appeared in the temple eight years before its destruction and pronounced judgment upon the people in words taken from the same passage in Jeremiah; and it may have been during the lifetime of Jesus

6. The command not to take a wife "in this place" does not necessarily imply what we mean by "celibacy."

that, according to Jewish tradition, Rabbi Zadok began his fast for the salvation of the temple.[7] Both Jeremiah and Jesus certainly anticipated a fairly imminent destruction of temple, city and state, verified respectively in 587 B.C. and 70 A.D. Needless to say, this understanding of the saying would not exclude a further meaning going beyond the historical situation of that time.

Before exploring other possibilities we need to look more closely at the saying as a whole in the context of Judaism at that time. The saying runs: "There are eunuchs who have been so from birth, and there are eunuchs who have been made eunuchs by men, and there are eunuchs who have made themselves eunuchs for the sake of the kingdom of heaven. He who is able to receive this, let him receive it." The first two classes occur frequently in Jewish writings. The common classification was into those born so and those who had been castrated. Neither of these classes necessarily entailed celibacy: the former could marry Jewish girls and the latter female proselytes or manumitted slave-girls. In normative Judaism celibacy was practically unknown. Marriage was, and is, regarded as a sacred duty in fulfillment of the command to "increase and multiply" which was interpreted distributively. We hear occasionally of rabbis who eschewed marriage in order to dedicate themselves to the study of the Torah—what we may call "wisdom-celibacy"—but it is interesting that Rabbi Ben-Azzai, who is reported to have done this, found he had to justify his decision in the face of criticism.[8]

7. The text from Josephus occurs in *The War* 6, 5, 3 and the other in the Talmud, the treatise entitled "Gittin," 56a. Josephus's report of the oracle of Joshua (= Jesus) ben-Hananiah is reminiscent of Jeremiah 16, 9, "I will make cease . . . the voice of the bridegroom and the voice of the bride." References in E. Stauffer, *Jerusalem und Rom*, Berne, 1957, pp. 82–83. It is interesting that in orthodox Judaism marriages may not be celebrated during the three weeks preceding the ninth of Ab (July–August) which commemorates the two destructions of the temple.

8. H. L. Strack and P. Billerbeck, *Kommentar zum Neuen Testament aus Talmud und Midrash*, I, Munich, 1956, 2nd. ed., p. 807.

According to the Talmud, marriage also has the object of promoting chastity and purity since these are considered difficult if not impossible to maintain outside of marriage. An unmarried man was therefore inevitably an object of suspicion unless there was some obvious reason for his remaining single. The dangers inherent in justifying clerical celibacy on the basis of the Old Testament and Jewish practice can be seen in the fact that, while the high priest had to abstain for seven days prior to the Day of Expiation, he could not perform the service unless he had a wife to sanctify his household.[9]

In sectarian Judaism the situation was somewhat different. As is clear from the well-known references in Pliny, Philo and Josephus, the Essenes eschewed marriage, though we need not pay too much attention to the reasons given by these outsiders, namely, that "a wife is selfish, jealous to an immoderate extent, an adept at corrupting her husband's morals and leading him astray by her constant enticements."[10] On the probable hypothesis that the community of Qumran was Essene this would apply also to them, but here we have a difficulty. If they practiced voluntary celibacy we would expect to hear something about it in their Holy Rule (the Manual of Discipline) but this scroll is entirely silent on the subject. In both the Damascus Document and the rule of the Community, moveover, we find a prohibition of sexual relations before the age of twenty, which would seem to imply that no prohibition applied after that age. Finally, female skeletons have been discovered in the Qumran cemetery, though no one seems to know to whom they belonged or how they got there.

Most scholars have concluded either that all the community practiced voluntary celibacy for a time or that a part of the community practiced it all the time. We cannot examine these

9. Isidore Epstein, *Judaism*, Harmondsworth, 1959, p. 156.
10. Philo, *Hypothetica* xi, 14; see Pliny, *Hist. Nat.* v, 15; Josephus, *The War* 11, 8, 2.

different proposals in detail but may refer to a recent alternative explanation put forward by a Swedish scholar, Abel Isaksson.[11] He holds that members of the community were permitted to marry and beget children (thus fulfilling the divine command) between the ages of twenty and twenty-five. If they wished thereafter to go on to full membership of the community, they had to remain celibate. We are not told how they disposed of their wives; perhaps the children were adopted by the community as oblates since there is provision for this in the writings of the sect.

What is important for us is the motivation of this choice of the celibate life, and in order to understand it we have to go back into the Old Testament and in particular to the ideology and practice of what is generally called "the holy war." We find no "book of rules" concerning the conduct of the holy war but two examples make it clear that sexual abstention was mandatory for those who took part in it. The first is that of David and his men at the time of their visit to the sanctuary of Nob (1 Sam. 21, 4–6). Here, by the way, it is interesting to note how from the time of Cyprian of Carthage this was used as a parade-text in support of priestly celibacy, or at least sexual abstention, on *ritual* grounds, since the priest gives David the holy bread only after he has ascertained that he and his men had been sexually abstinent for some time before. It will be remembered that Jesus used the example of "what David did" in subordinating ritual requirements (in this case sabbath-observance) to elementary human needs (Mk. 2, 23–27); one would have expected this to have some bearing on a specifically Christian approach to *any* kind of ritual requirement found in the Old Testament. In any case, David makes it clear that sexual abstinence was customary on this kind of campaign—"women have been kept from us as always when I go on an expedition; the vessels of the young men are holy even when it is a common journey; how much more today will their vessels be holy?" (v. 5). The second example is that of Urijah whom David tried to

11. *Marriage and Ministry in the New Temple,* Lund, 1965.

persuade to sleep with his wife Bathsheba in order to allay suspicion on himself, but who refused even when drunk since he too was engaged on such a campaign (2 Sam. 11, 7–13). Moreover, the nazirate, closely associated with the holy war, also involved sexual abstention. The Qumran War Scroll ("The War of the Sons of Light against the Sons of Darkness") makes it clear that the sectarians projected the ancient institution of the Holy War into the eschatological future and that it was in virtue of this that they practiced some form of celibacy. Within this ideological framework the monastery was seen as a camp with everyone at the ready for imminent conflict. Here there was simply no room for women and no time to be lost in the minutiae of family life:

> No young boy and no woman shall enter their encampment when they go forth from Jerusalem to go to battle until they return . . . any man whose sexual organs are not in a state of purity on the day of battle shall not join them in battle for holy angels are in communion with their host.[12]

We have here a contamination between the eschatological and the ritual which is understandable since the sexual taboo associated with the holy war in the Old Testament is certainly ritual. Sexual relations, or even involuntary seminal emission, disqualified one from taking part on the grounds that the campaign was a sacred action, one in which Yahweh himself participated personally or vicariously. The idea of angels taking part alongside the people of God in battle array reminds us of Jesus' refusal to call on twelve legions of angels at the crucial moment of *his* combat. What, at any rate, we find at Qumran is a permanent, no longer just intermittent, form of sexual abstention, and this in view of an eschatological conflict which was thought to be imminent.

Turning to the gospels, we see that John the Baptist, the son of a country priest, appears to be celibate, and some scholars have

12. 1QM 7. 3–7.

explained this and other aspects of his person and message by associating him with the kind of eschatological revival found at Qumran. Jesus himself was not only a relative of the Baptist but intimately associated with him for a time during the earliest phase of his public ministry. After John's arrest he took up his message and proclaimed it in almost identical terms. He may also have seen more clearly the inevitability of his own death after John was summarily executed—it will be recalled that Herod thought that Jesus might be John the Baptist raised from the dead (Mk. 6, 14). In the light of the actual historical situation at that time the reference to a third class of eunuchs additional to the two known to contemporary Judaism need not be interpreted either as purely theoretical or as an attempt by some group of early Christians to justify the practice of voluntary celibacy. Jesus states that "there *are* eunuchs who *have made* themselves eunuchs for the sake of the kingdom of heaven." This would more readily refer not to celibacy as we usually understand it but rather to voluntary separation from one's partner. In the absence of further evidence of Jesus' mind on this issue we cannot go beyond a possibility; but the practice—which we have seen to be probable—of precisely this kind of "celibacy" at Qumran and—as we shall go on to see—in the missionary activity of the early Church certainly supports it. What then of the celibacy of Jesus himself?

V

The question of the sexuality of Jesus is one which it is still almost impossible even to raise let alone discuss among church-going Christians. This was eloquently confirmed by the reaction to Canon Hugh Montefiore's suggestion, made with the greatest reverence and restraint, that Jesus may not have married because he was not "the marrying sort." The phrase itself may have been

31

unfortunate and ambiguous, but evidently what irked many of his critics was not so much the suggestion that Jesus' nature may have contained more of the homosexual than the heterosexual but the inference that it contained any kind of sexuality at all. Yet if he was human his body must have secreted both male and female hormones and if he was, as we take him to be, perfect man (though this itself is a difficult idea to grasp and formulate) we must suppose some kind of balance, not normally attainable, between *logos* and *eros,* or whatever terms we choose to express the polarities of the male and female elements in a human being. His all-embracing compassion, his frequent use of feminine imagery, the empathy which allowed him to enter into the suffering and frustration of women, his attitude to the prostitute who washed his feet and the woman guilty of adultery—these all show those qualities of relatedness and receptivity which characterize *anima* or *eros* in a man.

Here we come up against the modern difficulty of understanding and accepting the results of the christological debates of the early Christian centuries. The fact that these debates presupposed categories and definitions—especially about what human nature really is—which are no longer considered acceptable is only part of this difficulty. He was Man, but was he *a* man? To what extent if at all was he within the evolutionary process? May we legitimately enquire as to his psychological type or blood-group? These are only examples of the kind of question which we still find it very difficult to ask, even if we have gotten away from the crude idea of his humanity and divinity in separate watertight compartments. In practice, despite our formal adhesion to the creed which we recite together, when we think and speak about Jesus we are generally either Docetists or Arians without being aware of it. And in consequence our presentation of Jesus lacks both reality and the power to convince.

The ambivalence of our position is most obvious when we come to speak, or refrain from speaking, of the sexuality of

32

Jesus. We readily admit, because it is there clearly in the record, that he was familiar with anger, fear, even contempt, but not with that passion and force which we recognize to be at the center of our own lives. Is it because we believe that a truly sinless man must be without sexual experience or even sexual temptation? We may find confirmation of this in the silence of the gospels on any sexual experience of Jesus. We read of his sympathetic dealings with others who had come to shipwreck in this area of experience, we have certain sayings which show that he accepted and radicalized the moral demands of the Torah which set limits to the expression of sexuality. But to find any particular emphasis on the sexual we have to wait for the apocryphal gospels and collections of the kind recently discovered at Nag Hammadi which are deeply colored by Gnostic dualism. It is surely significant that much of the devotional fiction still popular among many Roman Catholics—such as, that Mary "knew not man" because she had made a vow of virginity, or that the Beloved Disciple was so because, unlike the others, he was a virgin—stem from this suspect corpus of pious fiction. Equally significant is the commonly accepted interpretation of the Virgin Birth according to which the sexual element had to be excluded right from the beginning if Jesus was to be perfect man, an interpretation which neglects not only the typological comparison with the "virgin daughter of Zion" giving birth to the messianic people (see Is. 66, 7–8) but the intention of the biblical writers to emphasize the exclusively divine origin of the Christ-event. It seems clear, on the basis of the biblical record, that Jesus, unlike some of his later interpreters, accorded no special significance to the sexual. As part of the goodness of creation it can be consecrated. Like anything else in man's nature it can become the sphere of sin and disobedience.

To realize this is already helpful and indeed necessary, but the basic problem of the celibacy of Jesus remains. It is still extremely difficult even to suggest that there may be a historical dimension to this question and that historically we cannot even be certain that he was unmarried. Though understandable, this revulsion is unfortunate since it makes it difficult if not impossible to ask oneself the question whether Jesus *had* to be single rather than married, and it is only by asking this question that some theological understanding of his celibacy—and, by implication, of the Christian practice of voluntary celibacy—can be reached. If we are to take the historical existence of Jesus seriously we cannot—to take one possibility—rule out on *a priori* grounds that Jesus was celibate because too poor to marry. We know that there were many unfortunate Galileans in this situation since Galilee was the most underdeveloped region in Palestine and the most affected by the constant guerilla warfare that was going on at the time. Sephoris, the capital, only a stone's throw from Nazareth, was burned to the ground by guerillas during the infancy of Jesus, and the whole of the period of the hidden years was marked by atrocity and counter-atrocity in which many would have found it impossible to bring up a family. If this is true, and we have no positive indication one way or the other, it would not exclude a voluntary acceptance of this condition.

With the question of voluntary sexual abstention we return to the saying about the three classes of eunuchs. How are we to understand celibacy "for the kingdom of heaven"? There are no grounds for believing that this class, which almost certainly included Jesus himself, eschewed sexual relations on ritual or cultic grounds. As we have seen, Jesus' attitude to these questions rules this out from the start. Nor have we sufficient reason to suppose that they remained unmarried to facilitate the exercise of a pastoral ministry. If this were so we would find it difficult to explain why nowhere in the New Testament is pastoral ministry ever associated with the celibate state. We may add that today, when Roman Catholics have more freedom of movement in ecumenical relations, the argument that celibacy facilitates pastoral ministry is not heard so often from its apologists. A more convincing explanation would be that those to whom Jesus here refers lived celibate in order to face the eschatological struggle ahead unencumbered by marital and family responsibilities. Paul states this explicitly in telling the unmarried that "in view of the impending distress it is well for a person to remain as he is" (1 Cor. 7, 26). Luke's version of the parable of the banquet (a familiar eschatological image) makes the same point indirectly since one of the guests turns down the invitation on the pretext that he has just married a wife (Lk. 14, 20). Luke also makes a significant addition to the sayings dealing with the renunciation of family ties as a precondition of discipleship. His version reads:

> If any one comes to me and does not hate his own father and mother *and wife and children* and brothers and sisters, yes, and even his own life, he cannot be my disciple. (14, 26)

> There is no man who has left house *or wife* or brothers or parents *or children* for the sake of the kingdom of God, who will not receive manifold more in this time and in the age to come eternal life. (18, 29)[13]

Now this would sound not only strange but repellent and immoral to Jewish ears (perhaps it still does to ours), since according to Jewish thinking a man who abandons his wife is responsible for the immorality or adultery into which she may easily fall as a result of his action. Jesus himself makes this point clearly (Mt. 5, 32). Some commentators, especially Roman Catholic, take it for granted that the reference to wife and children, which is not found in Matthew's version, implies the acceptance of a celibate life in the way we understand this term. This view, however, involves attributing to Luke some very careless and misleading editing since the first text obviously

13. Luke's additions are italicized. See Matthew 10, 37 and 19, 29.

presupposes that the disciple is married and the second refers to him as having *left* his wife and children. A more obvious explanation would be that nothing, not even wife and children, must stand in the way of the Christian missionary who sets out to proclaim the kingdom of God. We saw earlier that, according to a probable explanation, the members of the Qumran community left their wives and children "for the sake of the kingdom," that is, to prepare unimpeded for the great eschatological struggle ahead. It is clear that one of Luke's main objects in both the gospel and Acts is to reconcile the Christian mission with the primitive eschatological message. The mission is to be the preparation for the *eschaton,* and the hardships and persecutions which accompanied it, and of which Luke himself had firsthand experience, were the signs of the impending advent of the kingdom. If some of the apostles including Peter and the Lord's brothers were accompanied by their wives on their mission tours (see 1 Cor. 9, 5), we have reason to believe that others were not. Paul himself may have belonged to this group since we need not conclude, on the basis of 1 Corinthians 7, 7–8, that he had never married. It may be that he had married and left his wife to give himself totally to the mission. He appears to have been a rabbi, and we know that the duty of marriage was particularly incumbent on rabbis.

Luke's version of the sayings which we have quoted above not only provides the best context for understanding the eunuchlogion but shows the absolute necessity of not studying the celibacy question in isolation. What seems to be stressed is the readiness to break natural ties of any kind in order to dedicate oneself entirely to the urgent mission of disseminating and living out the revolutionary message of the gospel. What must be transcended in the first place are family ties as a whole. The first disciples called left their father mending his nets; others, as we have seen, left their wives and homes. In the case of Jesus himself we know too little about the period prior to his baptism in the Jordan to make the kind of generalization found so often in devotional literature. It is clear, however, that after this turning point he strongly resisted the pressure of family ties and made provision for his mother only when his mission had been completed and his death was imminent. The requirements of the mission also involved giving up a settled domicile and breaking business connections. This clearly flows from the Lucan form of the sayings and is confirmed by his description of the early Christian mission. Here we have a valuable indication of the essential link between celibacy and poverty which is not always given the emphasis it deserves.

We cannot comment here on the problematic nature of the monastic and religious vows of poverty, chastity and obedience except to note the paradox that, whereas they are generally presented as facilitating a flight *from* the world, the New Testament texts we have been looking at would lead us more naturally to see them as facilitating a flight *into* the world. Perhaps we should try thinking of the Christian who has undertaken these vows as the counterpart of the political revolutionary who gives up all the familiar comforts and reassurances of a family, a settled job and a home to dedicate himself totally to propagating and living out the revolutionary message, perhaps even taking to the hills or the jungle. The comparison will at least invite reflection on how far the Christian message has been "spiritualized" and thereby robbed of much of its revolutionary impact.

The question is bound to arise at this point whether the meaning of celibacy for Jesus, and for the dedicated celibate in the world today, can be exhausted by speaking of it purely in terms of preparing for the eschatological event or freeing oneself for a mobile mission with a view to this event. Both Jesus and Paul speak of the celibate life as a gift of the Spirit, and as such it takes its place with the other "gifts" which marked early Christian enthusiasm—speaking with tongues, healing, heroic renunciations, as well as other less extraordinary activities. These were

37

seen by Paul and other early Christian writers as signs of a new power breaking through into the closed, unredeemed world, the powers of the age to come already at work in this age. That this character of proleptic sign may also belong to celibacy is indicated in Jesus' answer to the Sadducees: "in the resurrection [the age to come] they neither marry nor are given in marriage, but are like angels in heaven" (Mt. 22, 30). This may not look very encouraging to us who do not generally look forward with keen anticipation to an "angelic" existence and for whom an appeal to some experience in a world other than this one carries with it an air of unreality. Of course, we will bear in mind that here as elsewhere Jesus is speaking the religious language of his own age and his own people and that that language is no longer ours. But perhaps here again Luke's parallel version of this casuistic discussion gives us a better clue to meaning. In Luke 20, 34–36 the answer of Jesus runs:

> The sons of this age marry and are given in marriage; but those who are accounted worthy to attain to that age and to the resurrection from the dead neither marry nor are given in marriage, *for they cannot die any more,* because they are equal to angels and are sons of God.

We may well have here the extension of a typically Jewish way of thinking to which we referred earlier. Sexual relations were forbidden before cultic acts, especially for priests but on one occasion for the whole people. This, of course, has nothing to do with the kind of celibacy which Jesus refers to. Though the high priest had to abstain sexually before the Day of Expiation he could not, according to the Talmud, perform the ceremony if he had no wife to sanctify his home. The underlying idea was that the sacred action performed in the *temenos,* the cultic enclosure, set up around itself a kind of magnetic field which repelled sexuality in any form. In Kingdom Come the *Shekinah,* the indwelling mystery, would be perpetually present and therefore sexuality would be perpetually repelled, that is, absent. Marriage, therefore, would be superseded.

Mention of the angels reminds us that for the Qumran sectarians the angels would take part in the eschatological war and in the new age which it would usher in. F. M. Cross suggests[14] that the anticipation of living like these angels in the new age, as spiritual beings without need of procreation, may have prompted the practice of celibacy among some of the sectarians. This would place the primitive Christian practice of some kind of celibacy even more firmly within the eschatological perspectives of first-century Judaism.

This interpretation is possible though not without its difficulties. Perhaps Jesus was simply affirming that sexual relations are proper to mortal men but have no part to play after death. This at least is a more accessible idea to us today. Given the way it has evolved, the species as a whole can overcome death only through sexual union, hence the deep and intimate relation at all levels between sexuality and death. For us, as part of the process, to engage in sexual relations is both a way of accepting death —implicit in the acceptance of the body—and of inflicting on it a local and provisional defeat. This explains the pathos of that scene near the beginning of the book of Genesis when, as death threatens on every side, the Woman cries out that she has gotten a child. One aspect of the relation between sexuality and death is well expressed by Richard L. Rubenstein in a *Playboy* discussion-panel:

The insights of both literature and religion speak of the relation between love and death. When we are involved in sex, we are involved in that activity out of which the human origins arise. We are also reminded of where we are going. There is a certain tragic sense connected with the sexual act. What is involved is not purely personal and voluntary. When we engage in sexual intercourse, we are serving forces beyond our own nature. Even

14. *The Ancient Library of Qumran,* London, 1958, pp. 72 ff.

what we desire is beyond our own nature. In sex we give our bodies to each other. I believe our bodies are all we have. When I give my body, I give my total self . . . but to accept my body is to accept my mortality. Paradoxically, to accept sex is to accept death. To accept sex is to accept the fact that our bodies are limited in time and ultimately brings with it the price we pay for entering time—namely, death.[15]

At any rate, the saying in Luke 20, 36, whether it comes from some early collection of Jesus-sayings or from Luke himself, implies that sexual union as we know it will in some way be taken up and superseded in the greater mystery of the risen life beyond the reach of death and therefore beyond the need constantly to defy death. Paul makes a similar point in arguing against the naïve and materialistic ideas about the resurrection of the dead in vogue among the Christians of Corinth. This, however, does not entitle us to conclude that Jesus saw celibacy as a proleptic sign of the kingdom in which marriage would play no part. Those who choose the celibate state do so *on account of* the kingdom (Mt. 19, 12), namely, in function of the ultimate purpose of God in the world which is the kingdom. This is something quite different. Much less can this text be used to downgrade sexual union to the purely biological level, as if it could not be the sign and sacrament of a mutuality which goes beyond the biological level of sexual exchange.

VI

In his recent study Schillebeeckx rightly points to a neglected factor in the celibacy debate, the inevitability of this way of life for one who has received the gift; true evangelical celibacy implies an "existential inability to do otherwise."[16] This means, as

15. May 1967, p. 72.
16. E. Schillebeeckx, *Celibacy,* London and New York, 1968, pp. 21 ff.

he goes on to point out, that while the church cannot oblige anyone to be celibate it can dispose of its own ministry by restricting it to those who have received this gift. This is in fact what the Roman church has done. He goes on to posit an inner affinity between ministry and celibacy on the ground that both are "gifts" according to the New Testament, both represent modes of self-dedication and availability to the community and the world as a whole. Moreover, the celibate, especially the celibate priest, is a sign of the transcendent nature and mission of the church.[17] On this question of innate affinity between celibacy and ministry I feel there are several questions which Schillebeeckx leaves unanswered. I would doubt, in the first place, whether his interpretation of the "eunuch-logion" in Matthew as addressed to the inner circle of apostles and disciples *qua* "ministers" can really serve to clarify the issue in the way he suggests. For one thing, as we saw earlier, "eunuch" is not synonymous with "unmarriageable"—eunuchs could and did marry. Moreover, if we interpret the saying as referring to the disciples having left their property and family including their wives, we have to reckon with the fact that, as far as the wife was concerned, this was not a definitive renunciation (see 1 Cor. 9, 5). It would be foolish to deny an innate appropriateness of celibacy to some forms of ministry, but is it appropriate to all—especially to the ministry of leading and coordinating the local church which was first and foremost a house-church? Certainly no sign of any inner affinity is detectable in the apostolic and sub-apostolic periods between the gift of celibacy and those of teaching, administrating and so forth which would generally have been exercised by church-leaders. May we then suppose that this affinity, which is merely latent in the earliest period, gradually came to the surface as a result of a deepening meditation on the New Testament data throughout the history of the church? This, of course, is possible in the abstract, but is it a

17. *Ibid.*, pp. 65, 111, 115–116; 98 ff., 106 ff.

satisfactory description of what actually happened? Schillebeeckx himself refers to certain pagan motives which were conscripted by church writers in defense of clerical celibacy which, never more than partial, was imposed in the face of considerable resistance. He does not, however, in my view, give sufficient weight to what was, historically, the strongest force working for the legal enforcement of a celibate clergy, namely, a process of re-sacralization greatly aided by hermeneutically unsound use of the Old Testament.

I do not think it is captious to state that, in reading a moderate and well-argued *theological* exposition of the celibacy question such as Schillebeeckx's, one is struck constantly by the discrepancy between the ideal and the real, between the theological principles to which one may in good part assent and the data of experience. This, of course, is no reflection on the authors who provide us with these expositions, but the whole point of this chapter is that theological reflection cannot be dissociated from experience, granted that the experience is representative and presented without bias. So, for example, the point is well taken that the church does not, and cannot, oblige to celibacy; all that it does is insist that if you want to exercise higher office in the church you must be and remain celibate (pp. 103, 116). Ministry in the church is restricted to those who already possess this charism. But, we may ask, is this what happened historically? As we have seen, and as would, I think, be generally admitted, the practice of clerical celibacy was greatly influenced by the monastic ideal of *ascesis* which included total sexual abstention. This was not an exclusively Christian phenomenon and gave rise to some serious ambiguities in the Christian context. It is one thing for a person to feel an irresistible need to express his faith-relationship to Christ by remaining unmarried and then, independently, to seek office in the church; quite another for a young person to be put through a long training for ministry in the hope that he has this gift. Of its very nature, the charism of celibacy can come only to a mature adult who has successfully dissolved the latent aggressive and sexual instincts of childhood and passed beyond adolescence (irrespective of his actual age). What then are we to make of the long process of conditioning implied in the retention of junior seminaries?—that they are to be retained is clear beyond a doubt from the recent encyclical.

It is likewise true that the purpose of remaining celibate is to allow for a greater degree of availability in the Christian minister. We have all known many fine priests, especially those engaged in a mobile type of mission, where this was eminently verified. But is it a fact of experience that this is always or even generally true? Wider ecumenical contacts have made it impossible for a Catholic honestly to advance this argument by contrasting the celibate Catholic priest with his married counterpart in other churches. If it is right to be guided by experience and observation I would personally have to conclude that the balance is tapped in favor of the married minister.[18] There is also the undeniable fact that being celibate may actually constitute a serious impediment to the priest's or minister's availability. To take one example from the Latin area, which includes, after all, a great number of Catholics, the vital requirement of pastoral visitation is either drastically curtailed or even done away with for fear of the celibate priest finding himself in a compromising situation or coming under suspicion. The result is of course that in these areas the pastoral clergy is essentially a sacristy-based corps dispensing the sacraments to those who care to come to the ecclesiastical filling-station.

The same thing comes through with damning clarity in Cardinal Pizzardo's communication to the cardinal-archbishop of Paris which put an end to the worker-priest experiment in that

18. Since we are speaking of a professional availability we may ask the question whether the fact of, say, a doctor being married greatly hampers his availability to his patients. This, of course, is not to deny that the specifically religious and Christian understanding of availability is not concerned exclusively with the expenditure of time and energy.

city a few years ago. In this we read that "the worker-priest is not only thrown into a materialistic atmosphere which is harmful for his spiritual life and often dangerous for his chastity, but he is also, as it were, led in spite of himself to think like his workmates in matters concerning trade unions and social questions and to take part in their demands. This is a most dangerous chain of causation which leads him very soon to take part in the class war."[19] This hardly requires comment.

Something similar can be said, again on the basis of experience, of aspirants to the ministry in their time of preparation. After having worked in both Catholic and Protestant theological seminaries I could not honestly conclude that students in the former are more available either for carrying out a local mission or for their own preparation for the ministry, acquiring the necessary academic and practical skills. In my experience married students in Protestant seminaries, even those with several children to look after, manage to get through just as much work, if not more, in the two or three years leading to the B.D. or the eighteen months leading to the G.O.E. as celibate Catholic students in the four years of their theological course of studies leading to the S.T.L. or whatever. There may be reasons for this quite unconnected with the fact of being married or unmarried, but we can at least question the assertion that, as a general principle, celibacy leads to greater availability. It just does not seem to work out that way.

One other and last example of ambiguity in the confrontation of theological reflection with actual experience may be mentioned. Schillebeeckx spells out the sign-value of celibacy under the headings: christological, ecclesial and eschatological. By living unmarried "for the sake of the kingdom of God" Jesus has shown us a vocational possibility which is still meaningful, and the one who accepts it indicates to the world in his person the tran-

19. For this whole question see *The Worker Priests,* ed. by J. Petrie, London and New York, 1956, pp. 147 ff.

scending significance of Jesus. By being celibate in and for the church he is also a sign of the transcendental mission of the church which is to be accomplished by personal union with Christ. By giving up the prospect of marriage he shows in a special if negative way the inner tendency towards the future inherent in the mystery of Christ.[20] This can clearly be true of the Christian, whether man or woman, who makes a mature and specific choice of the unmarried state. Whether it is true of the priesthood in the present cultural context of understanding is, however, not at all self-evidently true. By definition a sign must communicate reality within a specific cultural context, and Schillebeeckx himself points out towards the beginning of his study that while the whole way of thinking which produced the present forms and structures of the church is a thing of the past, the forms and structures themselves have remained. Here he puts his finger on a basic factor in the crisis of ministry in the church today.

VII

Due to an almost endemic Roman Catholic habit of thought according to which today's church is, at every point, the result of a rectilinear, irreversible and foreordained process stretching back to the beginnings, the reaction to our investigations so far might well be: all very well, but so what? Yet it should be obvious that the church's history is not really like this at all and that we still await a satisfactory theology of doctrinal development. If everything were irreversible, the very idea of church reform would be inadmissible, and not even the narrowest conservative would say that today. There have been developments in the church's life which have, very fortunately, been reversed. There have been laws which seemed like the laws of the Medes and the Persians which may not be altered and yet which have been altered and

20. *Op. cit.*, pp. 100 ff.

indeed suppressed. And in every case this has come about through a deeper scrutiny of God's will in Christ revealed in the Scriptures combined with a closer attention to the social, political and religious conditioning of the church's life and mission in different ages.

Practically speaking, the failure of the Roman Catholic church today to come to terms with its mission in the modern world is one of self-understanding. At the official level it is focused on a dual disability, to take the Scriptures seriously and to rid itself of a false mystique of authority, and the two are closely related. Both are emphasized by the confusion evident in the Vatican II *Constitution on Divine Revelation,* for in this document the vital question of the controlling influence of the Scriptures on the life of the church was left unanswered while the whole issue was confused by the easily identifiable interpolations of Paul VI, of the kind which also appear in the *Constitution on the Church.* In a world impatient of archaic institutional forms and ways of thinking which are simply relics of the past—as distinct from genuine tradition—this failure of self-understanding is hardly less than fatal.

There is a great difference between living within a tradition, which requires constant and radical reinterpretation in the light of present circumstances, and merely living on the overdrawn account of past forms, achievements and habits of thought. The difference is that the former can give creative shape to the future while the latter condemns one to drift. The immediate theological tasks are for the church to work out a more radical and scriptural form of self-understanding and to absorb the simple and direct New Testament teaching on authority. This last is crucial. I would suggest that the questions of birth control and clerical celibacy are signs that the Spirit is calling on Roman Catholics to make the great renunciation of going beyond themselves by giving up the ecclesiastical fundamentalism which has characterized their thinking increasingly over the last few centuries and which, despite some progress, is still with the church. We do not turn to the Scriptures (as I have been trying to do in this chapter) in order to appeal to Christ *against* the church; but we have to see that our loyalty to the church, rightly understood, entails the primacy of our loyalty to Christ. Perhaps the basic error has been that of identifying the church with the institutional form which it has come to have after two thousand years of the most varied experience during which the sociological and political structures of society have been profoundly altered. Suffice it to refer once more to the commonly accepted representation of the church in terms of *regnum* and *imperium*, as, for example, in Bellarmine's well-known comparison with the republic of Venice. This was the starting point for those apologists who, in defiance of the scriptural evidence, went on to identify the church with the kingdom preached by Jesus. To renounce the security which this way of thinking has given us will be little short of heroic. Yet all the signs are that it will have to be done and that time is no longer on our side.

To return, finally, to celibacy and the three aspects under which we have been talking about it. It is clear that asceticism was not the real motive-force behind the process which led to the all-inclusive law in the twelfth century. A desire for personal ascesis may lead individual Christians, clerical and lay, to remain celibate. Beginning very early in Christian history, some have elevated this into a *state of life* by embracing monasticism (later, religious life in general) and the vows associated with it. This indirectly influenced the process through the tendency, beginning in the fourth century, to take bishops from among the ranks of the monks. The idea of the monastic groups forming a Christian élite also inevitably, as we have seen, reacted on the secular clergy. It seems to me that the relevance of monasticism lies more in the fact that it contributed decisively to the idea of different Christian states of life. Because the secular clergy, for the reasons seen, were drawn into the sphere of attraction of

47

monasticism, they too came to be considered as embodying a state of life. The vow of celibacy undertaken at the subdiaconate stage, the promise to the bishop at priestly ordination and the less well-defined injunctions to practice evangelical poverty reflect the three originally monastic vows. The ensuing tension between a *state of life* and a pastoral and ministerial *function* has never been successfully resolved and is today more acute than ever. Monastic orders have been clericalized and are asking with increasing insistence why monks have to be priests; the secular clergy have been monasticized and are asking with increasing insistence why they have to be monks. And behind both questions there is the underlying doubt whether ministry in the church has to be considered as a state of life at all.

Obviously, some kind of asceticism or at least moral standard of life is appropriate to those who aspire to take part in the church's ministry. But here we meet the further paradox that whereas celibacy has now become a mandatory part of this, the standards required in apostolic and sub-apostolic times (see, for example, 1 Tim. 3, 1–13 and Tit. 1, 5–9) hinged on the ability of a prospective deacon, presbyter or bishop to manage his own household or, in other words, to be a good husband and a good father.

It is clear, therefore, that the basic motivation behind the process which led to mandatory clerical celibacy must be sought elsewhere. We have seen that the first attempts to legislate, at the Spanish council of Elvira at the beginning of the fourth century, aimed not at celibacy as we now understand it but at continence within marriage. It therefore had the purpose neither of encouraging the priest to greater moral heroism (not directly at any rate) since there is no mention of this in the acts of the council, nor of leaving him freer to minister to others since the poor man still had a wife and family to provide for. The reason is, quite clearly, that sexual relations were deemed incompatible with the administration of the sacraments, especially of course the eucharist. Here a decisive factor, surprisingly often over-looked in this discussion, enters into play, namely, the frequency of celebration of the eucharist. We saw that the high priest had to abstain sexually for the seven days prior to *Yom Kippur* (the great Day of Expiation), and this no doubt was true of other great cultic occasions in the Jewish calendar. Once the habit had been formed of appealing to this practice, documented in the Old Testament, on the ground that what is demanded of priests of the Old Law must, *a fortiori,* apply to Christian priests, it was inevitable that the celebrant of the eucharist could not approach this central act of Christian cult after having sexual relations with his wife. And once it had become the custom for either pastoral or devotional reasons to celebrate the eucharist daily the only logical conclusion was that the celebrant had to be totally abstinent. And so we come back full circle to the cultic world of the Old Testament and its demands which the early church, after an initial hesitation, had so enthusiastically rejected.

This raises the question of the viability of this subsumption of all reality into sacred and profane. We may ask whether this feeling for the sacred, this conviction that some objects, places and persons are, so to speak, ontologically sacred, that is, sep-arate, is a characteristic of primitive forms of religious ex-perience destined to recede with the development of higher and more spiritual forms of religious consciousness. Recent writing on secularization has, perhaps surprisingly, said little explicitly on the sacred and has simply taken for granted that the sacred view of the world is obsolete and that biblical religion culminat-ing in Christianity tends intrinsically and inevitably to supersede it. I would certainly agree with this but feel there is a need to speak explicitly and positively of the sacred and to integrate studies in the morphology of the sacred already carried out into our understanding of the present situation of the Christian churches vis-à-vis secular reality. The fact is that a tendency towards sacralization appears even in more evolved forms of religious expression, nowhere more than where people still think "religiously" of the Christian reality or suppose that it demands some form of "religious" objectivization—sacred places, persons, things and times. A good example, to which we shall return in a later chapter, is the *locus* of the eucharistic assembly during the first few centuries. All the terminology associated with the eucharist in the apostolic age is non-sacral and it was celebrated in the house of some Christian who was in a position to act as host (significantly, hospitality is one of the virtues required of bishops in 1 Timothy 3, 2). With the building of large city-churches and basilicas in the Constantinian age all this changed, and we find, in the mass for the consecration of a church, that the Entrance Hymn refers to Jacob's numinous experience in the ancient pagan sanctuary of Bethel—*terribilis est locus iste!*

A word of warning is, however, appropriate at this point. There is a sense in which sacralization has to be seen as an attempt to impose meaning on a world constantly threatened by disorder and the dark circumambient forces which endanger the organized life of society. In the ancient Near East, for example, the *akitu* or New Year Festival had the function of an annual return to the creative center, a reconsecration of a created order which was always felt to be provisional and menaced by disorder. Something of this comes through in the Easter midnight vigil. In this sense the sacred is more real than the profane in the same way that order is more real than disorder, and meaning more real than unintelligibility. If therefore we are speaking of sacralization or consecration as conferring meaning we must agree, with Eliade, that "sacredness is, above all, *real*. The more religious a man is the more real he is, and the more he gets away from the unreality of a meaningless change. Hence man's tendency to 'consecrate' his whole life."[21] The placing of the grains

21. Mircea Eliade, *Patterns in Comparative Religion,* London and New York, p. 459.

of incense in the paschal candle is symbolic of Christian consecration, but let us note that what is consecrated is the total
historical cosmos, the *pleroma* filled with the presence of the
risen Lord.

It will be obvious that the kind of sacralization criticized often
in this book is of a different kind. There is a fundamental
ambivalence running through the whole phenomenology of the
sacred. On the one hand it confers order and meaning, on the
other it is dangerous and unpredictable. Correspondingly, there
is a tendency both to consecrate the whole of life and to sacralize
certain objects, persons, places and times which become thereby
taboo—set aside from profane contact and use. The motive
force behind this is fear of the unpredictable, of what lies beyond
the conscious control of man; which is something quite different
from the total consecration of life and human values referred
to above.

Whatever else we may say, this concept of the sacred motivated
by fear and the sense of danger is no longer an ingredient of
the consciousness of modern man and has no earthly relevance
for the great majority of the people to whom the churches are
meant to minister. Why, then, do we perpetuate it? To sacralize
means to separate, and we separate or segregate because we are,
perhaps unconsciously, afraid. Is it not possible that the Christian
message of redemption is, in the first place, one of liberation, in
particular liberation from fear, including fear of the sacred?
We say that we are redeemed, and yet so much of our lives
as Christians is dominated by fear. Here, as it seems to me, Père
Audet raises a prophetic voice in his recent excellent study of
celibacy and ministry from which I quoted earlier on in this
chapter. On the relation between celibacy and sacralization he
says:

> The perception of sexual "purity" and "impurity" as well as the very
> different evaluations placed upon it over the course of history,
> belong to the most archaic depths of human consciousness, where

51

they are bound up with the most elementary structures of fear. The question is whether it is desirable for us to maintain these structures and cultivate that archaism indefinitely; whether the law of clerical celibacy, with all the very real greatness it has produced, is to continue indirectly to stand surety for one of the most evidently regressive elements in our entire inheritance as human beings.[22]

Elsewhere he reminds us that the sacred is not the same as the divine; and we may note further that the first Christians never seem to have wanted to describe the divine event which they had witnessed or experienced in terms associated with the sacred.

Nowadays it is considered more enlightened for Roman Catholics to speak of celibacy and virginity as forms of witness. The trouble here is that it is awfully easy to talk about witnessing in a way so smooth and self-evident that nobody dares ask the question: witnessing to what? An American nun complained to me once that she was always being told, in answer to difficulties which she experienced about her vocation, that her life was a way of "witnessing" but that no one had ever given her a coherent account of what she was supposed to be witnessing to—if she could get that straight she would be happy to witness all over the place. Can voluntary celibacy be understood as a sign of and witness to immortal life? to the future kingdom? to some transcending value *within* human life which "the world" tends to neglect?

If we begin with life beyond death or the future kingdom we run the risk of coming up against a stone wall, no matter how sincerely and urgently we try to communicate the sense of a reality which lies beyond the human power of verification. But the earliest Christian message speaks of a reality which is already present and subject to human experience here and now. Through the Spirit, the presence of the risen Lord is experienced in the

22. *Op. cit.*, pp. 149–150. This book was refused an *imprimatur* in France, which further illustrates the point about fear.

community and its worship; the Christian can already experience here and now something of "the powers of the age to come" (Heb. 6, 5). This power or "spiritual energy" (the suggestive term used in the *New English Bible* translation) is manifested in the miracles of the Lord and those which were experienced in the early churches, as well as in the spiritual gifts of which Paul speaks so often in his correspondence. In a certain sense it would be a logical deduction, and one in keeping with biblical thinking, to speak of the person who performs the healing or speaking with tongues or whatever as himself a sign since he is, so to speak, the vehicle of that mysterious power and energy. If it is legitimate to class the practice of voluntary celibacy among the gifts of the Spirit, then to live celibate can be considered a sign of or witness to the reality of the kingdom to come.

While admitting this, however, we should add that it is dangerous to over-dramatize celibacy in this way. In doing so we run the risk of isolating it in a way which would be both unscriptural and unhistorical because we have no evidence that the celibate was ever seen in this light in the early period of Christianity and because since then other influences, which we have been talking about in this chapter, have radically altered the emphasis. We could give it credibility only by placing it firmly in the context of the entire Christian community as a sign to the world. The new Christian reality is a brotherhood and sisterhood of love as a sign to mankind, divided by fear and hatred, of what it is destined to become. The style of life which any Christan in whatever situation adopts has to be referred to this. For most, the married life will be the best way of opening oneself to love and growing in it in a way which can achieve a genuine value as sign. The New Testament and early Christian history show that this was also true of many, indeed most, engaged in various kinds of ministry including presidency of the eucharistic assembly—especially since it was a house-assembly. Others may feel called to the celibate life as for them the best way of growing in love and

53

opening themselves radically to others. We do not normally choose a style of life because of its sign-value but because we believe that this is the best way for us to become the kind of persons we wish to be. This is the real test of the choice—married life or celibacy—a point well made in a short essay by David B. Burrell of Notre Dame University entitled "The Other Side of the Celibacy Question":

> The only trustworthy sign of an authentic life is the extent to which one has learned to love. If celibacy provides the situation in which some can learn to love and grow in love in a fashion that is deeply their own, then it has earned its place. If it does not show itself in this way, then it merits no aspirants; and if it has not proven to be such for any individual person, then it has no further claim on him.[23]

What remains is the functional value of celibacy, celibacy *dia tes basileias*—on account of, or in view of, the kingdom. Early Christian witness certainly attaches this to ministry understood in the wide sense of the word as found in the New Testament, but never to pastoral ministry in the local church or the presidency of the eucharistic assembly. It was found specially fitting to one kind of ministry of the Word, that in which the itinerant missionary was engaged. Of course, not all by any means of the early itinerant missionaries renounced marriage or, if married, the company of their wives (see 1 Cor. 9, 5). Paul himself freely renounced either the former or the latter, but neither he nor anyone else at that time would have dreamed of disturbing the free order of the *ekklesia* by insisting that everyone engaged in the ministry had to adopt the same style of life and remain unmarried. I would not have anyone think that I am advocating a simplicist and naïve return in this respect or any other to the practice of the primitive church (in some respects very primitive, as one Anglican divine was wont to add); but that we have a

23. *The National Catholic Reporter*, September 6, 1967.

serious problem on our hands few would deny, and the considerations I have put forward in this chapter are offered in the belief that the thinking and practice of those who were so much closer than we are to Christ should have some relevance in solving it.

2. The Encyclical
Sacerdotalis Caelibatus

It might seem out of place and profitless for anyone who holds the views outlined in the previous chapter to attempt a commentary on the recent papal encyclical on priestly celibacy. Papal pronouncements of this kind are not generally calculated to convince those not already convinced or who believe that even in matters most deeply concerned with Christian faith, genuine dialogue, conducted without presuppositions, can be productive of real progress in understanding and real changes in the structures and life of the church. There are good reasons enough for commenting on documents which, however imperfect, express in some way a general consensus in the church, documents such as those which emanated from the Second Vatican Council. In the present case, however, we had a statement finalizing the issue at the very moment, the convening of the Synod of Bishops, when it seemed the time was ripe for a full and honest discussion of a problem which affects not just the few thousand priests directly involved but the whole community. Yet, despite this, good reasons exist for not passing over such a document in silence. For one thing, papal pronouncements of this kind can no longer be thought of as concerning just the closed circle of convinced Roman Catholics. The Second Vatican Council at least taught us the need to move out into real ecumenical dialogue and that questions of ministry and Christian styles of life are no longer purely domestic issues.

Put at its crudest, the question for the contemporary Roman

Catholic confronted with a document of this kind is whether it can be taken as a reasoned statement of a case which may be discussed and criticized, in the manner of a government White Paper or an Anglican Commissioners' Report, or whether it must be accepted in grateful silence as a long-awaited oracular utterance. The kind of language used and the way the case is here presented appear to favor the latter hypothesis. Thus, the objections to mandatory clerical celibacy are concisely stated at the beginning (§5–11) and are then disposed of on the grounds that those who present them "cannot receive this precept" or "are unaware of the higher logic of that new concept of life" (§12) or do not "know how to appreciate the gifts of God." The conclusion seems inescapable that the undivided church of the first three centuries (at least), the Orthodox church with its long unbroken tradition and the Reformed churches show a different approach to ministry and celibacy because they "cannot receive this precept" and are spiritually unaware with regard to this gift. A further answer to these objections is sought in the "solemn and agelong voice of the pastors of the Church" and the countless numbers both clerical and lay, male and female, who have embraced the state of celibacy. But the question at issue is the existence of a *law* of clerical celibacy, not the Christian's choice of the celibate state as a highly valuable style of life.

In the last section of the previous chapter I referred to two related failures of contemporary Roman Catholicism: to take the Scriptures seriously in the way they must influence the church's progressive self-understanding, and to get rid of a false mystique of authority which itself is anti-scriptural. This bears directly on the present encyclical and its subject matter. We have just seen that, despite all that the council said about episcopal collegiality and the witness of the Spirit in the whole church, it was promulgated before the first episcopal synod had any opportunity of discussing the question with the intent of foreclosing argu-

57

ment. Due to the absolutist self-understanding of the church which it presupposes it literally does not know what to do with the clear scriptural fact that neither Jesus nor Paul nor any other Christian writer of the apostolic or subapostolic age speaks in mandatory terms of the celibate life. Moreover, it sees the present discipline on this subject as the final end-product of a rectilinear and irreversible historical process. "It is *unthinkable* that for centuries she [i.e., the Roman Catholic church] has followed a path which, instead of favoring the spiritual richness of individual souls and of the People of God, has in some way compromised it, or that she has with arbitrary juridical prescriptions stifled the free expression of the most profound realities of nature and of grace" (§41). This is a type of statement which it is very difficult to comment on and elucidate. We may, however, ask whether it is equally *unthinkable* that the Roman Catholic church has for centuries followed the path of opposition to the development of the natural sciences, or given its tacit support to dominant Western capitalism or discouraged the reading and scientific study of the Scriptures. And if any change is not just inadvisable at this moment but *unthinkable,* what of the Curia which has also been with us for centuries? We may readily and gladly admit that celibacy has been of inestimable value to individual Christians in the past and still is to very many in the present. But here we are dealing not with the practice of voluntary celibacy in general—the value of which is beyond question—but of a *law* which achieved its present form as late as the twelfth century.

Starting with the series of oratorical questions in §3, it becomes clear that this document belongs to the category of affirmation (more precisely, reaffirmation) not argument, monologue not dialogue. It comes clean in §15 which states in a rather roundabout way that though the gifts of Christian ministry and voluntary celibacy are separate it is up to church authorities to decide which persons are eligible to the ministry, and it has already decided—more than eight centuries ago—that only prospective celibates need apply. The same is repeated in §62 which goes on to say that "in virtue of such a gift, corroborated by canon law [*sic*], the individual is called to respond with free judgment and total dedication."

The encyclical rightly plays down the idea of cultic apartness and purely ascetical motivation in favor of the imitation of the celibate Jesus. We even find the shadow of an answer to the question why Jesus himself was celibate. One line of argument appears to be that whereas "matrimony . . . continues the work of the first creation," celibacy is more in accord with the new creation and the new covenant from which it springs (§20). According to this new way, "the human creature adheres wholly and directly to the Lord, and is concerned only with him and with his affairs." The natural consequence of this would, of course, be that the celibate state is more fitting and desirable for *all* those who belong to the new creation, namely, for all Christians; and therefore that marriage is really a *faute de mieux* tailored to those who "cannot receive the gift." This obvious difficulty is met by linking the celibacy of Jesus with his function as mediator between God and men, a function which is passed on to "those whose fortune it is to share in the dignity and in the mission of the Mediator and eternal Priest" (§21). Apart from the difficulty that neither the New Testament nor ancient tradition links the celibacy of Jesus with a priestly office of mediation, we would have expected at this point some reference to the mediatorial function of the whole priestly community (see 1 Pet. 2, 9–10). This would have enabled us to see marriage and voluntary abstention from marriage as *complementary* life-styles embodied in the Christian community as a whole rather than using celibacy to accentuate the cleric-lay class distinction.

A similar failure to come to grips with incontrovertible scriptural data appears a little later on when "the consecrated celibacy of the sacred ministers" is taken to be the sign of "the virginal love of Christ for the Church" (§26). If we are to be true to scriptural witness we would have to say that Christian marriage rather than "ministerial" celibacy has this sign-value. Paul states this clearly in a well-known text (Eph. 5, 32), following a long line of biblical tradition.

It is important to note the combination in this document of an apparently scriptural orientation with an often last-minute failure of nerve or sincerity or courage in grappling with what the Scriptures actually say. One would not, of course, expect an encyclical letter to contain either a detailed exegetical treatment of the relevant issues or a close historical study of Christian thinking and practice in this area. What one may legitimately expect, however, is that the conclusions reached reflect the results of critical and scholarly studies of responsible exegetes and historians. Here there is something to be desired. We saw, for example, in the last chapter that Luke 18, 29–30 (the blessing of those who renounce home and family ties) cannot refer to celibacy as we understand it. A more careful consideration of this text might have led to some reflection on the celibate state as more appropriate to one particular form of Christian mission —the itinerant type of mission as practiced in the early-church period and, in various forms, down to the present. This would have provided a useful approach to a discussion of different styles of Christian living and their mutual interraction and, on the more practical level, of the functional aspects of celibacy. The encyclical hardly mentions these at all.

The history of the celibacy question is summarized in about a hundred and fifty words (§35–36). Here again, one would not expect a detailed and nuanced study of the question in this kind of document; but a selective treatment which gives the impression of a foreordained and inevitable progress towards the canonical situation which is with us today is hardly a satisfactory basis for further study of this critically important subject. We might admit that the time is not ripe for change or that the balance of probability favors the retention of the present ecclesiastical discipline as a whole. Arguments could be put forward to show that from the pastoral point of view the ordination of married men to the priesthood would not be appropriate in many areas of predominantly Catholic population—not, at least, at the present. The encyclical, however, goes well beyond this in absolutizing one particular line of historical development with the purpose of foreclosing argument. In doing so it excludes the possibility that the Spirit may be calling us to new forms of life, to a *metanoia* which involves retracing our steps, undoing what has been done, freeing ourselves from past forms in order to look clearly into a future to which God is calling us.

A historian not committed to the view of development implied in the encyclical would have no great difficulty in filling in the gaps and thus correcting the emphasis. He would feel obliged to add that while it is true, as the encyclical states, that many undertook the voluntary practice of celibacy in the first three centuries many others did not, and in fact a married clergy was the rule not the exception during this period. He would want to correct the impression that the earliest attempts to legislate were concerned with celibacy as we define it today by pointing out that what they forbade was the use of marriage by bishops and priests. The difference is not unimportant. He would feel obliged to deny categorically that the historical reasons for adopting this way of life "were always inspired by specifically Christian considerations" (§18). The tendency towards sacralization and the consequent deterrence of the sexual are not specifically Christian and in fact raise some serious problems in a Christian context, as we saw in the last chapter.

The full development and definition of priestly celibacy had to wait for the Middle Ages. It is well known that the fathers of the First and Second Lateran Councils (1123 and 1139), who declared that a cleric in major orders could not validly marry, were greatly concerned with the heresy of the *Nicolaiti* who not

61

only held an adamistic and utopian view of sexual relations but were much involved in simony. This certainly influenced the intransigent line taken by these assemblies. More important, the prohibition of clerical marriage in this period was not unconnected with the social evil of clerical benefices. Since, according to the feudal custom of primogeniture, the holding devolved by right on the eldest son, a married beneficed clergy would result in the breakup and alienation of clerical property. Hence it was important that clerics should not have legitimate offspring. This no doubt explains why in the acts of the Council of Trent clerical celibacy is treated under marriage and it is specified that the children of priests may not hold benefices. It would probably be safe to add that clerical concubinage was so widespread in the late medieval period that the law may well have been either dropped or greatly liberalized had it not been for the doctrinal attack of Luther on celibacy.

The decisive nature of the historical factor is accepted implicitly in the way the encyclical explains the different discipline of the Eastern church. This is "due to the different historical background of that most noble part of the Church" (§38). Later on, support for the Western discipline is found in the writings of the Greek church fathers, esepcially in those which exalt virginity. This, of course, raises the question why the Eastern church, more intimately acquainted with its own ecclesiastical and patristic tradition, did not draw the same conclusions from these writings that the Western church has done. Perhaps the reason is to be sought not primarily in the different historical background of the Orthodox church but in something specifically "different" in the history of the Western church. This, of course, does not alter the fact that the same tendencies were common to both. So, for example, the encyclical quotes from John Chrysostom: ". . . it is becoming that he who accepts the priesthood be as pure as if he were in heaven" (§39). A statement like this may seem so obviously valid that we do not stop to consider what it connotes. If, as here, it is used in support of the present discipline in the Roman Catholic church, it must imply that purity in its fullness is not open to the Christian living in the married state. We are therefore led of necessity to conclude with Jerome that in the presence of Christ's sacramental body all sexual union, including that within Christian marriage, is impure—*omnis coitus impurus.*

Much is said in the encyclical of celibacy as the final expression of a love which is "genuine, total, exclusive, stable and lasting" (§24). Here, despite the rhetoric, we have a real problem. It will hardly be doubted that voluntary celibacy can be part of a growth in affectivity and the capacity to relate meaningfully to others. For some it will be undertaken out of inner necessity precisely to realize this outgoing love. But this is just one of many examples in this document where the issue of mandatory clerical celibacy is confused with the values attaching to the Christian practice as such; and the question which remains to be answered is whether the present discipline promotes or hinders the achievement of this objective. At this point discussion is displaced by a series of rhetorical questions:

> Who can see in such a life so completely dedicated and motivated as shown above, the sign of a spiritual poverty, of self-seeking, and not rather see that celibacy is and ought to be a rare and very meaningful example of a life whose motivation is love, by which man expresses his own unique greatness? Who can doubt the moral and spiritual richness of such a consecrated life, consecrated not to any human ideal no matter how noble, but to Christ and to his work to bring about a new form of humanity in all places and for all generations? (§24)

If this is applied to the Christian practice as such as we can accept it without reserve. But if, as is apparently the case here, the life referred to is that of the priest on whom the celibate state is binding, we should want to ask some real as opposed to rhetorical questions. Does the mandatory tie-in of the celibate state with Christian ministry render either the former or the latter more difficult and ambivalent as the object of a specific and deeply personal choice and decision? Do the sacrality and immobility inseparable from the legal definition of a celibate priest make it in the concrete more difficult for many priests to "become what they are," that is, achieve real personal growth? Take the case, not uncommon, of one who has a real desire to serve in the church's ministry and who on this account accepts or goes along with the "rider" of celibacy without making it the object of a specific and personal decision. Because this touches what is most deeply personal in him it will, sooner or later, present him with serious difficulties in his struggle to grow as a genuine human being. Yet today, when the priest is seen less and less as a sacred symbol and more is demanded of him as a man, this growth is absolutely necessary. Moreover, we know a great deal more today than previously about the psychological preconditions of this capacity for altruistic love of which the encyclical speaks at this point.

We now realize, for example, that a basically infantile need for mother-security or for resolving the father-conflict may well underlie the attraction exerted on some by the still highly authoritarian Roman clerical system. Thus the answer to the question posed by the encyclical whether celibacy gives the priest "the maximum efficiency and the best disposition of mind, psychologically and affectively, for the continuous exercise of a perfect charity" (§32) will emerge only after a hard look at the facts and cannot be established on some abstract *a priori* theological grounds. It is here that the Synod of Bishops could have made a valuable and authoritative contribution to the debate had they been consulted before the writing of the encyclical. If the principle of collegiality laid down in Vatican II is to mean anything at all it surely must apply in the concrete to cases such as this.

At any rate, all the indications are that the debate will continue notwithstanding.

One aspect of the problem which, incidentally, the encyclical does not examine is the effect of the conflation of celibacy and ministry on recruitment to ministerial service in the Catholic priesthood. Even apart from the celibacy requirement a problem exists here. What kind of person is attracted to the clerical ranks in the Roman Catholic priesthood? To what kind of temperament is recruitment generally addressed? Commenting on the Terman-Miles experiments in masculinity and femininity carried out in the United States, R. F. Hobson remarks:

> An interesting, though perhaps not unexpected, finding is that the scores of clergymen, in this test, reveal that they constitute one of the least "masculine" (as defined by this test) of male professions or occupations. It might be asked whether or not this result indicates attitudes and characteristics which would be generally considered as suitable for the ministry, and in what sense a priest should be "masculine."[1]

Of course, a great deal would depend on whether one accepts the concept of "masculinity" postulated in the survey. Different criteria are adopted in different cultural *milieux*. To take an obvious example, there is a great difference between the attitude towards the Catholic priest in Britain and the United States on the one hand and that prevalent in Latin countries on the other. In the latter case the "*padrecito*" or "*pretino*" comes out badly precisely because masculinity is associated directly with sexual capacity and practice—even sexual athleticism. There may well be, in addition, a direct relationship between the concept of the priest as a sexual non-combatant and the kind of devotional *Kitsch* mainly originating in Latin countries centered on the image of a sexless, emasculated Christ.

1. In *The Archbishops' Commission on Women and Holy Orders*, p. 50. See P. Berton, *The Comfortable Pew*, Philadelphia, 1965, pp. 62–63, on the "passive-dependent" type.

The encyclical recommends that those who are discovered to be unfit for ministry in the church—either for physical, psychological or moral reasons—"should be quickly removed from the path to the priesthood" (§64). Perhaps we do not give enough consideration to the fact that those also must be excluded who, no matter how keenly they desire to share in the pastoral work of the church and are otherwise well qualified to do so, are not willing to sacrifice the normal instincts to marry and raise a family. Here we are far removed from the apostolic and sub-apostolic periods when aptitude for bringing up a family and governing the small community of the household were taken as basic criteria for the exercise of pastoral ministry in "the household of the faith" (1 Tim. 3, 2–5; Tit. 1, 5–9).

Part II of the encyclical deals with priestly formation. What is most obvious here is that the retention of the celibacy clause entails a whole process of testing and conditioning[2] in some respects not unlike that of a candidate for the Secret Service. The process is clearly envisaged as beginning at an early age—the subject is described throughout as "the youth" ("ardor and generosity are marvellous qualities of youth," [§69]), and the role of the teacher or educator is emphasized. There is frequent reference to the biological, psychological and hereditary characteristics of the subject (e.g., §63). A kind of blueprint is provided for "the progressive development of his personality through the means of physical, intellectual and moral education directed towards the control and personal dominion of his instincts, sentiments and passions" (§65). Everything is mapped out, at least in outline, in this process of arduous preparation for the exercise of ministry. The key-note is "guided liberty" (§70) and the end-product "a balanced personality, strong and mature, a combination of in-

2. The word actually occurs in the *Decree on Priestly Formation:* "In minor seminaries, which are built to nurture the seeds of a vocation, students can be conditioned to follow Christ the Redeemer" (§3).

herited and acquired characteristics, harmony of all his powers," et cetera.

For those of us who have seen in our own or others' experience how these good intentions so often rob the individual of his capacity to make genuinely personal and therefore meaningful decisions regarding a way or style of living there may well be something rather repellent about this well-meaning process of "guiding" the individual's liberty. The retention of the junior seminary system, clearly presupposed here as it is in the relevant Vatican II documents, still leaves plenty of room for the whole apparatus of hidden persuasion and pressure. Having set up this context, it is hardly any good insisting that "none of the real personal and social difficulties which their choice will bring in its train should remain hidden to the youth" (§69). The obvious question which will be asked here is whether a young adolescent placed in this situation can ever have anything more than a purely notional grasp of what the choice of celibacy implies. Here we can apply, *mutatis mutandis,* the comment of a sympathetic Protestant scholar on the *Decree on Priestly Formation:*

> It is altogether praiseworthy that a student be helped to understand that he is not called to dominion or honors, and that he be trained in priestly obedience, humility and self-denial, as other religious communities can also appreciate. But should not the document have spoken somewhere of the freedom and dignity of the individual and of the desirability of developing the diversity of the Spirit's gifts even among members of the sacramental priesthood? At this point the Decree reads too much like a composition of bishops for bishops, absent-mindedly withholding from their fellow-priests what they generously allow to laymen and even to those outside the Church.[3]

We have had too many examples of *guided liberty* in ecclesiastical and political history not to suspect that this kind is no real

3. Warren A. Quanbeck in *The Documents of Vatican II,* ed. by W. M. Abbott, New York and London, 1966, pp. 459–460.

liberty at all. No system, least of all an ecclesiastical system, can *give* a person liberty. True interior freedom is a task, something to be achieved. What we can, however, demand of an institution is that it provide the optimum conditions for the individual to fulfill this task. This requirement was expressed forcibly by Davis in *A Question of Conscience:*

> Just as individual development takes place within a social context and as part of a common becoming, so, too, interior freedom requires exterior freedom for its achievement. Exterior freedom consists in those conditions that enable people to be and become themselves, that allow them to express their ideas outwardly and execute their decisions, *that release them from oppressive threats and methods of persuasion which induce fantasy fears and play upon their emotional insecurity,* and finally that guide them with truth and do not deceive them by half-truths or falsehood[4] (italics mine).

Both authors, in different ways, point to what is still a radical weakness in the church, of which the "official" attitude to clerical celibacy is only one symptom.

The last part of the encyclical, entitled in the English version "Lamentable Defections," deals with the question of discharge from the priesthood. As is by now well known, it is still extremely difficult for a priest who has either not made a positive antecedent choice of celibacy or feels unable to make a subsequent choice to obtain honorable discharge. The only loophole provided by canon law is the case of ordination resulting from grave fear or force (canon 214)—both remote contingencies today. Opinions as to numbers vary since the Vatican office responsible publishes no statistics. A *Time* magazine report stated that some 4,000 cases had been reviewed between 1964 and 1966. Other guesses abound but none of them is verifiable.[5] The

4. *Op. cit.,* p. 215.
5. E.g., R. T. Francoeur in *Celibacy: The Necessary Option,* ed. by G. H. Frein, New York, 1968, p. 162.

encyclical refers to "a minimal percentage" of dispensations granted (§85). Later on it states that a dispensation is sometimes granted to those "whose priesthood cannot be saved, but whose serious dispositions nevertheless give promise of their being able to live as good Christian lay people" (§88). The assumption behind this statement is that those who apply would not, in general, be the kind of people one would expect to lead a good Christian life.

Understandably, the encyclical does not describe the interminable and humiliating process involved for a priest who decides to resign from the ministry. In this process two factors of overriding importance stand out: fear of scandal and fear of escalation. While it is clear that the resignation of any Christian minister can be accompanied by scandal in a real theological sense, the irony is that the whole process sanctioned by the document is scandalous in the eyes of most of the Christian world precisely because of the absence of the specifically Christian qualities of love, acceptance and humanness. As for the fear of escalation, the encyclical states quite candidly that the reluctance to grant dispensations is dictated by the need to *encourager les autres* or, spelled out, to "confirm good priests in their determination to live lives of purity and holiness" (§89). This invites the reflection that there may be something wrong with a system which has to resort to tactics of this kind to keep people in the ministry.

What happens when a priest decides to resign from the ministry? An application is filed which is addressed to the Pope but which is processed, together with several hundred others, by a Roman committee chaired by a cardinal to whom, of course, the petitioner is a stranger. The application is not acknowledged but in due course, perhaps as soon as three or four months later, it will be sent back to the local bishop who must interview the petitioner, ascertain the state of his health—especially his mental health—interrogate others who know him as to his probity of character and intentions, and so on. The petition is eventually returned to Rome together with the bishop's report and perhaps other letters of recommendation and testimonial. In some cases the report of a psychiatrist is deemed desirable. After a further period of indeterminate length which may run into years the decision of the Roman office will be conveyed to the bishop who will convey it to the applicant. It is perhaps true to add that the length of the delay will be in inverse ratio to the age of the applicant.

The applicant might conceivably submit to this protracted humiliation for his own good reasons, either to remain within his own ecclesiastical system or to enter into a marriage blessed by his church. But it is only too clear that the likelihood of many applying for a dispensation from the celibacy clause is greatly diminished by the fact that, once the application has been filed, the petitioner can have no idea in advance how long he will have to wait for an answer. He can only be sure of one thing, that the chances of a favorable outcome are slim indeed unless, apparently, he happens to live in Holland. In fact, relatively few do apply and fewer still wait out the long period until the verdict arrives.

Under these circumstances it would be true to say that the present discipline, confirmed in the encyclical, is an open invitation to anyone in this dilemma to find the shortest way out rather than going through "official channels." The state of confusion which can result can easily be imagined. Some will simply not feel able to leave the Roman Catholic church in which they have spent all or a great part of their lives and expended their energies. It has become so much a part of themselves that to cut themselves off would mean a deep psychological and spiritual mutilation. What can they do? One reaction might be to remind them that they should not have put themselves in this situation in the first place. This is, by and large, the attitude embodied in the encyclical. But a genuinely Christian attitude surely implies that we take people as they are, not as we think they should be or as they might have been had circumstances been different.

With the possible exception of the treatment of marriage cases, we have here the clearest symptom of structures and procedures which embody fear rather than love and which, despite the rhetoric of official pronouncements, are basically unchristian in sensitivity and orientation. The fundamental issue is, of course, freedom. The *Declaration on Religious Freedom* of Vatican II was certainly a welcome step forward, yet it would not be cynical to add that it concerned matters which are by now effectively beyond the control of the church. Dispositions within the church are another matter. We can only hope that we will not have to wait too long for the same principles to be applied in the latter as in the former case.

All the indications are that discussion will continue despite the appearance of this document. There is by now a wide consensus that we need a much simpler form of honorable discharge from the ministry for those who no longer feel able to continue in it. This should be treated at the local level rather than impersonally by a panel of clerics in Rome. It should be possible for one who leaves the practice of the ministry to continue as a layman within his own communion with all the rights of a layman including the right to marry if he chooses to do so. Would it also be too much to expect that the experience and talents of this growing number could be put to use for the benefit of the local church? We have only to mention this possibiilty to realize that it is unlikely to happen without a radical and therefore painful rethinking of the problem of which mandatory clerical celibacy is only a symptom. In the following chapters I want to indicate some of the issues at stake and suggest some lines along which I believe this rethinking ought to proceed.

3. A Place for the Erotic?

I

I have taken the line in the previous chapters that the celibacy issue is important not just in itself, in the effect it has on individual lives and the life and ministry of the church, but as a symptom of a deeper malaise. I know there is a growing weariness with the proliferation of writing on Christian sexual attitudes and the many attempts which have been made and continue to be made to update our theology of marriage. What follows is not a biblical theology of marriage. It is an attempt to fill in what appears to me a significant gap in the current debate, namely, the specifically biblical approach to sexual experience. To draw attention to some neglected aspects of this question does not imply a readiness to produce definitive answers. All I would say is that no solution will be satisfactory which does not take account of them.

To explore the possibility of a Christian theological understanding of the erotic would seem an unrewarding task. Composed as it is from end to end in an atmosphere of acute eschatological crisis and tension, the New Testament is reticent on the expansive possibilities of human life as such. According to the meager indications we have, Jesus himself was almost certainly celibate. Paul also may have been, though we have seen that this is by no means as certain as some exegetes have supposed. There is very little in the New Testament at all on the sexual, and what there is speaks more about the creative possibilities of sexual abstention than about the creative (not just procreative) possibilities of the man-woman relationship. True, as time went on, we find an increasing depth of focus on this and other aspects of bodily existence, but it did not take long for a pervasive anthropological dualism to complicate the whole process of thinking in positive terms of life in the body. The point hardly requires to be labored that these have been the terms in which, until recently, most Christian teaching on sex has been formulated. Suffice it to think of Augustine's distinction between the *ratio superior* in which, as he logically remarks, there is no sex (*ubi sexus nullus est*) and the *ratio inferior,* or Hugh of St. Victor's dichotomy between marital and carnal union, only the former of which has any real spiritual value.

It can hardly be doubted that the Christian failure to grasp this particular nettle is, for many people, the cause of the rejection of the Christian offer as a whole. Even very ordinary Christians feel this somehow, but perhaps it comes through most clearly in the reaction of the creative artist in whatever medium whose temperament makes him more sensitive to the possibilities of life in the body. One could refer at random to Joyce's *Portrait of the Artist as a Young Man* or Yeats's *Crazy Jane* cycle. In one of his letters Rilke puts the question to his correspondent (he is speaking of Christians):

> Why, I ask you, if people want to help us, we who are often so helpless, why do they leave us in the lurch at the roots of all experience? Anyone who assisted us *there* could be confident we would demand nothing more of him. For the assistance he would infuse into us would grow of itself with our life and would become greater and stronger simultaneously with it. And would never go out. Why do they not set us into our deepest mystery?[1]

Rilke, of course, wrote from outside the Christian experience, but we have no reason to suppose that dissatisfaction is confined

1. *Selected Letters of R. M. Rilke,* London and New York, 1946, p. 339.

to outsiders. Anyone who talks to people or even dips into the religious press will be aware that there is a widespread feeling abroad among Catholics that in the area of experience where they are most deeply committed as persons and at the same time most vulnerable, that of sexual relations (understood as within the totality of human relations), the church has left them in the lurch or, worse, led them into a bog. Of overwhelming importance though they are in themselves, the questions of celibacy and birth control, both covered over with a discrete silence on the council floor, are important as symptoms of the need for a radical rethinking in this area. But who will do the rethinking? It was left to an Oriental patriarch at the council to make the obvious point that it is those who, presumably, have no sexual experience who are legislating on sexual conduct for those who have. In this creative area all we can expect of church legislation is that it confirm the witness of the Spirit among those who are struggling to interpret the intractable data of experience within a Christian frame of understanding. Consequently, we should not be surprised that people are speaking out on these issues rather than waiting for some official guideline which, in fact, many of the more discerning have ceased to expect. According to the biblical tradition, to speak out is the first duty of the prophet (it is arguable that this is the primary semantic connotation of the word), but no one can speak meaningfully who does not first listen. Some of us still believe that we must listen first and foremost not to some still small voice within, not even *primarily* to ecclesiastical superiors (who in this case are for the most part either silent or ambiguous), but to the Word of God in the Scriptures. If we do this as believing members of the Christian community we may hope to contribute to the living witness of faith even if what we say is not at once endorsed by the whole church including those in authority.

Having said this, however, we return to the difficulty from which we began, that the New Testament and, in particular, the recorded sayings of Jesus are clearly inadequate as a code for sexual conduct or a basis for a positive assessment of sexual experience in general. Apart from the eunuch-saying, discussed earlier, the extant words of Jesus on this subject are confined to a critique of current Jewish casuistry on divorce. In keeping with his demand for singleness of purpose and radical obedience to the will of the Father, Jesus radicalizes the moral demands of the Torah and inexorably traces back sexual irregularity to its root in man's heart (Mt. 5, 27–28). It is hardly necessary to explain the relative silence of the tradition on sexual questions on the grounds that Jesus was "the great neutraliser of sex,"[2] much less on the basis of some fanciful reconstruction of his own psychological or sexual history. His message begins and ends with the kingdom: it is the coming of this kingdom which he proclaims when he first steps out of obscurity (Mk. 1, 15) and which he reiterates when standing before his judges a few hours before his death (Mk. 14, 62). In comparison with this everything else pales into insignificance. In virtue of this men are snatched away from their wives and families and become "eunuchs for the kingdom of heaven." Yet when Jesus rose from the dead the stars did not fall from the sky and the moon did not turn to blood. Life went on as before, and we find the same disciples who had left everything fishing quietly in the lake and going about from place to place with their wives.

As stated in an earlier chapter, it is this eschatological perspective in the gospels which we find difficult to interpret and transpose into categories meaningful for us today; and there are signs that this attempt at transposition was already well under way in the first age of the church. Eschatology as to do with the *direction* of existence, and we feel somehow that it is inadequate simply to speak in eschatological or teleological terms without at the same time allowing for an analysis of human

2. Tom F. Driver, "Sexuality and Jesus," in *New Theology No, 3*, ed. by M. E. Marty and D. G. Peerman, New York, 1965, p. 130.

(that is, bodily) existence as such. And when, as happened quite early, the primitive eschatological message was expressed in terms of anthropological dualism, what Bonhoeffer referred to as the right to bodily life was completely submerged. How is the idea of direction or purpose to be reconciled with the enjoyment of that right since, as Bonhoeffer again remarked (in the relevant chapter of his *Ethics*[3]), it is inherent in the nature of joy to be spoiled by any thought of purpose? Maybe at this stage we should turn to the Old Testament for enlightenment; not in the sense that what we find in the Old Testament is in any way normative for conduct or thinking in the area of sexual experience but insofar as it offers some kind of an analysis of experience and indicates how and at what point the divine redemptive act touches on that experience. It is hardly possible to extract from the Old Testament a treatise on the sexual; for one thing, Hebrew has no word for "sex" which would have made discussions of the kind that flourish nowadays difficult even if there had been any inclination to undertake them. But if it is impossible to elaborate a treatise or doctrine, it should at least be possible to point out some fruitful and positive approaches and at the same time dispel some common misunderstandings which have played their part in producing the impasse many feel exists today.

II

In the Wisdom writings, which are a reflection on and diagnosis of human existence, the role of the erotic is frankly accepted. This is important since in common experience diagnosis is necessary for redemption. Qoheleth enjoins on his listener to "live joyously with the wife you love," and the author of Proverbs

3. London and New York, 1963, pp. 155–166.

sees "the way of a man with a maiden" as the deepest mystery of all that he beholds. Sex is seen as a gift and procreation a task joyfully accepted. The Canticle may appear at first sight a rather embarrassing intrusion into the canon considering the surprising candor of the description of physical love which it contains. Originally composed in all probability as a song-cycle for a wedding which lasted a whole week as the Arab *wassf* still does, it is in the full sense of the term an erotic composition, but celebrates *eros* not as impersonal and predatory but as the supreme expression of mutuality—it is, in fact, in dialogue form. For the fully human love which it celebrates it claims the highest honor: "if a man offered for love all the wealth of his house it would be utterly scorned."

Both the potentiality of sex and the dangers inherent in its exercise form a basic motif of the earliest historical writings of the Old Testament, the Davidic Succession History (2 Sam. 9—1 Kings 2) in particular. Anyone reading this latter can hardly fail to be struck by the frank recognition of the role of the sexual in human behavior. Without wasting time on what is morally irrelevant—such as David being warmed in his old age by the Shunamite maiden (it was probably a way of discovering whether the old king was still potent) or Solomon's harem of spectacular size (the harem was a royal status symbol at that time)—we should note the balanced and sober appraisal of the role of *eros* in human relations. The same is true of the long patriarchal chain of sagas in Genesis. Here the writer deals plainly with the given facts of physical existence and for the most part refrains from moral judgment. He shows us these bedu sheiks as they really were, living with their full natural life undiminished by any preoccupation with "saving one's soul" or living with a part of one's mind in a future life. Their psychic energies were not siphoned off, as ours often are, by desultory reading, spectator recreations or excess cerebration. Self-transcendence was focussed on the union of the sexes, generation,

77

bringing children into the world. The most centrally important dramas of the Old Testament deal with generation, conception and birth.

There are ways other than sexual union by which man and woman can give and transcend themselves, but the Old Testament puts this full and affective self-giving sealed by matrimony squarely in the center. Sexual mutuality is *the* means of inter-personalization, an inverse proof of which can be found in the observable fact that all forms of sexual perversion, including extreme forms such as sadism, require a depersonalized milieu in which to operate. If our age is, as sometimes stated, basically antisexual it is because sex has been divorced from the context of inter-personal exchange and given a spuriously autonomous existence of its own, mainly through the exploitation of the media of communication. Attempts of the *Playboy*-type to evolve a "philosophy" of sex on this basis have helped only to emphasize the consequent inevitable trivialization. Precisely because. the Scriptures contain no kind of a "philosophy" of sex which would involve considering it as a phenomenon apart from the totality of personal relations, sexual partnership could become the image of the covenant relationship between God and his people. It is only if we place it against the background of religious thinking at that time that we can gauge the revolutionary boldness of Hosea's representation of the divine *agape* as *eros* and, moreover, in the light of the unsatisfactory experience of his own marriage. It is also important to note that in the writings of this prophet we have, for the first time, an attempt to deal with a culture which, unlike that of the Hebrews, gave a special religious significance to the sexual.

With this we come to a further point. Ancient Semitic civilizations in general thought of the sexual as somehow within the divine sphere. Hence the proliferation of creation-myths which represent the world as originating from the copulation or self-procured seed of divine beings. After the settlement in

Canaan the Hebrews came increasingly in contact with a more ancient and sophisticated Semitic culture in which the relation between sex and religion, rediscovered experimentally in our own day, was in special evidence. This contact must have posed for them the problem of whether and how the erotic was to be sacralized, and it is interesting to see how they attempted to solve this problem. The orgiastic rites practiced in Canaan evidently inspired in people who had recently graduated from a semi-nomadic way of life a mixture of revulsion and attraction. The revulsion can be documented in the legislation forbidding such things as cult-prostitution of both sexes, transvestism and the like. The attraction can be documented in the actual course of the history from which we see what little effect the legislation had. Of course, the Old Testament gives us only one side of the story. We now know that the practices condemned in the prophetic writings and the legislation had the purpose, for those who took part in them, of bringing sex within the sphere of the sacred. The fertility-drama followed a divine archetype, the cultic prostitutes mimed the part of the life-bestowing deity (they are called "holy ones" even in the Old Testament), and the whole thing had the functional concern of promoting the immanent forces of life and procreation—the fertility of the fields, cattle and women-folk on which the future of the community depended. The violent reaction on the part of the Hebrews against this way of sacralizing the erotic followed on the rejection of the idea of deity as a *Spendergott,* an immanent life-force, and of religion as having the purpose of inserting the community into the unchanging cycle of nature. According to Hebrew faith, God's action had already been experienced in a definitive way before they had entered the land. The decisive events—the call of Abraham, the giving of the law, the liberation from Egypt—took place outside the land. Hence the tension inherent in their faith between the covenant-God who had revealed himself at Sinai and the *baalim* who were in possession

79

when they arrived in Canaan. When Elijah feels the need to reaffirm his faith he makes a pilgrimage which takes him back to Sinai (Horeb) away from the land. This bears directly on how they viewed the strongly sexual orientation of Canaanite religion. The mutuality and self-giving in sexual relations were to reflect not an unchanging divine archetype but the relation of mutual self-giving established in an historical epoch between themselves as a people and their God. The sexual was therefore not allowed to become (what it can easily become) a means of what Aldous Huxley called downward self-transcendence and, ultimately, depersonalization.

In the experience of the sexual in antiquity we find a crucial case of the ambiguity which characterizes the sacred and the process of sacralization. Most ancient mythologies contain archetypes which illustrate both the creative and destructive potential of sex. The perception of the sacrality of sex arises from the fact that it is seen both as the basis of social institutional life and as potentially disruptive of the divinely authenticated social order. It is at the same time both institutionalized and outside the institution, a permanent threat to its stability. This explains the severity with which the marriage bond was protected (among the Assyrians even an unfounded allegation of infidelity was punished by flogging, forced labor and castration) and the existence of a great number of taboos concerning seminal emission, menstruation, abstention at certain prescribed times and similar matters. Sex as potentially destructive, formless, chaotic and limitless could, however, be encountered, accepted and integrated into the *equilibrium instabile* of the social order; indeed it had to be if the social order was to remain in contact with the primal energy by which it was activated. The old creation myths spoke not of a *creatio e nihilo* but of the world as formed out of chaos in a quite materialistic way. It was, in a sense, part of the constitution of the world and threatened continually to reassert itself over a precariously established cosmos. The sexual

80

imagery so often employed in creation myths expresses something analogous about the role of the sexual in society. The role of sex, even though feared because unpredictable and demonic, was always active.

From the point of view of comparative religion the most extraordinary thing about the Hebrews was that their god had no *paredros* or female consort, not at least officially, though popular religion generally insisted on providing him with one. This did not, however, imply that the sacred aspect of sex was abandoned; it was not abandoned but historicized. While the devotees of a more popular religious piety kept on setting up images of Anath or Ishtar or some other fertility-queen in the Yahwist sanctuaries—even in the Jerusalem temple—the prophets insisted that Israel alone was the consort and bride of Yahweh. While this implied that the sexual is open not just to sacralization but to redemption (which is what the history is about), it introduced a tension which is still with us, a sexual backlash which has never been absent from Christian history. Perhaps we need to stress not just the redemptive possibilities but the need to integrate *the shadow,* to actualize the potential creativity of the sexual.[4] The history of clerical celibacy illustrates, at any rate, how far we still are from an adequate understanding of the role of the sexual in Christian theology and life.

III

The story of the Man, the Woman and the Snake stands at the beginning of what is generally known as the Yahwist corpus. It is evidently offered not so much as a historical episode but a paradigm of the man-woman relationship and the dangers which

4. Perhaps the most imaginative expression of this need in modern literature can be found in the writings of Nikos Kazantzakis, especially his novel *The Last Temptation of Christ.*

beset it, and as such is a product not just of faith but of historical experience. The Man is represented as radically ordered to society, and the society of the Woman in the first place. As Plato in the *Symposium* attempted to express the origins of sexual attraction in the myth of the primitive hermaphrodite, so here the writer conveys it exquisitely in the myth of the ecstatic sleep during which the Woman is taken from somewhere near the Man's heart and presented to him as "a helper fit for him." A good example of how a polemical *eisegesis* of the Scriptures can cover over the deep and original religious sense of the text can be found in what Augustine makes of this phrase "a helper fit for him." In his *De Genesi ad litteram* he writes:

> If woman is not made for man as a help in bearing children, what sort of a help is she? If it was to work with him in tilling the land, there wasn't enough work for one let alone two! And even if he had needed help, surely a man would have been a lot better for that! The same goes for consolation when loneliness is a burden. How much more pleasant for life and conversation when two male friends [*amici*] dwell together than when man and woman dwell together![5]

There is clearly no room here for sexual relations as an expression of mutuality and tenderness. It was, moreover, Augustine's conviction, expressed elsewhere, that all sexual activity is inseparable from concupiscence (which is intrinsically sinful) and that if man had not "fallen," some way would have been found other than sexual intercourse for filling up the number of the elect.

There is, by now, no need to labor this point. The history of Christian thinking has been rehearsed and texts from Augustine quoted *in abundantiam* if not *ad nauseam*. In fact, we tend to get so snarled up on polemical issues that we easily miss the psychological depth beneath this apparently artless story on

5. *Liber VIII, 5.*

which so much has been written throughout the ages. For the post-Freudian Christian the orgiastic religion of Canaan, symbolized as it was by the Snake, would be a large-scale example of the incestuous link with the mother and therefore regressive (the Snake comes up behind his heel!). This link has to be broken before either individual or community can move forward on a line which goes, in Erich Fromm's way of putting it, from incest to freedom. The sexual drive can either lead one backwards into an existence closed in on itself, a false autonomy, or it can be the means of moving forward to a genuine liberation and a greater openness to others. What is true of the individual is true also of a particular society; and so we should have no difficulty in reading this story as a dramatic representation of the options open to Israel once it had achieved some form of self-identity in Canaan. The object of a nature-religion such as that practiced in Canaan was to insert the community into the unchanging processes of the natural cycle; it sought integration but at the lowest level. The Hebrew prophetic writer would see this as regressive in view of the call to go forward which he believed his people to have received. This explains the intransigence of the prophets against any form of symbiosis with baalism and also, incidentally, the absolute prohibition of any theriomorphic representation of the diety.

Seen in this light, the story in Genesis 3 reads as follows. The Snake represents the sum total of the possibilities open to man who chooses integration at the natural level. It is the encounter with these possibilities which threatens him at all times. The temptation to be like God knowing good and evil is, basically, to opt for autonomous, self-enclosed existence, living and dying to oneself, and to set about achieving it in the first place through the uncontrolled exercise of sexuality. On the level of personal experience this is certainly a credible explanation. I find a good example of it recorded by the psychologist Joseph Nuttin. In his book *Psychoanalysis and Personality* he writes:

To the child, sex is something inaccessible, a terrain jealously guarded by the grown-ups, *entrance into which is, moreover, forbidden by God.* . . . One patient told us that when he decided to do what was forbidden he felt so big and powerful that it was like being like God.[6]

This was the temptation, but the outcome, as is so often the case, was far different from what was imagined before the experience. The writer is at pains to show that the first thing they noticed when their eyes were opened was that they were naked. He wants to explain why nakedness, which would seem the most natural thing in the world, in fact causes shame. Shame is followed by backbreaking work, trouble with their (perhaps teenage) children, eventually a murder in the family. In one of his letters Luther takes this process of disillusionment even further and muses how Adam and Eve could have stuck it out together for nine hundred years. The central psychological fact is, however, the sense of guilt and remorse joined with the same sense of frustration and disillusionment which Gide's *Immoraliste* feels after the tragic death of Marceline. The community element, with which the writer is more concerned, is emphasized by placing the Man's action as first in an interlinked sequence of actions which progressively disrupts life in community, ending with the complete breakdown of communications in the story of the Tower of Babel.

IV

An intelligent Christian reading of the Old Testament cannot fail, therefore, to bring out the positive role of the erotic as the appropriation of the right to bodily life, the truest expression of mutuality and the image of the divine self-giving. We could add that, although the Old Testament does not have the myth

6. New York, 1962, p. 157.

of cosmogonic eros, the affirmation that man is made in the divine likeness clearly has something to do with his ability to create offspring "in his own likeness" (see Gen. 1, 26 and 5, 3). We find also the prophetic affirmation that Yahweh, not the fertility lord of Canaan, is the true giver-God. Over against the naturalistic religion of Canaan, which was prepared to sacralize homosexual practice and even bestiality, the Hebrew prophetic writings affirm, implicitly, that man is the only animal that can make a free gift of sex in order to bring into existence a mutuality which is at the root of community. We may add that we find in the Old Testament an affirmation of the humanity and creative role of woman going beyond anything which the sociological and cultural position of women at that time would appear to warrant.

It seems a pity that so little of this has gone into Christian thinking, and that where the Old Testament has been used in this area it has generally been to inhibit and deter. It is rather odd, for example, when one comes to think of it, that catechetical instruction on sexual conduct should for centuries have been subsumed under the sixth and ninth of the ten commandments. Quite apart from the fact that this leads to neglect of the specifically Christian understanding of the sexual, it does not take a very careful exegesis of the two recensions of the "ten words" which we have in the Old Testament to see that they simply will not bear the weight which has been placed on them. In the first place, the prohibition of adultery is aimed at social injustice, as can be seen in the fact that it is sandwiched between murder and stealing. Elsewhere in the Old Testament the death penalty is prescribed for both guilty parties in adultery. As in other ancient Semitic law codes, there is the death penalty also for the rape of a girl solemnly promised in marriage, but for the rape of a girl neither married nor promised in marriage there is only the penalty of having to marry the wronged party without further option. It is arguable that the *social* aspects and

85

implications of individual sexual behavior have not received sufficient emphasis in catechetical instruction among Roman Catholics. Again, the prohibition in the ninth commandment is against laying hands on the *property* of one's neighbor. It is a law aimed at protecting private property itemized as house, wife, cattle, servants. The evident divergence between this patriarchal view of matrimony and that prevailing today of marriage as a partnership will evidently raise problems in trying to give instruction on this basis. The way the law is couched may give some support to Marx's interpretation of the family as the result more of the acquisitive than of the sexual instinct. Jesus himself went behind the legislative codes and simply affirmed the sacrality of the primordial union of man and woman, appealing to the good rabbinical criterion of interpretation by which an earlier text—in this case Genesis 2, 24—prevails over a later one. Paul takes up genuine Old Testament prophetic thinking when he sees this union as the reflection of the divine covenantal self-giving and therefore as "a great mystery" (Eph. 5, 32). To our loss we have, here as elsewhere, snatched at the legal and neglected the prophetic.

Many examples could be given of a hermeneutically unacceptable use of Old Testament texts in the area of sexual teaching which, in some cases, has had almost disastrous consequences. So, for example, several scholastics have found arguments in the Old Testament in favor of clerical celibacy which no biblical scholar of repute would care to endorse today. Better known is the use made of the story of Onan, son of Judah, who avoided doing his duty as *levir* (brother-in-law) by a means which has won him a dubious fame in the textbooks of moral theology. We are told that he "did what was displeasing to the Lord" (Jerome, typically, has "he did a detestable thing"), and the whole context indicates that "what he did" refers to his refusal of social responsibility as then conceived, with special reference to the malice he evidently bore his dead brother (there is no

reason to believe that he had to remain unmarried after per-
forming this duty). Much more important has been the Christian
attitude to the homosexual. Havelock Ellis charged the church
with responsibility for the savage repressive measures taken
against the homosexual, and it is at least true that policies
pursued in this matter by Christian legislatures have been determined with reference to certain well-known biblical texts.
The death penalty for homosexual practice, abolished as recently
as 1861 in England, passed into European civil codes from that
of Justinian (who believed that homosexuality was the cause of
earthquakes) and was imposed with the Old Testament death
penalty in mind. It seems that this latter aimed above all at cultic
male prostitutes of the type found in Canaan who, as the history
attests, featured intermittently in Hebrew religious practice down
to shortly before the Exile. And we shall recall finally (what is
by now well known) that the men of Sodom were punished
not just for their addiction to unnatural vice but for their flagrant
breach of the sacred and time-honored rule of hospitality. This
stands out even more clearly in the very similar incident in-
volving the men of Gibeah recorded in Judges 19, 12–26.

Perhaps no one has stated the main criticism of the "standard"
Christian teaching on the erotic more succinctly and pointedly
than the non-Christian Dr. Alex Comfort. In his *Sex and Society*
he writes:

> The traditional view of Christian civilizations has been that all
> forms of sexual activity are by nature suspect, and that only those
> that make up a bare minimum, necessary for the purposes of re-
> production, are permissible.[7]

It is hardly any use arguing that this is not the scriptual and
therefore cannot be the Christian attitude to sexual experience.
The fact is that due to historical influences of the kind that lie

7. London, 1963, 2nd ed., p. 17.

87

behind some aspects of Augustine's teaching, together with mis-representations of scriptual data of the kind illustrated above, the whole emphasis has been changed. On the subject of scrip-tural interpretation we should mention the influence of the Vulgate on the formation of thinking in the Western church. Until quite recently this was the only version, either in the original or translation, to which Roman Catholics had free access. As all know, the Vulgate translation was the *chef d'oeuvre* of Jerome, a great man in many ways but a man whose attitude to women and sexual matters in general was demon-strably pathological. Catholics now accept his translation of Judith, for example, as canonical scripture, but it appears that Jerome did not. In fact, he tells us that he lost little time trans-lating it, dedicating to the job "just a little head-scratching." The tenth chapter of this book describes the heroine's seduction of Holophernes. Anyone acquainted with Jerome's views on female adornment will not be surprised to learn that he introduced into this passage some modifications of his own. The best Greek ver-sions tell us that she bathed, perfumed herself, had herself a hair-set, wrapped a turban round her head (the Douai version has "a bonnet") and put on her best jewelry; "she made herself as beautiful as possible in order to capture the looks of the men who should see her." In place of this last phrase Jerome has: "the Lord also gave her more beauty because all this dressing up did not proceed from sensuality but from virtue."

This is censuring on a small scale, as is that in Esther when she set out to win the heart of Xerxes, but symptomatic nonethe-less. The case is different with Tobit. The hero of this pious tale, it will be remembered, was due to marry Sarah, but it transpired that seven former prospective husbands had met a mysterious death in the bridal chamber before being able to consummate the union. Tobias was, therefore, naturally somewhat appre-hensive, but by following the rather odd prescriptions of his travelling companion he succeeded where the others had failed.

The most important item of advice was to rise from the marriage bed and pray with her before consummating the union. This he does in the Greek text and both live happily ever after. When, however, we turn to the Vulgate, we are surprised to find the advice considerably amplified. Raphael says:

> For they who in such manner receive matrimony so as to shut out God from themselves and their mind and give themselves up to their lust as the horse and the mule which have not understanding—over these the demon has power. But when you shall take her, go into your room and for three days keep yourself continent from her and give yourself to nothing else but prayers with her . . . and when the third night is past you shall take the virgin with the fear of the Lord, moved rather by love of children than by lust.

We should accept frankly, in the first place, that there is in the sexual drive and the orgasm which is at the center of sexual union a demonic element which we cannot and must not leave out of account in our moral assessment of sexual relations. It is part of an ancient wisdom to accept this and do nothing to belittle it. The Old Testament certainly shares this view, at least implicitly, in setting up around sexual matters a strong fence of protective legislation into which even more ancient taboos have been assimilated. The author of Proverbs asks:

> Can a man carry fire in his bosom
> And his clothes not be burned?
> Or can one walk upon hot coals
> And his feet not be scorched? (6, 27–28)

At the same time, Jerome's view seems to lead to a complete disjunction between procreation and lust with no room for any kind of positive evaluation of sexual experience in general apart from a specific understanding of marriage. This is consonant with what we find elsewhere in his writings as, for example, that the only good thing that can be said of marriage is that it produces virgins. The influence of this way of thinking was not restricted to those curious exorcisms of the bridal bed and bridal chamber in the Middle Ages; it has played a role in ways more or less indirect and subtle in the formation of attitudes. Some of these we are just beginning to overcome.

V

For all its priests, wise men and prophets, the Old Testament world is often violent, tumultuous and brutal. But the sacrality of the center of man's affective life, his bodily existence, is always affirmed and its primacy jealously guarded. To contemplate this is already in itself a kind of release for us in the Western Christian tradition who have inherited such a heavy load of emotional sexual guilt. It is true that what is central for the Christian is the divine *agape* experienced in the depths of his being. It is also true that the Christian pattern of life through death means that friendship with God comes only through the fire of judgment on the old self. What, however, we have to believe at this juncture is that *eros* is not thereby relegated to the periphery but that rather it too is open to redemption within the totality of man's being.

4. Congregation and Ministry in the Old Testament

I

In view of the fact that the Old Testament, usually in the manageable form of selected proof-texts, has had such an important part in theological discussion and assertion on the nature of the church and its ministry, it is surprising that we have had to wait so long for any attention to be focussed on the hermeneutical problem involved in this whole process. The Christian use of the Old Testament has raised acute problems right from the very earliest days. During the ages of faith down to the time of the Enlightenment it was thought legitimate to detach Old Testament texts or passages from the historical situation in which they are rooted, and regard them as Word of God of independent and autonomous value as such. This has had an almost incalculable effect on Christian thinking in many crucial areas; one example was given in the last chapter but we might also think of the justification of wars of extermination and crusades with reference to the holy war of ancient Israel or the insistence on laws of ritual purity with reference to certain aspects of Jewish practice. Not only was there no awareness of the historical reality of Israel but, more important and fatal still, there was no firm basis for evaluating the Old Testament in its relation to the New.

With regard to the subject under discussion here, these drawbacks are very obvious to the modern theologian who reads through the endless polemical literature of the Reformation and Counter-Reformation periods to do with priesthood, ministry, clerical celibacy and the like. As is well known, the standard Roman Catholic dogmatic and catechetical approach has stood until recently in direct relationship to the polemically orientated exposition of the Counter-Reformation period as it is found, for example, in Melchior Cano's *De locis theologicis.* This is being rapidly superseded but we still do not know what to do with the Old Testament. We know that Christian faith does not *need* the Old Testament but we also know that the Old Testament cannot be dispensed with, as Marcion discovered in the second century. We are aware that the allegorical approach, so much favored by the Alexandrian school and church writers down to the Enlightenment and often heard from pulpits down to our own day, does not provide a satisfactory answer. Apart from the fact that this was not a biblical or Christian approach, it did not provide a way of elucidating the primary meaning of biblical passages and could easily degenerate into an exploitation of the Scriptures without any sort of criterion apart from the purely subjective insights of whoever used it. Also, by speaking predominantly of heavenly correspondents to earthly realities (in the manner of Plato's world of *ideas*), it drew the attention away from the concrete reality of the history of Israel and the promise which it contains.

Even if we supposed that theologically the Old Testament was unrelated to the New we could at least accept it as having a highly relevant *exemplary* value. Here we have a well-documented period of over twelve hundred years in the course of which a community came into existence as a federation of tribes, passed to a monarchy, lost its national identity and was reconstituted on a theocratic model by favor of or in spite of the great powers which succeeded each other in the primacy of power in the Near East between the sixth and first centuries before Christ.

We have ample opportunity of studying here, for example, how the function of prophet or priest is, in the course of time, subject to the process which Max Weber called routinization, the sociological aspects of a religious community in the process of formation, the reaction to prophetic preaching of different social classes in the community, the emergence of élites, especially a priestly élite, the growth and organization of denominations within the community, and so on. This kind of study, purely detached from any hermeneutical preoccupation, can hardly fail to be of value for understanding the same processes at work within the two thousand years of Christian history. For example, the gradual emergence of a Christian priestly élite with a well-defined class- or caste-consciousness and equally well-defined qualifications for entrance into it is parallel in more than one way with the same process at work in the post-exilic Jewish community.

But of course the Christian theologian can hardly be satisfied with such a detached attitude to the Old Testament. It is not just that the New Testament cannot be understood without the Old (think, for example, of Jesus as the Servant and the Son of man, or the word *"ekklesia"* which is the translation of an Old Testament word); the fact that the Christ-event is represented as the fulfillment of the promise which the Old Testament history contains make it imperative to think of an immanent relationship. The unique element in Israel was not just the decisively historical orientation of its thinking, as opposed to the mythological cyclic pattern found, for example, in Canaan. In addition we have to see this history as determined in its course by a divine promise arising out of a radical commitment of God to a particular community.[1] We are, of course, unable to verify

1. In keeping with this is the remarkable fact that in the earliest stages the deity is associated not with a locality, as was then common, but with a social group. See Albrecht Alt's well-known essay, "The God of the Fathers," in *Essays on Old Testament History and Religion,* London and New York, 1966, pp. 1–77.

this by the application of historical method; what we have before us in reading the Old Testament is the result of a prophetic insight into and interpretation of the apparently fortuitous succession of events. In the light of this postulate of a divine promise, prophetic thinking challenges the world to render a meaning and significance, and this challenge is addressed in the first place to the world of experience, the experience of men in society. According to the New Testament witness this promise has received its final and definitive fulfillment in Jesus Christ— "all the promises of God find their Yes in him" (2 Cor. 1, 20). In this sense the Christ-event witnessed by the early community and celebrated in its worship is the goal (*telos*) of Old Testament history.

Once we have stated this, however, we detect an ambiguity in speaking of Christ as the fulfillment of the Old Testament. We might, for example, be tempted to think of Old Testament history as following an ascending line which reaches its apex in Christ and is thereby fulfilled. This would certainly be incorrect since Old Testament history is made up in great part of a confession of failure and, in any case, no such linear movement is detectable. The fact is that Christ is not only the goal (*telos*) but the end or supersession (*eschaton*) of the Old Testament history. The promise is fulfilled not within a rectilinear historical continuum beginning with the establishment of Israel and ending with Christ but rather in the form of a final judgment passed upon Israel and its history. Take the crucial point of the relation of the Christian community to the historical Israel. The apostolic community speaks of itself as "Israel,"[2] yet this term refers not to a historical continuity of the Israel of history (which Paul designates as "Israel according to the flesh," 1 Cor. 10, 18), but to an eschatological reality established in the death and resurrection of Christ. The old covenant which dominated

2. Galatians 6, 15; Philippians 3, 3; Romans 9, 6 ff.; James 1, 1. See other terms such as "the people of the covenant," "the people of God," "the elect."

the existence of the historical Israel had been irretrievably broken, the historical kingship had been swept away, the old criteria for membership in the People of God—especially circumcision—had been abrogated; in short, the historical Israel had been superseded.[3] In this sense fulfillment includes supersession; and the relation of Israel as an ethnic or socio-political entity to the divine purpose in history has been dramatically altered.[4] This in its turn implies that judgment has been passed on the whole religious and cultic life and activity of Israel and that we simply cannot think of Christian religious institutions and functions as continuing those of the Old Testament. We could make this clearer for ourselves by looking at the way the author of the Epistle to the Hebrews understands Christ as high priest. As we shall see more at length later on, Jesus is not only typified by the high priest of the old order, especially in the celebration of the great Day of Expiation, but he supersedes both him and the whole cultic world which he represents and in virtue of which his office exists. In a similar way, the representation of Jesus as epitomizing the function of prophet throughout Israel's history (see Acts 7, 37) means that prophecy of the old order is superseded. This does not mean that either the prophetic or priestly element is to be absent from Christianity. What it does imply at the least is that both have been radicalized in Christ and that we cannot, for example, simply suppose, with Peter Lombard, that there exists an unbroken link between the Aaronic priesthood of the Old Testament and Christian priests.[5]

In this question much confusion has arisen through failure to define satisfactorily and distinguish between what used to be referred to in the time of both Catholic and Protestant orthodoxy

---

3. Some of these points are developed by R. Bultmann in his essay "Prophecy and Fulfilment" (in *Essays on Old Testament Interpretation*, ed. by Claus Westermann, London and New York, 1963, pp. 50 ff.), though he leads to conclusions which I would be unable to accept.

4. See Romans 9–11.

5. *Sent.* IV, d. 24, 9.

as the senses of Scripture. In the last two or three decades we have seen a renewed interest among Protestant biblical scholars and theologians in the possibility of a typological approach to the Old Testament.[6] This possibility is based on the premise that the whole of the history is a divine history, a history, that is, which is brought into existence and guided by the divine Word. This idea of God actuating human history is very difficult to grasp since we conceive of God as beyond history, and think of our history, the history of "the vehement, visible earth," as immediately present to God at every moment of its unfolding sequence. Yet it is beyond question that we find this typological approach within the Old Testament itself. A centrally important example is that of the Exodus. The Exodus was an event which happened at one precise moment of the history of the world and will never happen again. Yet continued reflection upon this event within the Hebrew community bestowed upon it a paradigmatic value, and so we find the anonymous prophet of the exilic period speaking of the return of his people to their land as a new exodus, and in the New Testament the redemptive death of Jesus is also described as an exodus (Lk. 9, 31). Since the Christ-event is conceived in the New Testament as the goal of Israel's history—and indeed of all history—it was natural that foreshadowings of the final all-consummating event should have been found in the Scriptures which the early Christians recognized as their own. The God who raised Jesus from the dead is the God of Abraham, Isaac and Jacob (Acts 3, 13), the God who has spoken to us in these last days by the Son is the God who of old spoke through the prophets (Heb. 1, 1). Since the goal of all the divine activity is the redemptive act in Christ, the end is somehow present at every moment of the history; hence the legitimacy of scrutinizing the history for correspondences in the

6. See especially the essay of G. von Rad, pp. 17 ff. of the collection mentioned above (n. 3).

events and the words which record them to the final event, the last word spoken which is the Word Incarnate.

For our present purpose we have to note that typological correspondences could also be found in the religious institutions of Israel and the various offices which went with them. So, for example, the passover animal could be a type of Jesus at the moment of his death (Jn. 19, 36) and the high priest entering the inner sanctuary once a year a type of Jesus entering once for all into the presence of the Father (Heb. 9, 6–12). But this kind of correspondence was possible only because of the radical discontinuity between the old and the new; and *new* here means *final* in the sense that only what is final is of ultimate significance. In the final event of Christ is contained and revealed the ultimate meaning which gives to everything which had happened before its real significance, namely, the significance it was meant to possess in virtue of the end or goal. From the Christian viewpoint, therefore, to consider anything in the Old Testament without reference to this final point of determination is necessarily to misunderstand it.

The hermeneutical problem which the Old Testament presents to the Christian reader has first to be stated in order to avoid the kind of misunderstanding which has plagued discussion of Christian ministry all along. Having made this point, we can pass on to a study of one or two aspects of ministry in the Old Testament which are, in my view, of particular relevance today.

II

One point which we must get clear at the start is that we are talking about different ministries, prophecy and priesthood in particular, within a definite community. These ministries must therefore be defined in function of the kind of community which they serve. This means that we can dispense with general meanings and definitions within the wider context of the history of religions as, for example, the origins of priesthood and its sociological and anthropological aspects. It also implies that we should first look more closely at the community or community-ideal in function of which the offices or ministries existed.

If we define Israel historically as the federation of the twelve tribes we must conclude that it first came into existence in Canaan, on the soil of Palestine. We have to remember that the historical consciousness of later Israelites projected back into the distant past their own view of themselves as a community united in worship and in the observance of a common norm of life laid down in the covenant-law repeatedly recited and accepted in their assemblies. The early traditions of Israel are, we can say, a precipitate of the faith of a worshiping and believing community throughout many centuries of its history, and we can detect in the way these traditions have come to us evidence of how later Israel thought of itself. The tribal federation or amphictyony[7] remained as a sociologically identifiable reality for about two centuries down to the monarchy. With the monarchy there came a crisis, since an hereditary insitution seemed to cut across the old charismatic principle and the question arose for many whether Israel could maintain its traditional identity. Charismatic appointment seems to have continued in the northern kingdom down to the time of Omri but threatened political chaos; in the south the introduction of the dynastic principle with David could come about only as the result of a great deal of theological rationalization and re-interpretation of the ancient traditions. It was, however, successful and gave a de-

7. This term is used by Martin Noth, followed by many others, by analogy with the early Greek and Roman amphictyonies, but we should note that an amphictyony is strictly a federation of cities not tribes. The term could therefore more appropriately be used of the Philistines or Gibeonites (Jos. 9, 17) than of the Israelites.

cisive orientation to the writing of a national history which, we have to remember, comes to us predominantly from Judahite and Jerusalemite sources. With Deuteronomy, usually associated with the reform of Josiah, we have a perhaps utopian attempt to re-assert the ancient traditional pattern. During the Exile the prophetic idea of the *remnant,* those who overcame the crisis of identity and the temptation of idolatry, determined the meaning given to "Israel." In the post-exile community the priestly and scribal voice articulates the self-consciousness of a community set apart from the world, living by the written word of the covenant-law as a gift made exclusively to Israel.

Throughout this long history "Israel" always remains, ideally, the same reality; but it is not difficult to see how, with the passing of time, the emphasis changes. This is most clearly the case with the community-concept presupposed in the Priestly writings. Here we have the tendency of an élite, set aside both by its intellectual status and sacral character, to identify itself with the community-ideal as a whole or, alternatively, to set itself apart from and above the community. We find a tendency to determine membership of the community by criteria of law-observance, especially the observance of the ritual law, and we begin to find phrases such as "the community *and* the priests." One consequence of this can be found in the terminology employed in the Qumran writings where the laity is simply designated as "Israel."

This tension throughout the history between an ideal Israel and the molding of the actual community by historical circumstances and different—and often conflicting—views about community-structures and community-life is of great importance, the more so that it is often neglected in the kind of discussion in which we are engaged. Basically, Israel's existence is determined antecedently by the divine election. In the scene of the burning bush Yahweh says to Moses: "I have seen the misery of my people" (Ex. 3, 7)—and as yet there was no people! This means that the source of its existence lies beyond herself, in the antecedent decision of God in favor of *this* community. As the Deuteronomic preacher put it: "It was not because you were more in number than any other people that the Lord set his love upon you and chose you, for you were the fewest of all peoples. But it is because the Lord loves you that he brought you out with a mighty hand" (Deut. 7, 7–8). Israel is not only determined by this antecedent event; we can say that at every point of its existence in history it is not so much an institution as an event. This could give us an important clue towards a better understanding of the church. The word *"ekklesia"* used in the New Testament is the Septuagint translation-word for the *qahal,* the assembly, used in those texts which speak of the community gathered together for worship—particularly in Deuteronomy. In both Greek and Hebrew the noun has a strong verbal and therefore temporal sense. It refers as much to the coming together as to the entity which results from this.[8] We can view it not so much as a static institutional entity but rather as a continual re-actualization of the antecedent divine event of election. In keeping with this, the gathered assembly celebrates and makes present the event which constitutes it as a community—whether we are speaking of the covenant-celebration of the Old Testament or the new covenant of the eucharist. Hence the *ekklesia* is, in the first place, the eucharistic assembly wherever it happens to come together (see Paul's use of the term precisely in this sense in 1 Corinthians 11, 18).

One important conclusion suggested by this analogy between *ekklesia* of the Old and New Testaments is that the Christian church, like Israel, must always be prepared to be destroyed and remade by God's Word. It never stands in its own right as a

8. See Deuteronomy 4, 10; 31, 12. 28 where the verb "gather together" (*ekklēsiasomai*) is used; the phrase "the day of the assembly" (e.g., Deut. 9, 10, LXX: *hēmera ekklēsias*) and 1 Corinthians 11, 18, "when you come together as a church" where, however, another word is used.

self-authenticating and self-perpetuating institution. It would be safe to say that until recently Roman Catholic ecclesiology, which was essentially a rationale of the Roman Catholic church's understanding of its current structures, made it impossible for us to see the church as standing under the judgment of God's Word. In the Old Testament there are many successive interpretations of what "Israel" really means. At each stage there were strong and articulate elements in the community which wanted to absolutize the current situation and confer definitive legitimization on those who held office and exercised power within it. The prophetic voice at each stage protests against this and recalls that the source of the community's life lies beyond the community itself. It puts continual pressure on the community to remain open to a future which it does not create for itself but which belongs to God, a future in which it may even be called upon to disappear—as in fact was the case at the Exile. The relative absence of this kind of prophetic witness after the Exile must surely be seen as an important factor in the evolution towards a highly institutionalized state-church against which the hasidic movements of the second century B.C. and Jesus himself protested by dissociating themselves from it.[9]

In the inter-testamentary literature and the New Testament the question as to the identity of the true Israel is central. We find here several groups representing themselves as the true embodi-

9. The way in which the Qumran "schismatics" (this term is used by G. Vermes, *The Dead Sea Scrolls in English,* London and New York, 1962, p. 16) dissociated themselves from what they regarded, with some justification, as a corrupt institutional set-up is instructive. They would have no contact with the temple clergy, not directly at any rate, and took no part in the organized liturgical life of normative Judaism. To judge by criteria found in later rabbinical writings they would certainly have been regarded as heretics but it is difficult to say whether such clear-cut norms were followed during the life-span of the sect. But they dissociated themselves only in order to be able to fulfill the ideals and commitments of the convenant-people in a way which they evidently believed to be the only one open to them, and they did it while reproducing on a smaller scale the organizational life of the historical Israel. There may be a useful if partial analogy here with what happened at the Reformation.

ment of the covenant made long ago by God with a people, the *remnant* spoken of by the prophets, the community through and in which God would establish his kingdom in the latter days. Even though it did not take place all at once, the rejection of the state-church of Israel by the early Christian community shows that it identified itself as the focal point of the new and eschatological covenant, at which point the whole human race responds inchoately to the will of God manifested in Christ. In keeping with this, *the church is nothing else than the world responding*. Ethnic, political, social and cultic barriers are thus broken down. There is neither Jew nor Hellene, slave nor free, male nor female (Gal. 3, 28), no more circumcision (Gal. 5, 6), no more pride in ethnic descent (Gal. 3, 7)—only a new creation. The former requirements for entry into the assembly are abrogated as are the ritual laws of pure and impure.[10] The church, then, is not a new institution, a new state-church or whatever; it is the mediation into the world of the new covenant and promise, new (in the sense of final and decisive) at whatever point it touches on man's historical experience whether in the first or the twenty-first century. Only when we have grasped this can we go on to speak of how this is to be embodied in structures, ministeral functions and the rest.

III

Israel entered history as the result of a decisive breakaway from established political and sociological patterns and this breakaway came about under the impact of a revolutionary new faith or, more exactly, of an old faith newly interpreted.[11] Though in the Old Testament as elsewhere the deity is often simply a col-

10. See Deuteronomy 23, 1–8 and cf. Isaiah 56, 3–5; Acts 8, 27 ff.
11. Most scholars would now admit that Yahwism was pre-Mosaic but achieved a new significance when taken over by Israel.

lective representation of a projection of values cherished by the society with which it is associated, Israel appears to have had a unique conception of a historical destiny deriving from a source which cannot be explained purely in terms of the society's own will-to-survive or will-to-power. Following on this we find that though Israel had much in common with other social groups in its organizational life and evolution, there is always strong pressure against absolutizing any hierarchical or governmental structure within the community. Unlike the Egyptian monarchy, which reflected the eternally hierarchized order of a divine world, Israel was always prey to a future into which its god inexorably summoned it. This summons into an unpredictable future communicated through prophetic preaching meant that Israel could never absolutize its own self-consciousness or embody that self-consciousness in a permanent hierarchical structure.

Characteristic of all the organizational life of Israel is what Max Weber called *charisma*. In the founding period the basic *charisma* was that of Moses since he was closest to that source from which Israel recognized her existence as a society to spring. Yahweh had spoken to him "clearly and not in dark speech" (Num. 12, 8). Every revolution begins in the charismatic impulse of some inspired individual and usually has no difficulty in organizing itself in the earliest period during the lifetime of the revolutionary leader. The trouble begins only when it becomes necessary, as it does sooner or later, both to subdelegate and to transmit this original, self-authenticating authority. In the Old Testament traditions dealing with the earliest period of Israelite history both subdelegation and succession in office are described as charismatically brought about. Moses had the same problem as every other revolutionary leader of not allowing the primary impulse generated by the revolutionary idea to be swamped or tamed by a bureaucratic organization using it for its own ends, especially to justify its own self-perpetuation. He complained that he was not able to carry the burden of the people alone:

103

Why have you dealt ill with your servant . . . that you lay the burden of all this people upon me? Did I conceive all this people? Did I bring them forth that you should say to me, "Carry them in your bosom as a nurse carries the suckling child"? (Num. 11, 11)

What follows is clearly the result of a prophetic re-interpretation of Israel's past. Seventy "elders" are chosen and placed around the Tent and Yahweh "took some of the spirit that was upon him [Moses] and put it upon the seventy elders; and when the spirit rested upon them they prophesied" (Num. 11, 25). We may note that in a parallel account of the same incident the people choose their leaders and Moses "ordains" them (Deut. 1, 13 ff.), which is not without relevance for the appointment of leaders in the church. The "prophesying" simply means that they gave evidence in some perceptible way of being spirit-possessed and that therefore the transference had really taken place. Then, as often, an unpredictable element intrudes. Two men who had not been officially "ordained" give evidence of being spirit-possessed and Joshua, speaking for all institutions which fight shy of the unpredictable, asks that they be suppressed. Moses answers: "Are you jealous for my sake? Would that all the Lord's people were prophets that the Lord would put his spirit upon them!" (Num. 11, 29).

In another passage, also from an early source, we find Moses advised by his father-in-law on how to apply the principle of subsidiarity. He himself is the mediator of the divine purpose (read: the revolutionary idea) and the source of that impulse which is to extend horizontally as long as the community exists and vertically down through all the ranks; "you shall represent the people before God and bring their cases to him" (Ex. 18, 19). He must himself choose leaders who can instil his own spirit and fervor into the community organized in groups (cells) of ten which fit into a larger framework of hundreds and

104

thousands.[12] These lay leaders must be trustworthy and incorruptible, filled with the spirit of the leader and capable of transmitting it to the group confided to them. In this way it was hoped that the original impetus which brought the community into existence could not only be transmitted to every single member but also survive the dangers inherent in any form of institutionalization.

We hinted a moment ago that the big test of a revolutionary movement comes in the generation after the founder's death or, perhaps more exactly, in the few years immediately after the revolution achieves its first objective. This is well illustrated by the history of the two most important revolutions of modern times. Everyone knows what happened between the death of Danton and the crowning of Napoleon and between the death of Lenin and the emergence of Stalin as undisputed autocrat in Russia. Though remote in time the analogy is nonetheless significant. Our earliest sources insist that succession to office must be charismatic, not automatic. The essential paradigm would perhaps be the succession of Elisha to the prophetic office of Elijah by the conferring of a double share of his spirit (2 Kgs. 2, 9–10). Hence the unmitigated opposition of the prophets both to an hereditary and dynastic monarchy and to the priestly dynasties at the local shrines and later in Jeruslem. This way of thinking has certainly gone into the account of how Joshua succeeded Moses. Moses laid his hands on his head in a gesture symbolic of the transference of the spirit (Deut. 34, 9), but this does not imply a quasi-magical idea of office of the kind which often lies behind the way some ecclesiastics speak of the "grace of state." It remains for Joshua to show forth in his own ministry, which is a continuation of that of Moses, that he too is "a man of the spirit" and is capable of acting with wisdom. An in-

12. Originally, this may have depended on the organization of the military levy incumbent on the tribes. The Qumran community adopted the same organization, no doubt in view of the eschatological war.

teresting parallel to this brief notice in Deuteronomy can be found in the Priestly version of the "ordination" of Joshua in Numbers 27, 15–23. Here Eleazar the priest appears side by side with Moses in an official act of cult similar to that of the ordination of the Aaronite priests (Lev. 8), and it is suggested that the presence of the high priest was necessary for valid commissioning. We shall comment later on the significant shift of emphasis implied in the phrase "Eleazar the priest and the whole congregation."

In the thinking of the Deuteronomist school the community is one indivisible unity constituted by the divine election. It is an exclusivist group insofar as definite qualifications are laid down for membership which bar *inter alios,* the illegitimate or mutilated and a variety of non-Israelite ethnic groups (Deut. 23). Different functions or offices are defined with close reference to the community-ideal which Deuteronomy contains. This is true of the monarchy (17, 14–29), of the priest-levites (18, 1–8), prophets (18, 15–22) and those who exercise more specialized ministries such as judges and scribes. A fact which is so obvious that it might go unnoticed is the absence of any reference to the cleric-lay differentiation. We find the term "layman," in a sense analogous to that in which it is used in the churches today, for the first time in the Priestly writings. Layman here is defined in a negative sense as a non-priest, one who does not belong to a priestly family. (When one comes to think of it, it is difficult to see how "layman" could be defined in any other sense since there cannot be laymen until there are priests.) Both the Hebrew word "*zar*" and the Greek translation-word "*allogenēs*" bear this out since taken literally both mean stranger (the Revised Standard Version sometimes translates "outsider"). Here we have implied the concept of a sacred world into which only those specially qualified and commissioned may enter and from which all others are excluded.

Different examples could be given of how this differentiation works out in practice. Thus certain foods are taboo to all but priests (Ex. 29, 33) and those drawn into the sacred sphere which the priest inhabits (Lev. 22, 11 ff.). The oil used in ordination may not be poured on the bodies of "ordinary men" (Ex. 31, 32). In liturgical passages expressions such as "the community and the priests" begin to appear, signifying that the old canonical concept of one people standing foursquare before God had been deeply modified. We even find the death-penalty imposed on any layman attempting to gatecrash into a priestly family (Num. 3, 10)—a radical solution to the "problem of vocations"! In many cases the old traditions are revised and corrected to fit them into the priestly schema. Thus Aaron is in some cases put side by side with Moses in decision-making, it is often he rather than Moses who mediates between the people and God, and the mediation is carried out as much by professional techniques as by prayer and intercession. The position of the priest in the community is authenticated by what a disinterested reader could only term magical practices as, for example, the walking-stick of Aaron which, when put in the Tent, produced blossoms and ripe almonds. The ceremony of ordination (Lev. 8) is particularly instructive in this respect. The congregation (*edah*) simply looks on and approves. It is informed that "this is the thing which the Lord has commanded to be done," and there is no point of the ceremony at which it has anything more to do than acquiesce mutely in what is going on. Great attention is given to the faultless carrying out of liturgical rubrics—the smearing of blood on the tip of the right ear and the big toe of the right foot, the eating of the correct portions of the ram of ordination and the like. The ordination lasts seven days and the *ordinandi* are commanded not to leave the door of the Tent for the entire period lest they should die (v. 35). This strongly penal note runs throughout the Priestly strand, and includes summary execution for purely ritual offenses. It is in the Priestly strand that we read of those distressing cases where offenders literally drop dead. All this evidently implied a great shift of emphasis. Whereas in the early, canonical community-model the individual Israelite was really at home, here we have the phenomenon of "dubious belongingness"[13] which seems inevitably to accompany the domination in the community of a priestly class. This is not unconnected with a concept of the deity as *unpredictable*, which is precisely why priestly mediation is deemed not only appropriate but necessary. And since it is difficult to enter into covenant-relationship with an unpredictable partner, the whole basis of Israel's life before God was thereby threatened at its roots.

IV

It can be argued that priest and prophet, who stand in such strong and even violent contrast at a later stage of the development of Israel, arose from one undifferentiated function. The Hebrew word for priest, "*kohen*," is identical with the Arabic "*kahin*," meaning "soothsayer" or "seer." Once the Hebrews began to settle down in Canaan a parallel process of specialization and differentiation was inevitable and this would have been greatly forwarded by the loss of political identity on the part of the Levite tribe and their consequent specialization in priestly functions.[14] At the same time, if we compare the traditions preserved in the Old Testament about the early period of Israelite history with those of other nations we can hardly fail to be struck by their markedly unpriestly character. In the earliest traditions, dealing with the patriarchs in particular, mediation with the divine world is not, except in exceptional cases, through

13. The phrase is Talcott Parsons' in his illuminating introduction to Max Weber's *The Sociology of Religion*, London, 1965, p. xxxvii.

14. See W. Eichrodt, *Theology of the Old Testament*, London and New York, 1961, pp. 392 ff., and T. J. Meek, *Hebrew Origins*, New York, 1960, pp. 119 ff., for the origins of Hebrew priesthood.

priestly persons and techniques. In passover the formative and constitutive religious event is traditioned within the family circle without any mention of a specific religious functionary. In the covenant ceremony the whole people gathered in cultic celebration is described as "a kingdom of priests and a holy nation" (Ex. 19, 6), since it is through Israel that God has decided to draw near to the world of the nations.[15] We have seen one or two examples a while back of how later Priestly editing has attempted to align this picture with an Israel in which the priesthood had already achieved dominance, but it is not too difficult to distinguish the original image from the superimposition.

One of the theological focal points of debate at the Reformation was the relation of priest and prophet in the Old Testament. For the Reformers, and for many still today, the protest of the prophets against what one author has termed "the levitical corruption of Israel's religion"[16] was absolute and unconditional. There was no room for both—one or the other had to go. The first revelation to a prophet on Canaanite soil which has been preserved contains a condemnation of what has always been regarded as one of the least attractive characteristics of a priestly caste—venality, the "three-pronged fork system" (1 Sam. 2, 13). This is not a mere accidental side-effect since an essential characteristic of missionary and charismatic prophecy as opposed to the institutionalized office of prophet or priest is that the former is non-remunerative.[17] Samuel was brought up in the priestly milieu of the Shiloh sanctuary but after his call broke away from the priesthood which survived the destruction of the sanctuary and set out on his own course; and this may well have been a decisive point in the process of differentiation between the

15. See M. Noth, *Exodus,* London and New York, 1962, p. 157, and, for a rather different explanation, W. L. Moran, "A Kingdom of Priests," in *The Bible in Current Catholic Thought,* ed. by J. L. McKenzie, London and New York, 1962, pp. 7–20.

16. H. Schultz, *Old Testament Theology,* Edinburgh, 1892, p. 36.

17. See Max Weber, *op. cit.,* pp. 47–48.

great prophets whose sayings have survived and the organizational priesthood. The first of these prophets, we recall, was also at pains to point out that he was not a paid professional (Amos 7, 14).

Throughout the history we read all the time, at least down to the Exile, of these prophetic eruptions into a closed world of cult, sacrifice and piety, challenging the assumptions upon which the whole thing was based. Starting with Amos the impression is overwhelming. In reading their outbursts we may well ask whether they were not engaged in what one of his disciples praised Freud for doing, opposing religion in the name of ethics:

> I hate, I despise your feasts,
> I take no delight in your solemn assemblies.
> Even though you offer me burned offerings
> I will not accept them, . . .
> And the peace offerings of your fatted beasts
> I will not look upon.
> Take away from me the noise of your songs,
> To the melody of your harps I will not listen;
> But let justice roll down like waters,
> And righteousness like an ever-flowing stream. (Amos 5, 21–24)

> When you come to appear before me,
> Who requires of you this trampling of my courts?
> Bring no more vain offerings;
> Incense is an abomination to me.
> New moons and sabbath and the calling of assemblies—
> I cannot endure iniquity and solemn assembly.
> Your new moons and your appointed feasts my soul hates;
> They have become a burden to me,
> I am weary of bearing them . . .
> Wash yourselves, make yourselves clean! (Is. 1, 12–16)

God is weary; God is sick and tired of that endless charade.

It is a remarkable fact that the Priestly and scribal circles to whom we owe the final form of the Jewish scriptural canon allowed these and similarly emphatic passages to remain. No doubt, one explanation is that the predictions which Amos, Isaiah and others aimed against the cultic community were so dramatically verified. From the last two verses of Psalm 51, which were certainly added in the post-exilic period, we can see that these circles interpreted the strong anti-cultic and anti-sacrificial language which the psalm contains as being directed against a current perversion of the sacrificial system and not against the practice of sacrifice as such; and this was no doubt their view of the passages quoted above. It would be an over-simplification to think of prophet and priest in the Old Testament as absolutely antithetic. The basic factor in the antithesis is that priesthood of its nature is subject to routinization and institutionalization, to becoming a caste set apart from the community as a whole with the tendency to identify, often in an ambiguous way, the interests of the community with its own. Priesthoods also of their nature are self-perpetuating, either by being hereditary, as in the Old Testament, or by certain qualifications imposed on prospective candidates which demand total subjugation to the priestly ethos, as in Catholic Christianity.

There is no simple way of stating what happened to Israel as a covenant community once a highly organized priesthood had achieved religious and (following on this) political preponderance. We can use words such as professionalization, clericalization, routinization, specialization,[18] sacralization, but each of these will give expression to just one aspect of what was a complex process which has to be studied within an equally complex historical context. Anyone who undertakes such a study will inevitably find himself thinking of similar tendencies at work in

18. T. C. Vriezen, in his *An Outline of Old Testament Theology*, London and New York, 1958, p. 263, speaks of ministerial priesthood as "a specialisation of a function originally belonging to the faithful themselves."

111

the history of the church. In this respect the issue is sharpened by Walter Eichrodt—by no means insensible to the positive value of the priestly *Weltanshauung* in the Old Testament—who summarizes as follows:

It is also the priesthood which can provide *the most serious obstacles to the development of a healthy religious life.* A rapid florescence of the priestly class is precisely what encourages it to separate itself from the community and become a caste, thrusting itself between the secular and religious life of society, and proving instead of a mediator more of a hindrance to direct intercourse with God. The caste's lust for power makes use of its control of worship to bring the congregation into complete dependence on the priest for the satisfaction of its religious needs, and because the cultus is thus compelled to subserve the acquisition of moral and material power it deteriorates, becoming exclusively secularized and losing its religious content. Furthermore, the high value set on tradition turns to a rigid adherence to forms long superseded, stifling any new religious growth; and for this reason the influence of religion on the shaping of public life is either directed along false lines or completely neutralized.[19]

Eichrodt is not polemicizing against the character of individual bearers of the priestly office, much less hinting at a deliberate and concerted plan on the part of the priesthood to seize power. The process described in the kind of terms used above works out in a variety of ways which however converge to form a different kind of society from either early Israel or the early Christian church. So, for example, the emergence of a highly organized professional clerical class seems always to produce an overkill of religious rationalization and an all-pervasive code-morality fortified by a well-developed penal system. In this respect a comparison between the Priestly legislation in the Old Testament (especially in the area of cult and ritual) and Roman Catholic canon law would no doubt be instructive. This necessarily works

19. *Theology of the Old Testament,* Vol. I., London, 1961, p. 465.

against the freedom of the individual member's personal response to God and contributes to the condition described above as "dubious belongingness." Moreover, it excludes wherever possible anything disruptive, eccentric and spontaneous—qualities which characterize the non-professional prophet and his message. This in its turn affects the whole concept of "religious life." Mediation becomes more and more a question of technique, more and more streamlined and efficient. Eichrodt puts it as follows:

> Hard on the heels of a crippling of the element of spontaneity in religion follows the degradation of God's ordinances of grace into a mechanical system of priestly techniques; and in place of a reverent obedience—finding in cultic experience the spur to joyful self-surrender—comes the desire to activate the resources of divine power to one's own advantage, and a presumptuous confidence in one's ability to manipulate God's salvation.[20]

It will be of great advantage to the "dubiously belonging" Christian of today, especially the Roman Catholic, to take note of the Old Testament historical witness and its relevance for the interpretation of his own history. In the present chapter I have, for the most part, been looking at the Old Testament as providing a sociological and cultural context for the study of community and office or function within the community, with special reference to that of prophet and priest. Despite the fact that the Old Testament world is no longer ours and the prophets and priests of whom it speaks are dead and gone, it still retains an exemplary value which gives it relevance for our present situation. Even if the Jewish Scriptures had not been appropriated by the Christian church and thus had no intrinsic relevance for Christian experience apart from their exemplary value, the very fact that the phenomena of prophecy and priesthood have occurred in Christian history would make it worthwhile to learn from

20. *Op. cit.,* p. 434.

113

the Old Testament. But of course the church has, from the beginning, laid claim to the Jewish Scriptures and made extensive use of them in giving expression to her consciousness of her own identity and mission. This raises problems of a quite different order which we will go on to look at more closely in the next two chapters.

5. Priesthood and Prophecy
in the New Testament

I

Vatican II had much to say about priesthood, some of it very good and to the point. Within the context of updating the Roman Catholic church as it now is, the program laid out in the *Decree on Priestly Formation* looks promising: it is to be undertaken by individual countries (chapter 1), vocations to the priesthood are to be encouraged (chapter 2), studies in major seminaries are to be updated even though the standard Thomist approach is not to be jettisoned (chapters 3 and 5) and the spiritual formation of potential candidates has to be deepened (chapter 4). What is at once obvious, however, is that nothing at all is said about the basic scriptural understanding of priesthood and no question is asked about the problem of ecclesiastical structures. In other words, the decree is a liberal but not a radical document.

The contention in this chapter is that the time has now come for a radical reappraisal rather than a merely liberal updating. To the liberal Roman Catholic of the post-conciliar epoch what follows will necessarily at first seem painfully naïve. I can only ask him to bear with me at least to the end of the chapter. The distinction between the radical and the liberal in church matters is that while the latter promotes reform within existing structures the former asks questions about the structures themselves. One

115

way to do this, and by far the more common even among Catholics today, is to question the relevance of, say, priesthood or parochial and diocesan organization on sociological or cultural grounds. While this may obviously have value it is not primarily what I am concerned with here. Theologically, the weak link of Vatican II liberalism can be located in the confusion especially evident in the *Constitution on Divine Revelation* on the subject of the relation of Scripture to the life of the church. The constitution accepts the Scriptures as constitutive of the church's life. The New Testament writings came into existence within Christian communities and at the same time are normative for the church's self-understanding, but the question of how this authoritative record must affect the life of the church here and now is not answered. It would not be unfair to say that before the council official Roman Catholic theology exploited the Scriptures, especially the New Testament, with the purpose of absolutizing existing institutions and conferring definitive legitimization on the present Roman Catholic church's self-understanding. Nowhere is this more in evidence than in the scholastic treatises on the nature of the church. To say that this scriptural hermeneutic has by and large lost credibility would be putting it mildly. A more honest approach would place before the church of today a choice between two possibilities: either to say that the Scriptures of the apostolic and sub-apostolic ages are merely the record of one historically conditioned response and self-understanding with no direct authority for us today, or to detect in them a word of God addressed directly to us which places our own self-understanding as a church and our institutional life under a continually present judgment. To accept this latter, as I do here, will not imply that we take the structures and institutional life of the early church as mandatory for us living in a totally different kind of world. What it will imply is that we detect in these writings the primordial Word which summoned the church into existence in the first place, in virtue of which alone it existed then and exists now, under the judgment of which it stood then and stands now.

At this point we should recall the lesson of Israel's history discussed in the preceding chapter.

Israel is called into existence and constituted by a Word of God spoken antecedently and addressed to the historical Israel anew in each phase of its existence.

The institutional form which Israel takes at any particular time—whether it be tribal federation, monarchy or priestly and sacral community—does not contain its own immanent self-justification. The Word addressed to Israel through the prophets even calls for the destruction and disappearance of Israel as a society structured in a particular fashion in order to make way for a future which God is preparing but which is not at the time open to scrutiny.

God's covenant with his people is permanent and contains the promise of an indefectible presence within history to the end. That the institutional form in which this covenant is embodied is not and cannot be permanent and self-validating is implied, as we have seen, in the prophetic idea of *the remnant*. To speak of a *remnant* is to speak of a future in which Israel will indeed continue to exist but in a way different from the present.

The relevance of this understanding of Israel's history for the Church at this point of its existence hardly needs spelling out. No one with his eyes open can fail to see the straws in the wind which is blowing through the Roman Catholic institution at the present time. Can this vast power structure operated by a clerical élite survive? Ought it to survive? It seems obvious to me that the unique and individuating element in the Roman Catholic ecclesiastical system is clerical élitism. Official documents in which the self-understanding of the church is canonized are all redacted by clerics; most of the charismatic gifts listed in the New Testament are now subsumed in clerical orders; religious orders and congregations are almost always founded by and always directed by clerics. Ethical norms, as we have said before, are dictated by clerics even in those areas where, presumably, they have no direct experience, as in family life and sexual relations in general. And of course canon law, which covers every area of Christian life, emanates exclusively from clerical circles. It may be significant here that of 617 canons dealing with *Personae* as opposed to *Res* 574 have to do with clerics and religious and only 43 with the laity.

If this situation is granted, it seems to me urgent to examine the structures of priesthood and clericalism in the church in the light of the New Testament and guided by the kind of hermeneutical approach I have tried to outline above. The urgency of the task arises out of two considerations. The first is that until something is done about this there is no earthly hope of anything approaching union between the Roman church and the sister-churches which continue to draw their inspiration from the Reformation. In the four years which have passed since the closure of the council we have had a long ecumenical honeymoon, but even ecumenical honeymoons cannot last forever. There is now some unfinished agenda to work through. The second consideration introduces an interesting paradox. In an essay on the *Decree on Priestly Formation* Bishop Alexander Carter says very well that "to live in the world and to be an instrument there of Christ is the very nature of the priesthood."[1] A sound exegesis would suggest that this is precisely the sense in which the New Testament describes the Christian community as a royal priesthood (1 Pet. 2, 9). Yet it is precisely the historical ministerial priesthood which has made it difficult and at times impossible for the church to be a church-for-the-world. Yves Congar has put it well by saying that a clericalist religion (of the Roman Catholic kind) is a religion without a world. Why this should be, or even whether this has to be, are questions which I leave to others. For the moment, I would prefer to turn

1. In *The Documents of Vatican II*, p. 435.

to the task alluded to a moment ago and begin by looking again at what the New Testament has to say about priests and priest-hood.

II

Judaism at the time of Jesus was very much a priestly society. As the gospel record testifies, the high priest had enormous influence. The ordinary priesthood, divided into twenty-four orders, was a closely-knit organization. Though their primary function was cultic, the country priests must have had some influence on the life of the common people. According to Jeremias, they made up about one tenth of the total population of the country.[2] In view of this, it is worthy of note that Jesus has very little to say about priests and priesthood. He refers to the action of the priest of Nob in giving David the bread of the presence to eat (Mt. 12, 4), defends his violation of the sabbath on the original ground that the priests also violated it by their cultic functions performed on the sabbath (Mt. 12, 5), and sends the healed leper to the priest who was from early times the official diagnostician of leprosy (Mk. 1, 44). But these references are purely laconic and by the way, and it remains true that Jesus shows remarkably little interest in priests or the priestly in general. He never refers to himself as a priest and nowhere in the New Testament is any Christian referred to as a priest. To say that this was to avoid any confusion with Jewish priesthood is hardly an adequate explanation. The Qumran community was very careful to distinguish itself from official Judaism and yet it had priests. The plain fact is that the cleric-lay distinction simply did not exist. In the well-known Pauline lists of ministries or *charismata* (Rom. 12, 6–8; 1 Cor. 12, 8–11; 28–31; Eph. 4, 11) no priestly or cultic office features. We are told, in Acts 6, 7, that many priests

2. J. Jeremias, *Jerusalem zur Zeit Jesu,* Band II, 1, 1929, p. 60.

embraced the faith, but there is no indication that they exercised a priestly ministry after their conversion and there is no indication elsewhere of a priestly element or priestly personnel in the life of the early communities.

In the context of contemporary Judaism Christianity appears as a lay movement which had to face continual opposition from the temple priesthood during the first generation of its existence. Jesus was put to death on an alleged charge of blasphemy against the temple as was Stephen whose point of view must have been shared by very many in the early church. A comparison with the Qumran community is very instructive in this respect. This latter was composed of clergy (priests and levites) and laity (referred to simply as "Israel"). The overseer (*mebakker*) was in name and function not unlike the Christian "overseers" (*episkopoi*) whom we find referred to in Philippians 1, 1 and the pseudo-Pauline letters of the sub-apostolic period. He was the guardian of faith and his main tasks were instruction and pastoral care. He was to "love them as a father loves his children and carry them in all their distress like a shepherd his sheep." There was in addition a supreme council—a sort of *curia* —composed of three priests and either nine or twelve laymen. The decision-making appears to have been in the hands of the priests since we read that "everything is determined according to their word." The laity were, at least ideally, divided into basic cells of ten and to each cell a priest was assigned. The charismatic element, so prominent in some of the early Christian communities, was largely absent at Qumran. The modern Roman Catholic, inured to a more or less benevolent gerontocracy, will find something to applaud in their mandatory retiring age fixed at sixty since "God has ordained that their understanding should depart even before their days are complete."

One thing about the figure of Jesus in the gospels which, though prominent and obvious, is not often emphasized, is that he attacked the organized, cultic and priestly religion into which

120

he was born. A lay figure, he condemned the priestly caste—the Hasmonaean priesthood—and the particular brand of institutional religion which it represented. The purification of the temple fulfilled the prophecy of the post-exilic Malachi (3, 1 ff.), whose theme is the cleansing of the sons of Levi and the entire sacrificial system. In the eyes of the representatives of that religion he was a rebel and a heretic and he died, ostensibly, as a victim of that same priestly caste.

Seen from this point of view, Jesus continues in the tradition of the great prophets of Israel who denounced a culture-religion which acquiesced in and thereby furthered an unjust social order.[3] In different ways he is represented in the earliest tradition as a prophet. It is as a prophet with a mission that he is anointed with the Spirit and with power; he prepares for his mission by a period of indeterminate length in the desert where the prophets had always been at home. Like Amos, he comes from the desert to the apostate city to speak the word which he finds in him. Like Elijah and other prophetic figures he associates others in the charism of his vocation. The people recognize him instinctively as a prophet, the prophet from Galilee (Mt. 21, 10; Lk. 7, 16; 24, 19), and Jesus accepts this designation in the saying about a prophet dishonored in his own country (Mt. 13, 57; Mk. 6, 4). It was even thought that he was a reincarnation of one of the great prophets of old (Mt. 16, 14; Mk. 6, 15; 8, 28). According to one well-attested tradition, he is identified as the prophet promised to Moses (Acts 3, 22–23; 7, 37; Jn. 4, 19; see Deut. 18, 15–18), which implies that he was thought of as recapitulating all of the prophetic witness in the Scriptures. He also, finally, shares the fate of the prophetic protestor at the hands of a society which does not find it convenient to listen to what he has to say: "I must go on my way today and tomorrow and the day following; for it cannot be that a prophet should perish away from Jerusalem" (Lk. 13, 33).

3. See especially Amos 5, 21–24; Isaiah 1, 10–17; Jeremiah 7, 1–4.

It has been rightly said of Jesus that "he takes his images from the secular world rather than from that of the priestly ministry."[4] As we saw a moment ago, there is only one occasion when he refers clearly to contemporary cultic practice—when he sends the healed leper to the priest in order that he might be able to resume his normal place in the community (Mk. 1, 44). Beyond this, however, there is evidence of a positive desacralization in his teaching with regard to Jewish cultic practice. Laws regarding food are spiritually valueless, David is recommended for eating the sacred bread reserved to the priests, and the laws of ritual purity governing membership of the chosen people are set aside to the extent that, as he affirms, the most pariah elements in society will enter the kingdom in advance of the moral theologians of that time. It is also quite clear that he took up a critical attitude to the crucial question of sacred times and places, the first with regard to the sabbath in particular, the second to the temple than which nothing more sacred could be conceived. The temple-saying and the interpretative *pesher* attached to it in the Fourth Gospel (2, 19–22) imply that there is no longer a sacred locus apart from the risen Lord and the community attached to him in faith. It was by no means simple opportunism which led his adversaries to seize on this saying and make use of it to bring him down. Sacralization is associated at the deepest level with localization, attachment to a sacred place; hence to attack *the* sacred locus was to attack their very existence as a sacral community.

Confirmation of this basic attitude of Jesus can be found in the way cultic terminology is used throughout the New Testament. Words like *"thusia"* (sacrifice), *"leitourgia"* (liturgy) and *"latreia"* (worship) undergo a highly interesting transposition. They are taken from the static world of Jewish liturgical practice and given a new significance in the context of the Christian life

4. See G. Schrenk, *Theological Dictionary of the New Testament*, ed. by G. Kittel, Grand Rapids, 1965, Vol. III, p. 263.

as a whole and the mission to the world which is an inseparable part of it. The Christian's self-offering to God is a "spiritual worship" in which his body is presented as a "living sacrifice" —as opposed to the offerings of dead animals (Rom. 12, 1). Spreading the gospel is a "liturgy" or "priestly service" (Rom. 15, 16). Even the death of the Christian can be understood as a sacrificial libation since in death he pours out his life as a free offering to God (Phil. 2, 17; 2 Tim. 4, 6). We shall suggest later on that this gives us a valuable clue to the specifically Christian understanding of priesthood.

It may be objected at this point that all of this goes beyond the evidence, that both Jesus and his first followers continued to frequent both temple (see Mt. 5, 23) and synagogue and to worship on the great feast days of the Jewish calendar. While this is certainly the case, it is evident that for Jesus and the early Christians the old cultic order had been in principle superseded. Temple worship belongs to a past age now over and done with and the only temple now is the temple of his body which is also the Christian community (see 1 Cor. 3, 16–17; 2 Cor. 6, 16). This is particularly clear in the conversation with the Samaritan woman—whether or not Jesus actually spoke as here recorded —in which he looks forward to a time when the Father will be worshiped in spirit and truth (Jn. 23–24). His abstention from any participation in the sacrificial system sprang from a motive different from that of the Qumran community which regarded the temple priesthood as illegitimate and corrupt. God's new and final act has shown up the whole cultic approach of Judaism (and of paganism too) as inoperative and ineffectual and has thereby superseded it.

A further implication of the struggle between Jesus and the priests should be noted, namely, that it shows up his mission as one of liberation from an impossible spiritual burden and a religious routine which had become to a great extent devoid of inner meaning. What is now important is the movement of the spirit from within, not conformity to a rule from without. In incidents like the eating of the grains of wheat on the sabbath and sayings about the complicated food-laws then binding, the perceptive among his disciples began to detect a new principle in operation. The priestly and scribal theology held to a fixed sacred order which was *there,* established and imposed from above, into which each individual had to fit like a chip of marble into a mosaic. It was an established order which applied to every detail of the daily round throughout the whole of life to the grave and beyond. On the moral side, each action was isolated, absolutized and judged in the light of a legal system of amazing elaboration and complexity. The new principle, on the contrary, introduced a flexibility into human conduct and relationships. It flowed directly from the prophetic mission of Jesus, in keeping with the great prophets whose charismatic impulse gave them a deeper insight into the roots of moral conduct. It gave people room to breathe and feel their humanity.

III

If we are not to write all this off as a pretty academic exercise or vaporize it by loose and ill-defined talk about development, we will have to admit that it means something—all the more so that, as a matter of historical fact, Roman Christianity has produced a clerical and cultic set-up not unlike that against which Jesus and the early church protested. This, perhaps, is due to obscure but endemic forces at work in any kind of religiously motivated group. Thomas Trotter of Claremont School of Theology has noted that "whereas Protestantism began as an anti-clerical movement, by and large today, at least in America, it is a movement of the clergy."[5] But if the New Testament provides the

5. Quoted in *Time,* March 24, 1967, p. 76.

basic form and pattern of Christian life in common, and Christian ministry in particular, then whatever variations come into existence through the play of cultural and sociological forces must in some way conform to this basic pattern. Karl Barth takes this further in pointing out that the lists of *charismata* or ministries in the Pauline letters are already variations on a basic form and reveal in their multiplicity and essential unity the real nature of Christian ministry.[6] This will easily be understood if we regard the *charismata* as expressions of the one *charis* with which the community is endowed, and the ministries as articulations of the function of the community in its relation to the world and of its character as a caring, loving and forgiving community in its life before God. This must obviously raise some painful questions for Roman Catholics who are prepared to take an honest, critical look at the shape of ministry in their church today.

The relation of the multiplicity of ministry to the essential unity of the Christian community was a crucial question for Paul and still is for our understanding of ministry today. Paul expresses it by the metaphor, familiar in the world of his day, of the body and its members. Christians are baptized into *one* body (1 Cor. 12, 13); there is one body and one Spirit, one Lord, one faith, one baptism (Eph. 4, 4–5). The unity which sustains and gives meaning to the many diverse ministries in the community derives from a relationship to Christ the one. At this point we have to be very careful in the way we talk about this relationship. We have been too prone in the past to speak of the church as a continuation or extension of Christ, as, so to speak, taking up where Christ left off. This obviously will not do at all. The primary function of the Christian community in the world is to witness to the reality and meaning of Christ as the one through whom we have been reconciled to God and brought into a new fellowship with him. This makes it impossi-

6. *Church Dogmatics*, Vol. IV, 3, Edinburgh and New York, 1962, p. 860.

ble right away to absolutize the church or put it beyond the reach of judgment and criticism. At the same time, it provides a norm for the *ecclesia semper reformanda,* namely, the efficacy with which it is actually witnessing here and now to this enabling power and freedom which comes from the ever-present Christ. Only when we have spoken of the church's mission of witnessing should we go on to speak of it as embodying this reconciling presence and living out the reality of its witness. Among the gifts or ministries enumerated by Paul there are those, obviously the most important, which have to do with witness: wisdom, knowledge, faith, miracles, prophecy, discernment of spirits, tongues, the interpretation of tongues, teaching, the apostolate, exhortation, evangelization.[7] The others, more directly *"dia-konic,"* depend for their purpose and meaning on this witness: healing, helping, administrating, serving, almoning and pastoral care.[8] All of these do not so much *continue* the mission of Christ as *reflect* it in its essential nature since Christ is not merely, and not primarily, the one who came to minister to others but the means of our reconciliation, the one mediator between God and humanity.

At this point we have to ask what place there can be for priests and a priesthood in this "model of ministry." As we have seen, no Christian is referred to as priest in the apostolic and sub-apostolic periods. There is not even the remotest reference to anything priestly in the lists of ministries enumerated by Paul or anywhere else in the New Testament where ministry is spoken of. Jesus himself was not particularly friendly to the Jewish priesthood and priestly ideals. The story of the man who fell among thieves recorded by Luke (10, 29–37) implies not only a searching criticism of these ideals—insofar as the priest and

7. 1 Corinthians 12, 8–10. 28–30; Romans 12, 8; Ephesians 4, 11. Wisdom, knowledge and faith have to do with insight into and communication of the Christian reality. Discernment of spirits with the presence or absence of the spirit of Jesus in others (see 1 Cor. 12, 3).

8. 1 Corinthians 12, 9. 28; Romans 12, 7; Ephesians 4, 11.

levite could justify their passing by the wounded man on the ground of religious scruple—but, at a deeper level, a new idea of fellowship to which those ideals were hostile. Here and elsewhere in the gospels we perceive that a new idea of human relations is coming into existence which would dispel the dubious belongingness inseparable from the priestly ideal. There was simply no more room for it.

Having made this point with all possible clarity we can pass on to note that the New Testament witness associates priesthood with both the mission of Jesus and that of the church in its relations to the world. According to Hebrews, Christ is designated by God a high priest after the order of Melchizedek (5, 5–6; 7, 17. 21) and is the great priest over the whole household of God (10, 21). This must be understood to mean that in Christ the priesthood of the old order is not continued but radicalized and superseded. By his death the old order is destroyed. Since the new act of God has rendered the old covenant and the law that went with it obsolete (8, 13; 10, 1), the priesthood of the old order must also share the same fate. There is no more room for a routine of sacrifice and a self-perpetuating priestly office since what these were unable to achieve has now been achieved once and for all in the total self-giving of Christ's death. To perpetuate the old order in its religious institutions, with all the very concrete reassurances which they brought with them, is simply no longer to believe in Christ and the power which God has communicated through him.

When we come to think of it, the message delivered by this anonymous Christian of the early years raises a problem so embarrassing for the church-institution that it took the upheaval of the Reformation for it to be seen clearly as it is. The writer clearly does not deny that the life in common to which Christians are called requires some degree of organization and institutional life in the widest sense of that term. But to re-assert and re-establish the old order with its cultic personnel and cultic routine, to forge again the link which had been so decisively broken, is to deny the finality of what has happened. What is only a danger for the community addressed by the author of this treatise was very soon to become only too real in the history of the church. Even though the infidelity was never total, it reflected in its institutional life a growing failure of perception with regard to its own identity as a community witnessing to the finality of Christ.

If we are going to take the history of the early church seriously and accord it any importance in our thinking today about the church and its present structures, we should take note of one interesting fact, namely, that the first Christians identified themselves as the true Israel and yet rejected contemporary Israel as an institutional model. By laying claim to the promise and the covenant they took upon themselves the role of the prophetic *remnant*, by which was implied that the promise would indeed always be embodied in a community but in a way quite different from the present. When we first meet this idea of a *remnant*— as far back as the eighth century B.C.—it is already a way of leaving the future open for God, of not absolutizing any institutional form of life as a definitive embodiment of the covenanted word of God. The Qumran community also speaks of itself as the true Israel, the people of the covenant, the elect of the Lord, and yet, differently from the early Christian community, reproduces the institutional pattern and gives a preponderant role to the priesthood. Surprisingly, few have noted this fact and fewer still have attempted to explain it. I would suggest that the reason is to be sought in the difference in eschatological orientation between the two communities. For the Qumran schismatics the end-event is still in the future though imminent. For the Christians, on the other hand, the end is already present, a conviction expressed very clearly in the first recorded sermon (Acts 2, 16 ff.). The Qumran community awaited the coming of both a royal and priestly messiah; they believed that "the final leadership of the chosen of God would rest in the hands of the Priest and the Layman."[9] The Christian heretics, on the other hand, attributed to Jesus, as embodying the final, all-encompassing reality, the characteristics of both royalty and priesthood, and in so doing radicalized and *superseded* the institutions which these figures represented. This explains why the early Christian community differed basically from the Qumran sectarians in not having a clergy-laity differentiation. According to early Christian thinking, the whole community is without distinction both priestly and royal—"a royal priesthood" (1 Pet. 2, 9)—even though no individual is ever designated as priest.

Outside of Hebrews the only Christian appropriation of the priestly idea in the old order is the designation of the new Israel as a "royal priesthood" (1 Pet. 2, 9) with reference to the covenant-address at Sinai (Ex. 19, 6). On the original meaning of this expression there is a considerable literature which will not detain us here. Everything indicates that it has been taken up in the New Testament to express one aspect of the relation of the baptized community to the world. In the first epistle of Peter, which some take to be a baptismal address, the community is called a priesthood insofar as it witnesses to, mediates and embodies for the world the reality which brought it into existence ... "that you may declare the wonderful deeds of him who called you." This interpretation is confirmed by Paul's reference to "the priestly service" of proclaiming the gospel of God, "so that the offering of the Gentiles may be acceptable, sanctified by the Holy Spirit" (Rom. 15, 16). Here the idea of priesthood is stripped of all purely ritual and cultic connotations; we have to return to the basic category of *mediation* which lies behind the idea of priesthood. The Christian community as a whole has to mediate the new event of reconciliation to the world. The whole point of being a Christian rather than a Jew or a devotee of some other

9. G. Vermes, *op. cit.*, p. 49.

cult is that now one has free *access*[10] where formerly one could only approach God through religious professionals and the various techniques of mediation, placation and intercession which they deployed. As Paul put it, once again transposing the technical language of ritual and sacrifice, "you who once were far off have been *brought near* in the blood of Christ" (Eph. 2, 13). By this means, as he goes on to explain, the dividing wall has been broken down and the purpose of God to create a new humanity in the body of Christ has been revealed. As the nucleus of this new humanity, freed from the age-old religious bondage, the Christian community is a sign to the world of what it is destined to become. Herein lies its essential character as a priestly society.

I hope I have been able to convey some idea of how carefully we have to evaluate those passages in the New Testament which take up and re-interpret liturgical and cultic expressions inherited from the Jewish scriptures. We shall see some examples later on of what happens when due attention is not paid to this interpretative process and the paradoxical way in which this kind of language is used. The Revelation to John (or Apocalypse) has always been the happiest of hunting grounds for fundamentalists and literalists, as everybody knows. It was put together as an apocalyptic tract for the instruction and consolation of the churches of the Asia Minor seaboard during a time of great crisis—probably the persecution under Domitian. The seer unfolds before our eyes a heavenly liturgy at one point of which the worshipers sing a new song in praise of Christ who has created out of the raw material of unredeemed humanity "a kingdom and priests to our God" (5, 10). The meaning is that God has extended to the baptized franchise into the new Israel.

10. This term (*prosagōgē*) is also taken from cultic and sacrificial terminology found both in the Old Testament and Greek antiquity. In Romans 5, 2; Ephesians 2, 18; 3, 12, and elsewhere where the corresponding verb is used, the idea is that approach to God is now by faith rather than by cultic practices.

The baptized community can now share in the worship of God as the old Israel stood before him at Sinai. We should note that wherever the Christian community is referred to as a priesthood in this document the idea of a kingdom also occurs, which shows, of course, that here as in 1 Peter the author has in mind the covenant-text of Exodus 19, 6. It would not be illegitimate to read into this text the conviction that baptism confers a distinct authority on the individual member and that this authority is inalienable and non-transferable. If I may burden this discussion with one more philological observation, I would ask the student of the New Testament to note how this authority connotes a breaking away from the old cultic restraints enabling the Christian to approach the ultimate Mystery with confident openness. In more than one text the idea of a new *access* to God through Christ is coupled with this concept of an unlimited confidence. It is further significant that the word used to express this idea, namely, "*parresia,*" also denotes a basic freedom of man in society, either the society of the world at large or that of the Christian community.[11] Luther summed up very well the meaning behind this, to us, strange juxtaposition of priesthood and royalty in the dictum with which he began his tract on *The Freedom of a Christian:* "A Christian is a perfectly free lord of all, subject to none; a Christian is a perfectly dutiful servant of all, subject to all."[12]

IV

A liberal Roman Catholic reaction to this reading of the New Testament on the priestly element in the church would no

11. On this confident access to God see especially Ephesians 3, 12 and Hebrews 10, 19. Literally, *parresia* means free speech, the right to say everything (that needs saying).

12. See *Luther's Works,* ed. by H. J. Grimm, Vol. 31, Philadelphia, 1957, p. 344.

doubt give great importance to the priesthood of all the faithful but would hardly go far beyond this. Thus Vatican II's *Constitution on the Church* sees the Church as reflecting the triple office of Christ as priest, prophet and king (§10). The participation of the ministerial priest in this office differs "in essence, not only in degree,"[13] from that of the layman, by virtue of which "he molds and rules the priestly people by the sacred power he enjoys." Having made this perfectly plain, the document moves on to exhort the laity to a greater consciousness of their dignity as sharing in the priesthood of Christ, as members of a priestly community (§34). The supposition behind this and similar writings—such as the popular treatise on the subject by Bishop Emil-Joseph de Smedt[14]—is that the priestly mission of Christ is shared fully and primarily by the hierarchy and ministerial priests and only secondarily by the laity. In other words, the point of departure is not the Christian community as a whole but those in it who have been endowed with *power* to "mold and rule" the rest. Despite the sincere liberalism of the council fathers I would still want to ask whether this can lead to anything but a perpetuation of clericalism and élitism, quite apart from the question whether the laity will be much enlightened or heartened by this description of themselves as a priestly society.

I can only submit at this point that my own thinking about the early Christian witness leads me to ask some questions which carry beyond this liberal position. Even where no satisfactory answer can be given at the present time a question may still be asked, even if it only enables us to ask better questions in the future. Neither I nor anyone else knows what the church will

13. This phrase is, of course, meaningless as it stands. The ministerial priesthood either belongs to the same order as the priesthood of all the faithful or it does not. Other examples of this kind of hedging in the council documents could be given.

14. *The Priesthood of the Faithful,* New York, 1962.

look like a century or more from now, whether it will be recognizably the same church, whether it will still have a priesthood, whether some of the questions being asked now will have been answered. Even a superficial acquaintance with the history of theological thinking in the church counsels caution against finalizing and freezing the present situation and, in particular, the current self-understanding of the Roman Catholic church. When Luther published his *Babylonian Captivity of the Church* in 1520 he was already regarded as completely beyond the pale of orthodoxy, yet many doctrines and practices which he attacked in that tract are under attack today from responsible Roman Catholics— the current understanding of papal infallibility and transubstantiation, for example—while his protest has, in some cases, been officially ratified, as in the case of communion under both kinds. A more recent protestor also feels it necessary to go beyond a liberal reform carried out within existing structures. On the subject under discussion Charles Davis writes:

> Reform of the priesthood raises the whole question of the social structure appropriate to the Church in a secular world. What should be the shape of the ordained ministry? Is not a more diverse distribution of functions called for? Need the ministry be a permanent state of life? What is the relation of the Christian ministry to secular society and secular commitment? Why should worker-priests be exceptional? Should not the imposition of celibacy go? To answer these and other similar questions requires a rethinking of the relation of the ministry to the Christian community and of the Christian community to the secular world. These questions go deep. For that reason the Decree on the Ministry and Life of Priests, issued by the Second Vatican Council, is too platitudinous to be very helpful. It is in fact a typical example of that avoidance of the real problems by an escape into the spiritual which has been the trap for many a reform. Not an idealization of the established order, but a questioning of it will alone serve to meet the present situation.[15]

15. *A Question of Conscience,* p. 84.

For the moment I would like to dwell on some purely theological questions which underpin our present understanding of priesthood in the Catholic church, leaving practical issues to later.

The first of these questions concerns the relation between ordination and ministry. Accepted teaching demands that we read the injunction of Jesus at the Last Supper, "Do this in remembrance of me" (1 Cor. 11, 24; Lk. 22, 19), as the constitution of the Twelve in the priesthood and consequently as the ultimate authorization for a sacrificing priesthood in the Church.[16] This would seem to presume either that only the Twelve were present on this occasion—a presumption accepted without question in Christian art—or that, if others were present, the words were in any case directed exclusively to the Twelve. But our earliest sources record the intention of Jesus to celebrate a passover with his *disciples* (Mk. 14, 12; Lk. 22, 11), which implies a wider group of participants than the Twelve. This may well be confirmed by the post-resurrection story of the two disciples, not of the Twelve, who recognized Jesus in the breaking of bread, which shows at the least that Jesus was accustomed to gather for meals with the wider circle of his followers. The first Christian assembly after the Resurrection consisted of about one hundred and twenty brethren including the women (and possibly children), which would point to the same conclusion. But even if we supposed in a more or less arbitrary way that the command was addressed to the Twelve, would it not also envisage the whole community represented by the Twelve by the very fact that they *are* twelve? And are not all Christians commanded to perform this memorial by eating and drinking together "until he come"? In his own forceful way Luther complained that "they have sought by this means to set up a seed bed of implacable discord, by which clergy and laymen should be separated from

16. See Canon 2 of the twenty-second session of Trent, Denzinger, §949.

134

each other farther than heaven from earth, to the incredible injury of the grace of baptism and to the confusion of our fellowship in the gospel. Here, indeed, are the roots of that detestable tyranny of the clergy over the laity."[17] The situation has changed somewhat since Luther wrote but we still have the right to ask whether this argument can honestly be advanced by a Catholic exegete today in support of this thesis.

In no area more than ecclesiology have Scripture texts been used by Catholic theologians in an arbitrary fashion, as possessing autonomous and independent value. Thus, if we appeal to the so-called Petrine text (Mt. 16, 18–20) in support of the papal position (though even the hardiest are beginning to realize that this is not so easy), we must also refer to that later text which ascribes the binding and loosing to the whole community of the disciples (Mt. 18, 18). We may add that the explanation of "binding and loosing" in terms of the exercise of authority by an ordained rabbi may well be a false lead since we can have no assurance that the rabbinical parallels adduced are valid for the time of Jesus or even that rabbinical ordination by the *semikah* (laying on of hands) goes back that far. Further, the giving of the Spirit, in John 20, 22–23, followed by the conferring of the "power" to forgive sins also occurs in the presence of the community of the Lord's followers. Since the author of this gospel represents the Ascension and Coming of the Spirit as taking place on the same day as the Resurrection, this may well be interpreted as another version of the Christian Pentecost. Luke's concern with chronology and the calendar has clearly led him to spell out and "unpack" the one salvific event in successive phases culminating in the giving of the Spirit. The least we can ask for here is that the authorization given to certain members of the community to signify that the sinner has received God's forgiveness be viewed in the context of the entire church as a

17. *Op. cit.*, p. 112.

forgiving community. James exhorts his Christians to confess their sins to one another (5, 16), showing thereby that the community embodies Christ's own mission of forgiveness.

In his *Address to the Christian Nobility of the German Nation* Luther refers to the teaching on the indelible character of the sacrament of order as "contrived talk and human regulation" and states in *The Babylonian Captivity* that it has long since become a laughing-stock.[18] The problem of understanding this teaching is no easier today than it was four hundred years ago and yet it still remains basic to the whole Roman Catholic understanding of priesthood. If the question is asked—and it has been asked of me often over the last few years—why we need a special order of persons to preside over the eucharist, we can either speak of the practical advantages of having a full-time "president" or simply appeal to Christian history and tradition. But if we feel obliged to offer a theological answer we have to come back to this *character* which the sacrament of order confers. If, however, our questioner persists and asks us what on earth this character or indelible seal on the soul really means we may be in trouble. The word itself, first used by Augustine, does not in this context bear any of the connotations which it has for us today. Augustine used it as a loan-word from Greek, in which language it stands for an impression or stamp made upon something. A similar Greek word is used in some early Christian writings to describe baptism, following on those passages in Paul which speak of Christians as sealed by the Holy Spirit (Eph. 1, 13; 4, 30; 2 Cor. 1, 22). The difficulty comes when we transfer this idea, clearly appropriate for baptism, to the Christian ministry, with the implication that, as a result of the character of order, one is placed in a state *a quo non possit recedere*.[19] Why should we think of an authoritative delegation to ministry in the church as conferring on the person concerned a new ontological status

18. *Luther's Works* (see n. 12), Vol. 44, p. 129; Vol. 36, p. 117.
19. Thomas Aquinas, *Summa Theologiae*, III, Suppl., q. 35, a. 2.

136

quite irrespective of his own psychological disposition, his state of mind or the stage of development which he has reached? Why can we not have a temporary ministry even while admitting the obvious advantages of a full-time coordinator of activities in the local church who would also preside over the eucharist?

It seems clear to me that the principal cause for this insistence on a life-long dedication to sacred ministry is precisely that, as a result of complex cultural factors, the ministry came to be thought of as predominantly sacred. Whereas New Testament terminology for the ministry is sociological and secular we find Cyprian of Carthage speaking of it in the middle of the third century as first and foremost "a service of the altar and sacrifice."[20] This must be correlated with the increasing tendency to speak of the eucharist in terms drawn from the liturgical and sacrificial vocabulary of the Old Testament and even of pagan religions. We may note in passing that Aquinas draws his *rationale* of celibacy precisely from this source—"continence is encumbent on them [priests] in order that they, who have to do with holy things, may be pure."[21]

One interesting and significant aspect of the rationalization required to justify priestly ministry as a permanent state of life is the use of the scriptural phrase "a priest *for ever* (after the order of Melchizedek)." Anyone who has gone through a Roman Catholic seminary will have had this quoted to him at regular intervals with reference to the state of life he proposes to assume. It occurs in Psalm 110 with reference not to a priest but a king of the Davidic line based on the historical fact that the Davidic kingship was at least partially modelled on the Canaanite kingships, particularly that of pre-Israelite Jerusalem with which Melchizedek is clearly associated. The author of Hebrews refers it to Christ in the sense that the priestly concept he represents, unlike that of the Old Testament levitical priesthood, is non-

20. See J. P. Audet, *op. cit.*, p. 136.
21. *Summa Theologiae* III, Suppl., q. 37, a. 3.

hereditary, non-sequential and non-transferable. This is quite clear from the contrast between the two priestly types in Hebrews 7. The Old Testament priesthood was priesthood *for ever* in the sense that it was professional and remunerative, a lifetime job. In direct antithesis to what it is generally understood to mean, the phrase implies that Christian priesthood cannot be like this at all.

Anyone who thinks seriously about this problem is bound to come upon a number of strange paradoxes and contradictions of this kind. Let me refer to just one other. Wherever in the New Testament we read of different forms of ministry in the church we come upon the idea of service and humility; yet the entire concept of priesthood and the priestly office is stated within the category of *power*—power to mold and rule the priestly people, the power of order and of jurisdiction, the power over the Body of Christ both sacramental and mystical. We can, of course, blunt this paradox by applying the kind of rationalization which Roman curial theology has had to develop in order to survive. But I suggest it would be more fitting to let the historical record speak for itself and ask the honest question whether what has arisen in Roman Catholicism is essentially different from the priestly power-structure which arose towards the end of the Old Testament period.

V

In the light of all this one can hardly avoid asking the question outright: is there any place for a priesthood in a church conceived on the apostolic model? An answer to this question must start out from a right understanding of ministry. The purpose of the various ministries is to enable the church to be what it is, to articulate its life and mission. This comes about by an embodiment of different aspects of the life and mission of the church (which are the same) in particular persons; the healer represents the church in its mission of healing, the prophet embodies the mission of the church as a prophetic community, and so on. Understood in this way, the ministries mediate the reality of the church as signs. Now since the church is also a priestly community, a "royal priesthood," why should there not be priests who mediate this aspect of the church's reality and existence by their function and manner of life?

As long as we remain on the level of the abstract we can hardly deny this possibility. Difficulties begin to emerge, however, when we ask how this embodiment and signification are to take place and what such a person must be or do in order so to embody and signify the church as a priestly society. Let us remember that all ministries are determined by their relation to the basic focal point of unity, our communal being-in-Christ. This is not a purely "spiritual" union of all who believe in Christ, much less a union of the like-minded. This unity becomes sacramentally visible in the local church in which all that the church means "happens," becomes event. Since the local eucharist is the center of the church in its character as event and in its mission,[22] it would seem appropriate to think of the president of the eucharist as embodying the priestly character and mission of the church. Even considering him as the one chosen by the community to preside rather than as a sacrificing liturgist or sacrament-dispenser, his office of convening the local church and thereby initiating its worship may well signify the community as taken up into worship with the heavenly Christ in the presence of God. Similarly, by pronouncing the form of absolution he may signify that through the present Christ God has extended forgiveness of sin to all who are gathered together.

22. In I Corinthians 11, 18 the eucharistic assembly is the *ekklesia;* the church "happens" when people assemble to fulfill the command of Jesus to eat and drink. "Schisms" in the church (1, 11) are reflected in the eucharistic assembly (11, 18).

The fact remains, however, that priesthood is not found among the ministries of the early church and that history teaches how difficult it is to avoid falling back into old patterns. If the church is to be the continual re-actualization of the eschatological Christ-event and yet operate in a society whose sociological structures change continually, the forms in which her mission is objectiv-ized must always remain under scrutiny. In other words, there must be a constant reaction against the routinization of the church's social and structural presence in the world, in particular against the threatening tendency to professionalism and élitism. Here the analogy referred to earlier may help. The two most important revolutionary movements of modern times, in France in the eighteenth century and in Russia just over fifty years ago, began by overthrowing an oppressive system and extending the promise of a new life to all who were willing to accept the revolutionary message. Yet in a remarkably short time there emerged in both cases a revolutionary élite which, acting in the name of the revolution, brought about a situation remarkably similar to that against which the revolution had been directed in the first place. While therefore admitting the possibility of the kind of embodiment described above, we must add that there is no place for professionalism and élitism and therefore no place for a priesthood in the sense of a professional class. This means in effect that we ought to aim at eliminating the differentiation into clergy and laity which has played the leading role in dis-solving that deep mutuality and belonging which was character-istic of church life in the beginning. It was not necessary then and I see no reason why it should be necessary now.

One further consideration is in order. Jesus is not represented as priest but he is as prophet. No Christian is referred to as priest in the New Testament but several are called prophets. Looking at prophecy from the purely sociological viewpoint, Max Weber has pointed out that it is of the essence of the prophetic "office" to be non-professional and non-remunerative.[23] This is true of the Old Testament prophets who, precisely because they were not professionals or officially appointed to a definite office, were able to "tell it like it is," to cut through institutional patterns and speak of the real Israel. This may help to explain the true function of prophecy in the early church and in our church today. In the New Testament, prophets occur in all four lists of *charismata* in the Pauline correspondence and their importance can be gauged from the fact that they come first in one of these lists (Rom. 12, 4) and second only to apostles in two others (1 Cor. 12, 28 and Eph. 4, 11). They are esteemed more than any other of the ministries including the *pneumatikoi* or pentecostals who had the gift of tongues. It is upon the apostles and prophets that the local churches are built up (Eph. 2, 20) and it is to the prophets that the mystery of Christ has been revealed in the Spirit (Eph. 3, 5). In the sub-apostolic period we find itinerant prophets going from church to church and treated with great respect. The prophets of the church for which the *Didache* was written were regarded as on a higher plane than administrators and we even find the sin against the Holy Spirit interpreted as doubting the word of a prophet (Did. 11, 3).

Christian prophets could come from any stratum of society. While many, probably most, had no position in the local community, some were church leaders as at Antioch (Acts 13, 1). Women prophets are found in Corinth (1 Cor. 11, 5) and in the Palestinian churches (Acts 21, 9), and probably in most of the early communities. They were called prophets because they were accepted as witnessing to the reality by which the church lives, below the level of structures, organizational techniques and methods. They cut across institutional patterns and were the chief

23. *The Sociology of Religion,* pp. 46 ff. It may be of interest to quote here his definition of priesthood: "the specialization of a particular group of persons in the continuous operation of a cultic enterprise, permanently associated with particular norms, places and times, and related to specific social groups," p. 20.

force of resistance against the endemic tendency to routinization and institutionalization. Two cases of this are particularly significant. It appears from 1 Timothy 1, 18 and 4, 14 that church leaders were sometimes designated by prophets, probably during divine service. In something of the same way, Paul and Barnabas were designated for the mission, also during divine service, when the Holy Spirit spoke through one of the brethren present (Acts 13, 2–3). In both cases the laying on of hands signifies the ratification by the community and its leaders of the prophetic designation, hence the tension is maintained between institutional and charismatic elements. Some indications here and there in early Christian writings, especially in the *Didache,* suggest that on occasion prophets also presided over the eucharistic assembly even though they had not been officially "ordained" to do so. These indications of a "charismatic eucharist" do not, admittedly, amount to proof, but are highly significant and raise the whole question of "ordination" in relation to the church's ministry. Are we really in a position to determine what constitutes a "valid" ordination and to exclude categorically those who do not comply, or do not appear to comply, with the conditions we lay down? And if ordination as we define it is an absolute datum to which no exception can be admitted, what about the apostles? Were they ordained? This is one of several areas where we have had too much certainty, and to admit this honestly will go a long way to healing division between the churches.[24]

Both prophets and charismatics faded into the background some time in the latter half of the second century and it is no accident that about the same time we find the beginnings of a priestly government here and there in the churches and the emergence of more clearly defined cultic forms. The tension was beginning to go out of church life and it is no exaggeration to

24. The practical ecumenical consequences of this are dealt with briefly by J. Edgar Bruns, "The Unity of the Church and its Ministry," *The Ecumenist,* January–February 1965, pp. 21–23.

say that only in our own time has the radically eschatological nature of the church been rediscovered. In trying to understand how this bears directly on the way we think of ministry, it may be useful to take another look at what happened to the earliest "model of ministry" during the first four centuries, and to this we now turn.

6. From Presbyter to Priest

I

WHAT must have appeared to outsiders as the most remarkable thing about the emerging Christian community was that it had no sacrificial apparatus and no priesthood and that, in consequence, it did not qualify as a religion. For those near at hand it was a splinter-group from Judaism; we recall that the Jewish lawyer Tertullus refers to it as "the sect of the Nazarenes" (Acts 24, 5). For those, like Tacitus and Suetonius, who viewed it from further afield, it was "a base and degrading superstition," one of the many that came from the East and flowed into Rome *sicut in sentinam,* as into a cesspool. Hence the charge of atheism levelled at Christians during the persecutions, a charge which was justified in that those who could understand what was really happening saw that the new faith meant the overthrow of the old religious assurances which undergirded life in society. Understood in its true sense, the supersession of Judaism with its ritual practices and personnel implied that religion *as such* was superseded, that "the *hieron* of man is brought to judgement as a human institution by the cross of Christ."[1]

From the purely historical point of view early Christianity arose as a Jewish sectarian movement similar to others that we know of in the first century of our era. It was also, as we have seen, a lay movement remarkably free in its relation to the cultic

1. G. Schrenk, in *Theological Dictionary of the New Testament,* ed. by G. Kittel, Vol. III, p. 270.

world of Judaism. It took over from Judaism several offices of leadership, in particular that of elder (*presbyter*) but, significantly, not that of priest (*hiereus*). Now the problem to be discussed is, quite simply, that in view of all this we would not expect a priestly ministry in the form of a definite *ordo* or caste to emerge and yet this is precisely what happened. Despite the fact that historians have covered the first four centuries of the church's history thoroughly and repeatedly and have analyzed the causes of this transformation at depth it might still be useful, in the context of what I am trying to say, to the situation we are in today, to have another look at one or two aspects of this process which are still of crucial relevance. After all, how we understand our history is an important part of how we understand ourselves, and there is still a great deal of misunderstanding to clear away.

One basic misconception, sometimes stated in a surprisingly naïve form, ought to be cleared away before we begin. It concerns history and tradition. Throughout its long history the church has been guided by the Holy Spirit promised to it indefectibly by Christ, and therefore it is antecedently impossible that it could go wrong in any really important and significant respect with regard to its life and mission. If, therefore, as a result of certain factors met with in its historical evolution, the church has taken a course—even one which leads it far away from what it was in the beginning—this must be ascribed to the prompting of the Holy Spirit present with the church. In its broad lines, therefore, the history of the church continues the primitive tradition by a process of explicitation. Even if it cannot be shown positively that either a doctrine (like the immaculate conception) or an institution (like the priesthood) has scriptural warranty, it can at least be demonstrated that the Scriptures do not exclude it.

Something was said in an earlier chapter apropos this confused approach to tradition and how the council had unfortunately produced little to dispel it. We can only point out here that this attitude, taken to its logical conclusion, renders church reform both unnecessary and impossible. What on these terms, for example, could we make of the officially sanctioned and promulgated teaching that there can be no salvation outside the church? The intrinsic theological absurdity of this position has been rationalized away by the scholastic distinction between the body and the soul of the church, in spite of the fact that historically, beginning with Cyprian of Carthage, this was not at all what was meant by the dictum *extra ecclesiam nulla salus*. And if we think this was just a question of clarifying terms and concepts we should remember that missionaries like Francis Xavier went to enormous pains to baptize vast numbers of pagans in order to save them from damnation, with the tragic result that, precisely in those areas which he visited, there is no significant Christian presence at all today. What on these terms, to take another example, can be made of the papal claim to political sovereignty pursued with vast patience throughout the medieval period and only abandoned in recent times? What of the doctrine of indulgences which the church managed to dispense with for over a millennium but which has been, since the eleventh century, repeatedly sanctioned in official documents and recently reaffirmed by Pope Paul VI?

All I am saying here is that the history (that is, the self-understanding) of the church cannot be absolutized. To close our minds on the past means in effect to close them on the future also, and this is a denial of all that our Christian existence means since the church is, in the first place, the church of the future, a future which even now God is preparing for her. It is no coincidence that the mainstream of scholastic theology, which saw its chief task as the rationalization of the church in its existing institutions and objectivizations, never developed a satisfactory eschatology apart from the *eschaton* of the individual Christian. It is also no coincidence that today, when scholastic theology is by and large discredited, eschatology stands at the center of theological debate.

II

Before attempting to analyze this remarkable transformation which began in the second century, was virtually complete in essentials by the fourth and was further rationalized and systematized during the medieval period, let us see what actually happened. As far as we know, the term "priest" is first used of a Christian minister by Polycrates of Ephesus writing towards the end of the second century.[2] A little later, we find Tertullian speaking of the bishop as *sacerdos,* but it is also he who reminds his readers that the difference between *ordo* and *plebs* (clergy and laity) does not go back to Christ and the apostles, adding, "are we laymen not also priests? Where three are gathered together, even if they are laymen, there the church is."[3] Origen also refers to the presbyters as priests, though this is probably an analogous usage deriving from his typological approach to the Scriptures.[4] By the time of Hippolytus, the terms *"kleros," "klerikos"* are already in common usage and the difference between deacons and presbyters on the basis of priestly ordination has been established, though the term *"ordinatio"* first occurs in Tertullian.[5] We may add that consecration, the anointing with oils, was only added to the rite of ordination in the sixth century,

2. Quoted in Eusebius, *Ecclesiastical History,* V, 24, 3. This, however, may be due to Eusebius himself, who refers to the clergy as priests: X, 4, 2.

3. *De Exhort. Cast.,* 7, 3. In *De Baptismo* 17, 7 he refers to the bishop as *summus sacerdos.*

4. See G. H. Williams, "The Ministry of the Ante-Nicene Church," in *The Ministry in Historical Perspectives,* ed. by H. R. Niebuhr and D. D. Williams, New York, 1956, p. 45.

5. On Hippolytus see G. Bardy, *La Théologie de l'Eglise de saint Irenée au concile de Nicée,* Paris, 1947, p. 287; G. Dix, *The Apostolic Ministry,* London, 1946, p. 217. On *ordinatio* in Tertullian see G. H. Williams, *op. cit.,* p. 51.

being taken over from the anointing of kings—evidently influenced by Israelite and Jewish practice. By the early fourth century the process of assimilation is complete in all essentials at least as far as the Roman church is concerned: the distinction between *clerus* (= *ordo*) and *laici* (= *plebs*), the use of the term *"laicus"* (layman) in the restrictive and negative sense as found in the Old Testament and in Roman canon law,[6] the presbyter as sacrificing priest.

The most significant result of this process is that *presbyter* is understood as synonymous with *priest*. In the rite of ordination as now used in the Roman church the *ordinandi* are referred to indifferently as *ordo presbyteratus* and *sacerdotes*. Parallel with this, there is no distinction between ordination and consecration. Both are combined in the one sacramental act in a way which we can only describe as ingenious: the matter of the sacrament consists in the laying on of hands which commissions them to the office of the presbyterate, the form consists in the words spoken by the celebrant some time later which are followed by the putting on of the priestly vestments and the charge "to change, for the service of thy people, bread and wine into the body and blood of thy son." The consecration of the hands with holy oil follows later still after the singing of the *Veni Creator*, and obviously has direct reference to the consecration of the bread and wine during Mass. What is interesting here from the scriptural point of view is the assimilation of two quite distinct rites. The first is the Jewish practice of commissioning to office by laying on hands (the *semikah*) which the early church took over either from contemporary or Old Testament practice (see, for example, 1 Tim. 4, 14; 5, 22) and which is found in the earliest period of Israelite history. The commissioning of the seventy elders by Moses is in fact mentioned in the ordaining

6. In canon 948 "layman" is given roughly the same meaning as *"zar"* in the priestly strand of the Pentateuch and, correspondingly, the Code goes on to define what he may not do.

bishop's inaugural address. The second is the consecration of the high priest which is reflected in the account of Aaron's consecration by Moses (Lev. 8) though, of course, the Catholic rite represents a much simplified version. We may add significantly that just as in the consecration of Aaron the role of the laity present is reduced to a minimum (Moses simply tells them that "this is the thing that the Lord has commanded to be done," Lev. 8, 5), so here, in the Catholic rite, we have the purely formal admonition to those present to come forward if they have anything to say with regard to the fitness of the candidate for the ministry. Of course, no one ever does.

It would be impossible to give here an exhaustive account of the transformation which took place during the early centuries and which resulted eventually in the rite of ordination as we have it. For many Catholics it has an air of inevitability, an irreversible process adequately explained in terms of homogeneous development of doctrine. For many others, however, there is the question of credibility. Today honesty and scholarship would compel us to admit that the New Testament evidence admits of several types of church government none of which points necessarily to a monarchic episcopate.[7] The churches founded by Paul seem to have been very loosely structured similar to that of Antioch which was presided over by prophets and teachers. Palestinian churches were ruled by a panel of elders based on good Old Testament precedent. There seems to be no essential difference between the functions of overseer (a purely secular term) and elder and the two offices could well have coalesced at a later point. A stage towards the emergence of the Ignatian type of monepiscopal government may have been the practice of appointing one of the panel of elders or overseers as

7. Both Philippians 1, 1 and Acts 20, 28 refer to overseers (bishops) in the plural. There is no evidence for either monepiscopacy or elders in the genuinely Pauline letters and none anywhere in the New Testament for a clergy. For details see H. Küng, *The Church*, London and New York, 1967, pp. 385 ff., 399 ff. (especially p. 402).

149

president, perhaps within a system of rotation. Several historical developments such as the need to combat Gnosticism and to offset the prestige of the charismatics had an important part to play in producing the situation which is already beginning to emerge clearly in the second century.[8] With the growing complexity of the organizational life of local Christian communities the bishops would have been obliged increasingly to delegate authority to the presbyters which would have included presidency of the eucharistic assembly. This process, which began fairly early in the second century, would have been accelerated in those churches whose bishops fled or went into hiding during the persecutions.

With the mention of presidency of the eucharistic assembly we come to a crucial aspect of the process we are discussing. Just as the terms for ministry in the apostolic period are non-sacral, so the eucharist is never explicitly designated by sacral and sacrificial language. The use of the terms *"synaxis"* and *"ekklesia,"* both of which refer to the community gathered together, shows clearly where the emphasis lies. The same for "the breaking of bread," since the one bread signifies the unity in spirit of those gathered together, a concept which finds beautiful expression in the thanksgiving prayer of the Didachist.[9] The same again for the term *"koinonia,"* signifying the common fellowship of those who come together to carry out the command of the Lord. Significantly, the term *"thusia"* (sacrifice) is not used of the eucharist in the New Testament period. Moreover, the eucharist was celebrated in the early days in a purely secular context, namely,

8. The charismatics were particularly strong in Corinth and in the churches of the Didachist and the author of Hermas. Tension between charismatics and presbyters in the Corinthian church resulted in some of the latter being ousted, thus occasioning the recall to obedience and order addressed to that church by Clement of Rome.

9. "As this broken bread was scattered over the hills and then, when gathered, became one mass, so may thy church be gathered from the ends of the earth into thy kingdom." *Didache* 9, 4.

in a house large enough to welcome the local *ekklesia,* and round the table at which the family took their everyday meals.[10] This was in keeping with the practice of Jesus who kept passover in the house of a friend or acquaintance in Jerusalem in accordance with the age-long custom of his people. There were, of course, no sacred vessels and no altar. A final consideration, often overlooked, is that the author of Hebrews does not refer to the eucharist when speaking of Melchizedek who offered bread and wine. This would be rather difficult to explain if it was common at that time to think of the eucharist as a sacrifice.

Though all of this needs to be said, it does not follow that the sacrificial element is absent in the eucharist as understood in early Christian communities. Catholic theology has rightly emphasized that the tradition attributes to Jesus a prediction of his own death as having redemptive value (Mk. 10, 45; 14, 24; see 1 Tim. 2, 6) and the fact that the passover which he celebrated is also represented as a covenant-meal clearly recalls the sacrificial meal celebrated at Sinai (Ex. 24, 8. 11). What we cannot, however, conclude from this is that the eucharistic sacrifice is a continuation of the sacrificial system of the old order. Again, it is not its continuation but its supersession. Let us recall that Jesus repeated the insistence of the prophets that what God desires is obedience rather than sacrifice (Mt. 9, 13; 12, 7), thus placing himself firmly in the line of that prophetic protest against conventional religious practice which we discussed in an earlier chapter. We have also seen how the sacrificial terminology of the Old Testament is spiritualized and re-actualized in the early church. This basic discontinuity is a central theme of Hebrews; Christ has offered *for all time* a single sacrifice for sin; by a single offering he has perfected *for all time* those who are sanctified (10, 12–14). This no doubt explains why early Christian writers speak only of the Christian offering, together with Christ, as a

10. See Romans 16, 5; 1 Corinthians 19, 19; Colossians 4, 15; Philemon 2.

"sacrifice of praise" (Heb. 13, 15; 1 Pet. 2, 9), quite different from the sacrifices offered in the temple. It is interesting to note that the first time we find the term *"thusia"* (sacrifice) used of the eucharist—in the *Didache*—it is with reference to the pure sacrifice of Malachi's prophecy[11] which implied condemnation of current sacrificial practice.

The application to the eucharist of sacrificial terminology, with all its attendant ambiguities, began fairly early. In 1 Corinthians 10, 14–22 Paul *compares* the eucharist with both pagan and Jewish sacrificial rites, though after speaking of the *altar* of Israelite worship he goes on at once to speak of the Christian *table* (10, 18. 21). It appears that the first to speak of a Christian altar was the author of the apocryphal Acts of John,[12] though Clement of Rome speaks of "the altar of God" in the temple with indirect reference to Christian worship. Both here and in Ignatius of Antioch, however, it is difficult to affirm that the language used goes beyond metaphor. The latter stresses the need for unity round the bishop and the "one altar" which he serves, but in both writers "the altar of sacrifice" refers to Christ himself.[13] We have seen a similar ambiguity in the way the author of *Didache* uses the term *"thusia"* (sacrifice) of the eucharist; and the same difficulty meets us when we turn to other writers such as Justin and Irenaeus, both of whom speak of it as the Christian sacrifice.[14] Vermes has advanced the interesting suggestion that this usage may have been influenced by contemporary Jewish theology of sacrifice and sacrificial ritual elaborated

11. *Didache* 14, 2–3. It may, of course, be questioned whether the author meant anything more than what is implied in the phrase "a sacrifice of praise."

12. Williams, *op. cit.*, p. 37.

13. Clement of Rome, *Ad Corinthos I*, 32; see 4, 12; 40; 43, 2, where he brings in the Old Testament sacrificial system. See on this E. Schweizer, *Church Order in the New Testament*, London, 1961, pp. 146–149. For Ignatius see *Ad Philadelphenses* 4 and *Ad Magnesios* 7 and his reference to the "sanctuary" in *Ad Trallianos* 7 and to "sacrifice" in *Ad Romanos* 4.

14. Justin, *Apologia I*, 65–66; Irenaeus, *Adversus Haereses IV*, 18:4–6.

on the basis of Genesis 22, the *Akedah* or binding of Isaac.[15] According to this understanding of the passage, Isaac freely offers himself to God as the representative of Israel; he offers his life to God and is given it back again so that he (Israel) may live entirely by grace and by the indefectible promise. In the same way Jesus offers himself totally, *pours himself out* (see Mk. 14, 24) to the point beyond which it is impossible to go, the point of death. In so doing he recapitulates the sacrifice of the whole Christian community. We can conclude that very probably the language used of the eucharist down to the end of the sub-apostolic period does not imply anything more than analogy with Jewish sacrificial rites and therefore does not betray the specifically Christian understanding of the once-for-all character of the sacrificial act of Jesus.

By the time of Cyprian of Carthage, writing in the middle of the third century, the situation has been profoundly changed. Not only can the eucharist be described as a sacrifice in the line of the Old Testament sacrificial rites but, more important, the Christian minister is engaged *primarily* in the service of the altar and sacrifices.[16] The line of development here is fairly clear. Where you have a sacrifice (thought of primarily in Old Testament terms) you need an altar and a sacred ministry to offer the sacrifice. The Christian ministry is now not just typified by the Old Testament priestly ministry but is its actual successor in direct line of descent. Once this door was opened the rest followed. Anything that is said of the Old Testament priesthood can be applied wholesale and indiscriminately to the Christian ministry, including the need for ritual purity and sexual abstention. This was bound to lead logically to the requirement of total sexual abstinence since by this time the eucharist was celebrated

15. G. Vermes, *Scripture and Tradition in Judaism,* Leiden, 1961, pp. 193–227. We have a fleeting but significant reference to the *akedah* in John 19, 17.

16. See *Epistolae* 1, 62.

daily. Hence the wheel comes full circle and we are back in the cultic and priestly world of post-exilic Judaism which the first Christians and Jesus himself had rejected so decisively. By the time of the great scholastics the situation had already been frozen into church law and there was no escape. So, for example, we find Aquinas arguing that since there were several orders—priests and levites in particular—in the Old Testament, *a fortiori* there must be several in the church, and that since continence was encumbent on them then with their imperfect rites, *a fortiori* it is on the minister of the Christian rites.[17] Despite the great progress made since then in our understanding of the Scriptures and in Christian hermeneutics we have not advanced appreciably beyond this position today.

Another aspect of this ambiguity ought to be mentioned, concerning the relation between the president of the eucharist and Christ as priest. It was in this context that the much abused phrase "*sacerdos alter Christus*" was first used by Cyprian, later to be taken up by Augustine,[18] though we should recall that it was modelled on an older way of speaking of the Christian as a replica of Christ, *christianus alter Christus*. The ambiguity lurking within this phrase is obvious. It could easily be taken to refer exclusively to the vicarious role of the eucharistic president, thus obliterating the important fact that in what he does he represents the whole worshiping community which is the priestly people referred to in the New Testament. Though the universal priesthood of the faithful was never lost sight of in the first four centuries,[19] not all ecclesiastical writers adequately expressed its inner relationship to the one, all-sufficient priesthood of Christ. Once you have a priestly caste firmly established and entrenched behind a barricade of legal enactment it is really quite pointless

17. *Summa* III Suppl. q. 37.
18. Cyprian, *Epistulae* 59; Augustine, *De civitate Dei* 20, 9.
19. E.g., Justin, *Dial. cum Tryphone* 116, 3, describes the Christian church as "the true, priestly race." Also Irenaeus, *Adversus Haereses IV*, 8:3; Tertullian, *De exhortatione castitatis* 7; Origen, *Exhortatio ad Martyrium* 30.

to speak of the priestly function of the entire community. We can have a shrewd idea that the covenant description of Israel as priestly meant precious little to the average Israelite during the period of priestly dominance in the post-exilic period, as little as the "priesthood of the laity" means to the average Catholic layman today. In this sense Luther's re-affirmation of this truth and simultaneous protest against a priestly caste-system (made from within the Roman communion) aimed at redressing a loss of balance which had had disastrous results in terms of the idea of church membership and of a completely clericalized eucharist.

One thing which will have emerged from the preceding is that a tendency to extrapolate into the Old Testament has been a prime factor throughout this whole process of transposition. No doubt it began by a natural process of analogizing, but its conclusions were nonetheless disastrous. So, for example, the author of the *Didache* refers rather oddly to Christian prophets as "our high priests" (13, 3) and Ignatius, while admitting the radical newness of the gospel, speaks of the bishop as the high priest and the presbyters as priests of the second order (*Phil.* 9). The most remarkable addiction to Old Testament analogies is to be found, however, in Clement of Rome. We know too little about Clement and his background to be able to hazard an explanation of his extraordinary interest in the rites and ministries of Judaism even when writing to a church (that of Corinth) which is generally considered to have been of predominantly Gentile extraction. Those who minister to the altar of God, he says, are the descendants of Jacob (Israel), namely, the priests and levites followed by the Lord Jesus himself (*1 Clem.* 32). Though he quotes from Hebrews he does not, oddly enough, refer to Melchizedek and, contrary to the statement in that letter (7, 14), seems to suggest a levitical rather than judahite descent for Jesus. He speaks of the need to carry out the liturgical rites in order and at the fixed times. They must be carried out only by the high priest, priests and levites according to their respective stations—an evident reference to the lack of order in the Corinthian community. He even alters the Greek text of Isaiah 60, 17 to prove the divine right of bishops and deacons.[20] With all this, he says nothing about the supersession of Old Testament ritual and ministry which is implied so strongly in Hebrews and elsewhere in the New Testament. Now it may be maintained that all he is doing is to adduce the existence of fixed order in Old Testament cultic life and ministry as an example to a particularly disorderly community which had just thrown out some of its presbyters;[21] but how dangerous this use of the Old Testament could be was to be seen clearly in the years ahead. By the fourth century it had become quite common to refer to the Christian ministry as the counterpart of that of the Old Testament. For Ambrosiaster the deacons are levites, the presbyters priests and the bishop the high priest.[22] Jerome states it quite clearly: "the traditions of the Apostles were derived from the Old Testament. Hence the same relative status of Aaron, his sons and the levites in the temple now belongs to the bishops, presbyters and deacons in the church."[23] Much later still we find Peter Lombard stating quite simply, in a text referred to earlier, that an unbroken line exists between the Aaronic priesthood and Christian priests.[24]

One fairly obvious explanation of this tendency which gathered force as time went on may be sought in the polemical needs of early church writers. They found themselves faced with the charge that Christianity was a new-fangled idea which could not compete *as a religion* with long-established cults. Some of them elected to meet this charge by hitching Christianity back on to Judaism and claiming that the Jewish scriptures contain a latent

20. "I will appoint their bishops in righteousness and their deacons in faith," *1 Clement* 42.
21. See Audet, *op. cit.*, pp. 125–126.
22. See Dix, *op. cit.*, pp. 320 ff.
23. Quoted by Dix, *op. cit.*, p. 329.
24. *Sent.* IV, d. 24, 9.

Christianity. The Christian church was present inchoately right from the beginning (*ecclesia ab Abel*) and its own rites and ministries are foreshadowed in those of the old order. While no one is going to deny lightly the legitimacy of this typological approach, the fact remains that the radical discontinuity between old and new was too often overlooked. And precisely because of the radical newness of the Christian message (and here, we repeat, newness means finality) we have to ask whether it is right to speak of the Christian faith as a religion.

Once the link between Judaism in its ritual aspects and the Christian life was reforged, it was not difficult to apply other aspects of the priestly theology and practice to the church. The need for centralization could be pressed on the basis of the deuteronomic and priestly postulate of cultic centrality, as in fact we find, at least inchoately, in Ignatius.[25] Appeal could be made to the dire punishment meted for disobedience to the priests in the Old Testament, and in fact Ignatius refers to the fate of Dathan and Abiram who dared oppose the priesthood (*Magn.* 3), while Clement seeks to re-establish order in Corinth by recounting how Moses settled the rivalry among the priests by means of the twelve gold rods (*1 Clem.* 43). He also emphasizes the need for ritual and cultic regularity by recalling the death penalty prescribed in the priestly legislation for certain faults (*1 Clem.* 41). Perhaps the decisive role in revamping this penal legislation and applying it to Christian living must go to the monks, especially those of the Celtic church. The moral and ritual legislation of the Old Testament provided a tool ready to hand in their self-imposed task of seeing that the moral law was known and observed by the great masses who began to pour into the church after the persecutions. They applied many of these laws in the first place to themselves in the form of a "holy rule" dictating their way of life. And since the most spectacular infrac-

25. *Magn.* 7; *Phil.* 4.

tions of this law always occur in the field of sexual behavior, the sixth and ninth commandments of the decalogue were conscripted to cover all possible sexual sins and were supplemented, where necessary, by the laws of ritual purity found especially in the priestly strand of the Pentateuch.[26]

III

While we are on this subject, we may be permitted to mention briefly one other aspect of this deep shift in emphasis which is not without relevance for the theme of this book, namely, the exclusion of women from the ministry.[27] I am aware, of course, that it is quite useless to raise this as a practical issue in a Catholic context at this moment. Despite the presence as auditors at the council of twelve laywomen and ten women religious and despite the fact the one council document refers to the unjust exclusion of women from some of their rights, only the most laconic remarks are made on the role of women in the church and, of course, the possibility of ordaining women to ministry is not so much as mentioned, even to be refuted. However, it has been effected with success in some Christian bodies and it has been discussed and argued in several Anglican reports, so we may hope that some day the subject may at least be discussed as a practical issue. For well-known sociological and cultural reasons it was not a live issue in the early centuries of the history of the church. By the time of Aquinas, however, we find the anomalous and rather amusing situation that, whereas boys and the insane could be validly ordained to the priesthood, women could not. We even find Anselm and other scholastics basing this

26. See the illuminating treatment of this subject in A. Mirgeler, *Mutations of Western Christianity,* London and New York, 1964, pp. 69–75.

27. For some illuminating remarks on the anthropological and cultural issues involved see G. Tavard, "Women in the Church: A Theological Problem?" in *The Ecumenist,* November–December, 1965.

prohibition on Old Testament grounds, which at least points to a real issue even if hermeneutically quite invalid. For of all major religions of antiquity Judaism was the only one without priestesses and its God the only one without a female consort—if we except the aberrant and heretical cult of Anath-Yahweh among the Jewish colonists at Elephantine (Assuan). At any rate, the reasons given by Aquinas for the exclusion of women from the priestly ministry do not look very persuasive to the modern reader. He argues from (a) the prohibition of Paul against women speaking in the assembly, quoting from 1 Corinthians 14, 34 and 1 Timothy 2, 12 (b) the fact that the tonsure is required for the priesthood and women cannot be tonsured since Paul says that it is shameful for a woman to shave her head, and (c) the fact established by Aristotle that woman is *in statu subjectionis* and therefore cannot embody the eminence of order which must belong to man alone.[28] The moral is that, while we may doubt whether the ordination of women is expedient and practical, we should not invent theological arguments to support a position on which we have already made up our minds. I will return to this question briefly in a later chapter but merely remark here that so long as women are not even allowed to approach the sanctuary during the eucharist (except *in extremis*), much less serve as deaconesses as they did in the early church, there is not much point in talking about the possibility of their being ordained priests. In other words, until we do some radical rethinking on ministry in general this possibility cannot even seriously be raised.

The exclusion of women from the sanctuary raises once again the question of the persistence of the sacred discussed at some length in a previous chapter. Here again, the influence of the Old Testament was determinative. Officiating priests were hedged in with all sorts of ritual laws, including the need for prior sexual abstention, in the exercise of their functions. There is no

28. *Summa* III Suppl. qu. 39, art. 1.

evidence from the apostolic or sub-apostolic period that these requirements were exempt from the general abrogation of the Old Testament ritual law. Yet, as we have seen, we find the requirement of sexual abstention—now total—coming back not for those who felt called to this kind of eschatological witness but for those ministers *qui sancta tractant,* who have to do with holy things. Etymologically, the sacred is that which is set aside. To speak in terms of sacred and profane is to imply that certain places, persons and things are removed from common use or activities by virtue of an inherent quality with which they are endowed. While to sacralize is a primitive and endemic tendency it easily becomes highly systematized once a priestly caste takes over. Now the really decisive point here is that, while in the old order the sacred or holy is reserved to the priestly and cultic sphere, with the coming of Christ it is extended to all who are united with him in faith. The entire Christian community is holy by reason of the common possession of the Holy Spirit in baptism. They are "the saints" (for example, 1 Cor. 1, 1), "a holy nation" (1 Pet. 2, 9), "holy brethren" (Heb. 3, 1). It is this "communalization" of the holy which brings with it the "communalization" of the priesthood[29] since the essence of the new fellowship is the common possession of the Holy Spirit. Hence consecration (that is, making holy) is no longer applied to priests but to the whole church and to each believer who accepts baptism. The Gentiles are consecrated (made holy) by faith in Jesus in the act of accepting baptism (Rom. 15, 16; 1 Cor. 6, 11). It can even be said that the unbeliever who marries a Christian is drawn into the sphere of the holy and thereby consecrated (1 Cor. 7, 14).

A further manifestation of the sacred-profane dichotomy is seen in the practice of consecrating buildings, that is, setting

29. I take this term from the illuminating essay of John A. T. Robinson, "The Priesthood of the Church," *On Being the Church in the World,* London, 1960, p. 76.

them aside for sacred as opposed to profane or common purposes. This tendency to "localize" the sacred is, of course, very ancient and generally not unconnected with the feelings of awe and fear aroused by a theophany or *kratophany* (a showing of mysterious and inexplicable power) experienced at the place in question. Jacob's numinous experience at Bethel provides a good example of this; after his dream he declares that it is an awesome place and proceeds to consecrate it by pouring oil on a stone. The Christian practice of consecrating churches goes back to the sixth century, at the time when it became popular to transfer the prestigious relics of the saints and martyrs to the churches and insert them in the altar. In the church of the first centuries, on the contrary, the only consecration was that which went with initiation, thereby preserving the specifically Christian insight that the only temple, the only consecrated building, was the community itself. As we have already noted, it is becoming increasingly difficult today to justify this dichotomizing of reality into sacred and profane not only on sociological and cultural but also—and this is my main point here—on specifically theological grounds.[30]

From the point of view of cultural and sociological development, sacralization is only one aspect of what with Dilthey we may refer to as objectivization or, with Max Weber, routinization. The first Christians thought of themselves as living *within* an event inaugurated with the resurrection and shortly to be terminated with the coming of the Lord. Coming to terms with the non-realization of the *parousia* implied adjusting to the *absence* of Christ, and so it was natural that in the course of time a more concrete system of mediation should come into existence. We may, perhaps, regard this as a regrettable tendency but it was natural nonetheless; but when it reached the point at which

30. An Anglican writer, Gilbert Cope, has argued this point persuasively in "Consecration Queried," in *New Christian* (London), 15 June, 1967, pp. 10–11.

the eschatological tension disappeared almost completely from church life it was no longer just regrettable but disastrous. Thus, though Christ is absent he is really present in the pope, his vicar on earth; the kingdom is present in the church; the new law for life in the kingdom is laid out precisely and in detail in the Code of Canon Law, et cetera. With this, the eucharist, the heart of the mystery, the new fellowship in Christ, becomes an *icon*, a sacred object which can be put on display.

Two other influences at work in this process of "objectivization" ought to be briefly mentioned before we conclude. They have to do in particular with the concept of "holy orders." In Philo we find· that the Old Testament priesthood is given special pre-eminence by being placed in a cosmic context. He refers to the high priest as "the high priestly logos in the temple of the cosmos" and even attributes cosmic significance to the priestly vestments.[31] Josephus is moving in the same direction when he speaks of the "eternal holiness" which the priest possesses as a result of his anointing.[32] Ignatius refers to the ordered hierarchy of the angels and principalities in making a point about the earthly hierarchy in the Christian churches (*Trall.* 5) and Clement, on whom the old priestly order seems to have exercised such a fascination, tends to insert church "orders" into the unchanging order of the cosmos, though his metaphors are more commonly military and political.[33] This approach reached its high point in Dionysius the Areopagite who outlined a complete hierarchization of the church's ministry in accordance with the nine choirs of angels divided into three orders. This way of thinking became standard once taken over by the scholastics, especially Aquinas.[34] We may recall that Luther, not without reason, regarded Dionysius as downright dangerous since he was more

31. For references see Schrenk, *op. cit.*, pp. 259, 272.
32. *Ibid.*, p. 269.
33. On Clement see Schweizer, *op. cit.*, pp. 146 ff.
34. For example, *Summa Theologiae* III *Suppl.*, q. 37, a. 2.

of a Platonist than a Christian. At any rate, the Platonism of Dionysius played a considerable role in both formulating and rationalizing the existence of fixed clerical orders in the church.

The second influence which ought to be mentioned, and which is even more important, was the strong appeal of the Roman *political* ideal of order on the church as it moved out of the persecution era and became first a legitimate religion under Constantine and later the only legitimate religion under Theodosius. This was, of course, accentuated by the historical accident of the pre-eminence of the Roman See. We have already noted that Tertullian applied the terms *"plebs"* and *"ordo"* to laity and clergy respectively. After the Edict of Milan the tendency to assimilate the various kinds of subordinate ministry in the Church to the *cursus honorum* or grades of promotion in the Roman civil service involved the obvious danger of thinking of church ministry in terms of a career. One result of this was that several of the ministries which in the New Testament period were distributed throughout the church and devoid of any specifically sacred character came to serve no other purpose than to punctuate the progress of the clerical student to the priesthood. Aquinas even attempts to distribute these "gifts" among the seven orders leading to and including priestly ordination. Anyone who looks at the list, *a fortiori* anyone who has gone through a Catholic seminary, will know how meaningless the four preliminary orders now are. Whatever its function was in the early period (it first appears towards the middle of the third century) the subdiaconate is now a purely liturgical office, the point at which the candidate first enters the sphere of the sacred from which he cannot easily withdraw. As for the diaconate, it is highly significant that the attempt to re-establish it as a ministry independent of the *cursus* has been thwarted by the inability to think of it otherwise than as a sacred office. The *Constitution on the Church* states that the duties traditionally associated with this office can in many areas be fulfilled only with

163

difficulty within the present discipline of the Latin church. It therefore proposes that it be restored as a proper and permanent rank, which means in effect that it be dissociated from priesthood. Older men, even if married, may be appointed as deacons with the approval of Rome. But if younger men apply they must be and remain celibate.[35]

If anyone requires proof of the difficulty involved in breaking with a basically irrational view of the sacred he will find it here. Clearly, the only reason why only older married men may be considered for this office is that one of the deacon's duties is to be, in the words of the document, "custodian and dispenser" of the eucharist and that younger men in the full exercise of their sexual power are for that reason unfit to handle the sacrament. Closely connected with this is the fear, probably quite justified, that once a married diaconate is fully authorized, mandatory celibacy for priests will come increasingly under fire. Meanwhile, the young who are not prepared to sacrifice the prospect of marriage but are anxious to serve look for forms of *diakonia* elsewhere and the church becomes increasingly unable to cope realistically with a mission in the world.

IV

It might appear from all this that I am advocating a disruption in the life of the church, a return to the primitive simplicity of early church life, the abolition of the priesthood, and so on. Let me then repeat what I said in an earlier chapter, that the way forward is not and cannot be a return to the forms and structures of early church life. The church is an organism with a continuous

35. "With the consent of the Roman Pontiff, the diaconate will be able to be conferred upon men of more mature age, even upon those living in the married state. It may also be conferred upon suitable young men. For them, however, the law of celibacy must remain intact" (§29).

life, not (in V. A. Demant's phrase) "a collection of uprooted, believing monads." It would be foolish to deny also that much progress in our thinking has been made in the last couple of decades, at least to the point where the kind of questions asked in this book can no longer be written off as wild and irrelevant. But the fact remains that, despite the enormous innate strength of social and religious conservatism, culture-Christianity, Christianity as we have known it, is breaking up. This may not be so obvious in the United States where church attendance is still very much tied up with either social status or ethnic loyalties;[36] it is much more apparent in Britain where it is highlighted by the growing irrelevance of an established church with an impressive plant and resources inherited from the past. Some, but not all, greet this gradual dissolution of the old structures with dismay. The Bishop of Woolwich sees it, however, as a subject not for despair but hope, and is prepared to state that "the great, and unexpected, hope is the rapidity in England with which the old is dissolving. Indeed, if it were not for the injection of vast sums from the Church Commissioners, our inherited system, with its thousands of consecrated buildings and full-time parsons living on their benefices, would in many areas have collapsed long since."[37] It is true that the Vatican power-structure has not as yet been subjected to the same pressures as has the established church in England. Despite promises of reform, the Curia is still manned and directed by ageing and, on the whole, conservative Italian clerics, and with some distinguished exceptions, the local churches, in the person of their bishops, have not had the courage and intelligence to get on their feet and establish their own identity. Where we may find hope here is in the fact that so many Roman Catholics, including priests, are unhappy within

36. Pierre Berton, in *The Comfortable Pew*, Philadelphia, 1965, shows that the same is true in Canada.

37. "Ministry in the Melting," in *New Christian*, 10 February, 1966, p. 11.

the present structures and have come to realize that we too, not just "the others," have been, in Kierkegaard's phrase, "playing the game of Christianity." Out of this unrest questions are being asked and subjects honestly and openly discussed which were until recently considered taboo. By its very existence this new honesty augurs well for the future.

In the present chapter I have concentrated on one cluster of questions the answers to which require honesty in our understanding both of our Christian past and our present situation. My conclusion is that we need a much broader understanding of Christian ministry which is impossible so long as we perpetuate the archaism of the sacred and embody it in "the sacred ministry" of the priesthood. It is only because I believe that this is in accord with the pattern of ministry laid down in the New Testament and early Christian tradition that I feel entitled to come to the conclusion. And if this does not make sense to many of my fellow Roman Catholics it makes sense in terms of the kind of world to which we are called to minister today and, above all, it makes sense ecumenically, that is, for the church of the future.

7. The Changing Role and Image of the Priest Today

I

The Catholic priesthood is a group of which a high degree of conformity is expected not only in terms of ideology but also of accidentals such as manner of dress, comportment and the like. I suppose it would be generally agreed that the social image or projection or *persona* must not be identified with the real self if health and wholeness are to be attained and maintained, and this would be especially true where pressure to conform to the image is strongest. The alternative is that by conforming to the image one soon becomes *hypocritical,* not necessarily in the moral sense but psychologically, by the very fact of this identification. Of no class of people is this so true as of the clergy. Like a masked actor the representative clergyman goes through the rehearsed motions and says the words he is expected by the audience to say rather than what he really wants to say or what he thinks he ought to say—presuming, that is, that he has something to say. He easily ends up by being a mask; and once the audience has accepted and approved the mask he had better keep close to the script since he is only what he is because there is an audience and also since, by being what he is, he is confirming the audience in their idea of what they themselves are. That, after all, is what he is paid to do as an actor. Let him depart from his script, throw away his carefully prepared sermon and say what he feels he ought to say and he may find, like the pastor in *The Night of the Iguana,* that he no longer has an audience.

This is a problem for clergy of any denomination, but it is also a problem for the Catholic priest, perhaps especially for him. Harvey Cox makes the point that the role of those people (preacher, priest, and so on) who speak professionally about God places them in a perceptual context where what they say can be safely ignored.[1] This is one obvious danger but it is perhaps not so great as that of a certain complicity between minister or priest and congregation by virtue of which a process of mutual reinforcement of identity takes place. Once this process is under way it can be almost impossible to diverge from the pattern and exercise any kind of prophetic function. Those who have tried it know best.

One practical conclusion is inescapable. The pastor who has been given responsibility for a congregation must exercise a prophetic role not only by refusing to conform to the image which many of the laity are only too willing to project on him but also by continually questioning his congregation's own self-understanding as a group witnessing to Christ in the world. Despite the bad press which he has had in popular biblical exposition Jeremiah might well be taken as an example of the prophetic pastor in the sense alluded to. Persecuted and probably expelled from his "congregation" at Anathoth, he was not afraid to carry out a one-man picket of the temple as the worshipers poured in to carry out their customary routine. "The prophets prophesy falsely, the priests rule at their direction, *and my people love to have it so*" (5, 31); "they have healed the wound of my people lightly saying 'peace, peace' when there is no peace" (6, 14); "prophet and priest ply their trade through the land and have no knowledge" (14, 18). The official spokesmen for God "steal my words from one another" (23, 30). This is just what happens any time religion degenerates into a routine,

1. *The Secular City,* New York, 1965, p. 247.

a concrete system of reassurances, a way of making one feel good inside. It is against this reduction of the Christian message to religiosity that the pastor has to protest, and this will generally involve him in protest against the role and image which have been laid down for him.

The priest who fits into the pre-established pattern and slips easily into the prepared role may find it very difficult to grow and mature as a human being. In many cases too much damage will already have been done before he comes to ordination. But even in the case of those who were fortunate enough to avoid the perils of junior seminaries and arrive at a psychologically free and intelligent decision about their choice of a career a question remains. Is it possible to become oneself to the depths of one's being and achieve full maturation while remaining within the officially sanctioned priestly ethos? While there are doubtless some who do succeed—insofar as it is possible for anyone to succeed in this—there are many more who obviously do not. Maturation demands a continual and painful process of self-discovery which is too often shut off by a false supernaturalism, especially if one is supposed to be a sacred person. A priest also lacks the opportunities for self-knowledge afforded by marriage and family life and he will be lucky to have lay friends who are on good enough terms to tell him the truth about himself. And yet without this self-knowledge he cannot break out of the established pattern into some kind of genuine inner freedom which is so necessary. "You will know the truth and the truth will set you free" is true not only theologically but psychologically.

With the mention of freedom we come to a crucial point in the current understanding of priesthood and all that it stands for. The New Testament is full not so much of a theology of freedom as of an enormous sense of relief and liberation. The great archetype of exodus has been fulfilled at last; the ancient religious bondage has been broken; we have passed over from

169

death to life. Theologians have discussed every aspect of the teaching of Jesus and Paul on freedom: freedom from sin, from death, from the law, from the old life. One such aspect often overlooked is that the Christian is also freed from religious routine, we might say from religious boredom. The trouble was that for some this was too good to be true—they kept on looking back over their shoulders at the old system they had left behind. At one point Paul positively snarls at the Colossians: "why do you submit to regulations? do not handle! do not taste! do not touch!" and says wearily to the Galatians: "you observe days and months and seasons and years . . . I am afraid I have labored over you in vain." To get the point, all we need do is contrast the enthusiasm of a Christian assembly as described in the early literature with the kind of experience we get in a typical big-city mass today. We have sold our freedom for a mess not of pottage but of mostly unintelligible verbiage.

Christian freedom is by no means irrelevant to the understanding of the current role of the Catholic priest and the possibility of superseding it. Bondage to religious and liturgical routine is symptomatic of unfreedom at the center of the individual and the community to which he belongs. Paul's main purpose in writing to the Galatian Christians was to combat Judeo-Christian missionaries who insisted on maintaining integral torah-observance as an essential element in Christian community life. Against these people who had infiltrated the communities of Asia Minor "to spy out our freedom which we have in Christ Jesus" he insisted that the Christian is called *to freedom,* that is, to achieve freedom as a task. Christ has set us free *for freedom* (5, 1) by calling us out of a fixed system of legal observance. A fixed point of reference outside ourselves which enables us to know what to do and not to do, what is right and what is wrong, provides a security which makes it unnecessary for us to embark on the difficult task of achieving inner freedom. Nowhere in the New Testament is the Christian promised security. Paul himself describes the end-state as the final realization of the new being in Christ experienced as absolute freedom, "the glorious freedom of the children of God" (Rom. 8, 21). In the light of this final purpose the Christian must live as a free man (1 Pet. 2, 16), free of all extraneous claims upon him (1 Cor. 9, 19) so that without any kind of constriction he can give himself to others in loving service.

Most of the difficulties experienced by the Catholic church in recent years, not least those connected with ministry, have arisen from the failure to recognize that freedom understood in the New Testament sense must always be a criterion for evaluating the quality and authenticity of Christian life both individual and communal. It can hardly be denied that the church has not been distinguished in the modern period for its promotion of freedom and has not always, perhaps not often, been experienced as a suitable structural context for the development of true interior freedom on the part of its members. This has been brought to our attention so often and forcibly in recent writings that it is hardly necessary to labor the point. Suffice it to think of the reaction to modernism, *la question biblique,* the reluctance to grant religious liberty to minorities in Catholic countries, the treatment of dissenters down to the most recent past either by the central bureaucracy or one or other of the bishops. The tendency to suppress liberty in the name of unity or purity of doctrine is of course always present in any kind of efficient organization of the dimensions of the Roman church, especially one which disposes of supernatural sanction. Erich Fromm has put it very well:

It is the tragedy of all great religions that they violate and pervert the very principles of freedom as soon as they become mass organizations governed by a religious bureaucracy. The religious organization and the men who represent it take over to some extent the place of family, tribe and state. They keep man in

171

bondage instead of leaving him free. It is no longer God who is worshipped but the group that claims to speak in his name.[2]

Some progress has, of course, been made. We have had the *Declaration on Religious Freedom* of Vatican II though this document is concerned exclusively with relations between the Catholic church and those, whether Christians or not, who do not belong to it. The principles laid down here would *per se* apply also to the church in relation to her own members but the relevant conclusions are not drawn. For example, it is stated that one of the basic principles establishing the right to religious freedom is the dignity of the human person; yet in practice this does not seem to apply to dissidents within the church. One may ask whether the current procedure of ecclesiastical courts in the solution of matrimonial difficulties can be said to respect the dignity of the persons involved. It is further stated that Christian freedom implies immunity not only from external coercion (which fortunately the church is no longer in a position to apply) but from psychological pressure as well (§2); yet such pressure is still used, sometimes in devious ways, to encourage absolute conformity. It may be, as the late John Courtney Murray suggested,[3] that once Catholics begin to realize that what applies to those outside the church applies also to themselves the ripples set in motion by this document will run far. More relevant to our present discussion is the fact that the same could be said of those engaged in the day-to-day pastoral ministry of the church. In this respect the growing discontent with and reaction against the established role and the total subjugation it demands on the part of many priests since Vatican II can be seen as a welcome and promising sign.

While freedom has its dangers, those arising from lack of freedom are very much worse. It would be foolish to use the language of melodrama in speaking of authoritarianism and unfreedom in the Catholic church, yet it is not difficult to see that these

2. *Psychoanalysis and Religion,* New Haven, 1950, p. 85.
3. See *The Documents of Vatican II,* ed. by W. M. Abbott, p. 674.

characteristics have contributed to a general impoverishment of the over-all quality of experience, a lack of spontaneity and warmth in human relationships, a failure to touch the depths of personal involvement. In the nature of the case, this would be particularly true of the priesthood and the kind of relationship which exists between priest and people. One symptom would be the "standard" practice of confession. Quite apart from the irrelevant categorizing of mortal and venial sins, exact specification of the number of times and purely nominal penances imposed, it is clear that many are driven to confess by a basically neurotic sense of guilt and the priest-confessor is willy nilly implicated in a process which postpones rather than advances true Christian maturity. There is here a lack of basic moral seriousness and it is not surprising that more and more people are abandoning private confession as a regular practice. Even apart from their role as confessors, few perceptive priests will not have sensed at some time or other that they are playing the role of ritual and moral scapegoat. Given the role imposed on him, the priest provides for many lay people an ideal alibi for an authentic and mature Christian life, especially if he himself lacks personal authenticity. The unspoken assumption behind the relationship implied in the role could perhaps be expressed as follows: your job is to tell me what to do, what my duties are (mass, confession, Catholic schools); I will do them—more or less—but, for the rest, my life is my own. Within this kind of relationship there is no room for growth and genuine Christian commitment.

What I am saying, briefly, is that for historical reasons the Catholic priest is in sociological bondage to a role which has a necessarily restrictive effect upon both his own personal authenticity and the over-all quality of Christian life in the Catholic community. This role both reflects and perpetuates sociological structures which are no longer generally conducive to the kind of full life of love, expansive self-giving and generous witness found in early Christianity.

173

II

The determination of roles is a decisive factor in the complex interactions which go to make up what we call society. The stability of society is, moreover, bound up to a great extent with functional consistency in fulfilling roles. To fulfill a role means to fulfill specific expectations in the "reference-group" to which the "actor" belongs,[4] and this demands adequate preparation in terms of professional competence and indoctrination in the ideology which sustains the role and gives rise to the collective expectations; in other words, a process of enculturation. Whether or not we accept the view that role-fulfilment is the decisive factor in the formation of personality, it is at least true to say that uncertainty about the expectations which one is supposed to fulfill in the society which forms one's reference-group is bound to induce deep anxiety and identity crisis.

Although all social roles, those of lawyer or doctor for example, involve the acceptance of a common ethos and therefore some degree of indoctrination in the widest sense of the term, this will be much more the case with the role of the priest or clergyman since here the expectations are much less ponderable. The need for "religion" is not nearly so well defined or, for that matter, so widespread, as the need for medical care or legal advice. It is therefore not at all inconceivable that a priest or clergyman who thinks he has a genuine role in society may in fact be responding to the expectations of a residual minority in the society to which he belongs and on their terms not his. This suspicion may have something to do with the sometimes rather frantic search for new roles by many of the clergy today.

It has always been true that social institutions and social

4. The term "reference-group" goes back to H. H. Hyman and is defined by T. Shibutani as "that group whose perspective constitutes the frame of reference of the actor." For this reference I am endebted to P. L. Berger, *The Precarious Vision*, New York, 1961, pp. 56 ff.

organization in general are impermanent and more or less provisional but it is only in this century that this has been clearly seen to be true. It is probably also safe to say that a good dose of self-deception has always been needed to accept any given society as permanent. Primitive societies, though hardly in a position to ignore the possibility of dissolution, always act on the supposition of permanence and assign fixed roles to certain individuals, the shaman or priest, for example. The great civilizations of the Euphrates basin were keenly aware of the ever-present menace of chaos as their extant literature attests and yet postulated the necessity of a fixed and divinely sanctioned social order. Here too the priest had an important role to play in the process of continual re-validation of the social order. The same can be said, *mutatis mutandis,* of the Roman Empire, the feudal system with its rigid hierarchy of social roles and the social class-system of modern Europe. The Victorian age in Britain provides one of the best examples of a society organized around the delusion of permanence and imposing a high degree of conformity in ethos and role-performance. The established church answered much the same expectations in this closely integrated social set-up as the priesthood of Sumer and Babylon and the state religion and its functionaries in ancient Rome.

It goes without saying, therefore, that religion has always played an important part in social consolidation chiefly by providing supernatural ratification and validation of social order and by being the bearer of the symbols of social integration. It is in this context that we have to situate the role of the priest or cleric as a professional man. Despite the distance in time and culture there is not such a great functional difference between the shaman or kahin of primitive societies and the torpid clerics of Trollope's Barchester novels. Seen in their social context, both have the function of reassurance by their very presence irrespective of whether they do anything very much. *So long as the delusion of permanence is maintained* no role is so fixed and

175

conventionalized as that of the priest or clergyman and in no case so much as in this are the consequences of disappointing social expectations so severe. Hence the need for a longer and more thorough preparation and indoctrination for carrying out this role. If society is to be free of anxiety as to its own self-understanding the bearer of the role can admit of no uncertainty, doubt or indecision. From him more than from anyone else a word-perfect performance is demanded.

One of the most important factors in the present crisis of the priesthood—and of the Christian ministry in general—is surely the gradual and painful dissolution of the myth of social permanence and the consequent difficulty of maintaining a meaningful role. Some are consicous of what is happening (and has been for some time) and are searching for new roles and a new relevance. Others carry on in serene assurance of their social role of reinforcement and disburdening. Others again sense that the old certainties are dissolving but prefer to live in the past and therefore in delusion. It would not be difficult to show how these different attitudes continue in uneasy co-existence in present-day America or Britain.

Since imaginative writing in general, and the novel in particular, reflect in one way or another the ethos of a society and the performance of roles within it, it would be instructive to investigate through this medium how the role and image of the clergyman or priest change from one age to another. While it is obviously impossible to do more than touch on this here one or two indications may be given. Where priests appear in the writings of medieval poets such as Chaucer, Dunbar and Langland they are usually being criticized either for the perversion or the non-performance of their pastoral role but the role itself is not questioned. In his *The Praise of Folly* Erasmus has some hard things to say about "the mob of priests" bent on securing benefices and stipends rather than engaging in pastoral care but the priesthood is still firmly part of a social hierarchy which goes from prince to beggar. In the world reflected in the broad mirror of the Shakespearean canon, clerics have a real if marginal existence. While the higher ecclesiastical dignitaries pronounce their blessing on "just" wars the lesser figures, like the friar in *Romeo and Juliet* and the "churlish priest" who refused Christian burial to Ophelia, maintain the image established in the writings of the medieval satirists and moralists. We see the vague outline in Shakespeare and other writers of his age of what will emerge much more clearly in the English novel of the eighteenth and nineteenth centuries: the cleric in the role of "validating the carnival,"[5] conferring legitimation on the given social structure without generally being taken seriously as a person. It was not until the structure itself came under serious criticism that the role itself was challenged.

It is, perhaps, not surprising that the most compelling portrayals of the Catholic priest in modern fiction are set in the context of Latin Christianity and that they are represented, in one way or another, as operating outside of the fixed role and the ethos associated with it. In different ways the Country Priest of Bernanos, the Whisky Priest of Graham Greene's *The Power and the Glory* and Abbé Calou of Mauriac's *La Pharisienne* carry out a redemptive mission in society in a purely individual and even eccentric way precisely by not responding to the expectations implicit in the role.[6] The country curé does not take the advice of his clerical friends. His death without the regular administration of the last rites in the company of a laicized priest implicitly questions the validity of the conventional role. Graham Greene's priest could only become even an unconscious instrument of "objective grace" by ceasing to be the complacent, conventional young cleric whose photograph adorned the wall of the police headquarters. Calou is first deprived of his teaching post by

5. This phrase is from P. L. Berger, *op. cit.,* p. 21.
6. These three works are studied briefly by Horton Davies in *A Mirror of the Ministry in Modern Novels,* London and New York, 1959, pp. 81–110.

suspicious superiors and later banished from his parish and suspended. Here too there is implied a condemnation of a conventional role-performance within a culture-Christianity no longer able to communicate life.

The same impression emerges from other works of Mauriac and of course much more so from those of writers outside of or hostile to the Catholic church (for example, Zola's *Germinal* or Joyce's *Portrait of the Artist as a Young Man*). The situation is different in the English-speaking countries where Catholics constitute a minority. There are no compelling figures comparable to the three above but only a number of stereotypes. The novels of Robert Hugh Benson, the imaginative reconstruction of the careers of priests during the Elizabethan persecution by Philip Caraman and the excellent biography of Edmund Campion by Evelyn Waugh may be taken to reflect the anxiety of one section of English Roman Catholicism in the face of social change and church reform. In America the type most dramatized in the novel and in films reflects the predominant Irish element in American Catholicism. In neither case do we find any clue to a meaningful role of the priest in the rapidly changing patterns of social life today.

III

One of the more positive aspects of Schillebeeckx's study of celibacy referred to in an earlier chapter is the importance he gives to the concrete, existential experience of priesthood. To take one example, priesthood was experienced differently at the time of the evangelical revival in the eleventh and twelfth centuries from the more cultic and sacral experience of the fourth.[7] We may regret that the author did not take up the question

7. *Op. cit.*, p. 63.

whether an entirely new experience of priesthood is emerging at the present time. As he remarks, forms and structures tend to outlive the thinking and experience which first gave them life. More precisely, what has through the ages been decisive in the theology and practice of priesthood is the sacral element and it is just this which has lost its hold today. If we live in the world at all it is quite impossible to think in terms of *a sacred person,* one set aside by reason of values which he possesses over and above what he is seen to be worth by his deeds and words. I know there are many priests who will be amused at the thought that they are sacred persons and many laymen who will be equally amused at the thought of having to treat priests as such. But this only serves to show that for anyone living honestly and authentically in society the official understanding of priesthood of the kind presupposed in *Sacerdotalis Caelibatus* must appear archaic and non-viable. We should not underestimate the importance of this discrepancy between the historic and "official" understanding of priesthood and contemporary consciousness. Not only is the idea of a sacred ministry still widespread in both the Roman and, to a lesser extent, the Anglican churches; it also bears directly on other important aspects of church life and provides the most effective barrier to progress and reform.

In view of the cluster of associations, mostly pejorative but at any rate intimately related to the sacred, which have gathered round the word "priest," we may ask whether it would not be advisable to follow the example of the early church and drop it from our vocabulary. This would be more than a verbal gesture, for by so doing we would signify our willingness to broaden our understanding of ministry and begin to disperse the concentration of functions in the historical priesthood. We would then be free to designate the rich variety of service available within the context of the Christian mission by terms borrowed from secular life (which is, again, what the early church did) or new terms appropriate to specific ministries or no terms at all.

179

The Vatican II *Decree on Priestly Formation* provides a good illustration of the difficulty involved in attempting to harness new insights in psychology and sociology on to the official under-standing of priesthood. This latter presupposes a basic self-under-standing which neither requires nor allows for a genuinely human development, human in the most inclusive sense of the term. Those who achieve human authenticity do so too often at the cost of increasing tension with the priestly ethos (as in the case of Abbé Calou and the *curé de campagne*) or, in an increasing number of cases, by decisively breaking away from it. At this point I may be permitted to quote from an article which I wrote a few years ago in *New Blackfriars* in which I attempted a rough description of the phenomenon of clericalism:

> It might seem obvious to state that the cleric is not exempt from the general rules which govern psychological behavior. This is often lost sight of—or at least obstructed—by a false super-naturalism which denies in practice, if not in theory, the influence of the ordinary human psychological and environmental forces at work upon the individual. One element which all psychologists would agree is necessary for balance and maturity is the ability to listen to others, to accept criticism, *to remain open*. The op-posite of this is fixing the situation at a certain level, setting up an invulnerable and impenetrable façade. Clericalism (in the pejorative sense referred to) implies a closed system leading to psychic impoverishment and a compulsive and superficial be-havior-pattern. When this is sanctioned, as it often is, by a fixist and tabloid morality whose ideal is complete security within the boundaries of the self, you have an ideal prescription for neurosis—which may have something to do with the disturbing number of clerics who suffer from nervous breakdown. This can, of course, be tragic, but is often the only road to salvation—pulling down a façade which, though resplendent with decorated marble and baroque angelry, can hide an interior in sore need of rebuilding.[8]

8. "On Clericalism," in *New Blackfriars*, July, 1965, reprinted in *Cross Currents*, Winter, 1967, pp. 15–23.

Etymologically, as we have noted, to be sacred is to be set apart. As embodying the sacred the priest is set apart not only from "the world" but from the rest of the Christian community. It would be instructive to contrast this cultic apartness built into the role with a quite different kind associated with ministry in the New Testament. At the beginning of his letter to the Roman church Paul describes himself as "set apart [aphōrismenos] for the gospel of God." The word he uses here could refer to ritual segregation. In 2 Corinthians 6, 17 it is used to express the need of the Christian to segregate himself from non-Christian religious practices, and occurs in a Scripture quotation which, significantly, has sometimes been used in support of clerical celibacy.[9] But here as later in the letter where he speaks of his evangelical mission as a "priestly service" (Rom. 15, 16) we miss the whole point if we suppose he is thinking ritually and cultically. What we have here is a positive desacralization of cultic language.

The apartness officially and in practice associated with priesthood is of quite a different kind. While it is obvious that there are many priests who find their own way to supersede it by virtue of an inner need for authenticity we would be foolish to suppose that it does not give rise to serious problems. Without referring to more or less severe personality disorders which can result from the static, sacral ideal and the isolation inevitably associated with it—obsessions and fixations of various kinds, chronic authoritarianism and the like—we would do well to note a phenomenon much more pervasive, namely the inability to communicate. The obvious seriousness of this derives from the premise that the Christian community is meant to be, in the first place, a system of communications and a focus of interpersonal relationships. It is still, for example, quite rare to find a Catholic eucharist which really embodies personal interchange between pastor and congre-

9. See E. Schillebeeckx, op. cit., p. 59, who gives some documentation apropos the use (or better, abuse) of this text. The text in question is, however, Isaiah 52, 11, not 51, 11 as here.

gation even to the limited extent of the former greeting the latter as they leave the church. It is also still quite rare to hear a sermon which really touches the personal interests and concerns of the congregation, one which really communicates. Perhaps the assumption is that "grace" has already been communicated in an objective way in the sacrament beyond the reach of verification in terms of human experience and that any other kind of communication is superfluous.

A further symptom of this inability to communicate on the personal level may be sought in the kind of language which we have become accustomed to expect in official Roman documents. A recent example is the statement of faith with which Pope Paul VI closed the Year of Faith which seems to belie everything that was said during the council on the need for genuine dialogue with modern man. Let us, however, look briefly at another example more relevant to the theme under discussion, the encyclical on priestly celibacy. In discussing this in an earlier chapter we noted how often it makes use of the stylistic feature of the oratorical question. By definition, an oratorical question neither requires nor allows for an answer. It does not address anyone in particular but simply implies that no further discussion is needed. Whatever valid observations the encyclical may contain are for the most part clouded in a maze of rhetoric— celibacy is a "brilliant jewel" to which it is purported to "add new luster," the present canonical dispensation is "a golden law," the celibate priest is "wholly and solely intent on the things of God and the church," and so on. This kind of language is not only quite useless as a medium of communication but actually insulting in that it reduces those addressed to the status of things rather than persons capable of response and serious dialogue.

This isolation and apartness are also writ in the larger letters of a clericalized church in its relation or non-relation to the world. Understood theologically, the being of the church, like that of the individual, is in its innermost nature *a being in the*

182

world. As long as it is conceived of as a sacred society it cannot communicate and creatively interact with a secular world since by definition the sacred repels the secular. And to return to the more immediate concern of this chapter, the crisis of identity in the priesthood today can be explained by the fact that the priesthood as an historical role belongs in a sacred and cultic society. Such a society existed in the Middle Ages and continued residually into the modern world, but it has been clear for some time that it is now in the final stages of dissolution.

IV

A conclusion which seems inescapable is that church ministry must liberate itself from sociological captivity to a role first assumed when the church became the establishment and still persisting in a political and social context which has changed beyond recognition. That such a liberation can only be achieved at the price of a radical rethinking of the church's place in society is a major theme of this book and will be pursued further in the last two chapters. To speak of the church as a sacramental community implies that it must be prepared to contradict the expectations current at any time in society. To celebrate the eucharist means to open oneself continually to the future and the eschatological fulfillment. To be a sacramental community means to be a sign to the world of what it is to become and is not yet. And since, according to early Christian tradition, the eucharist is also a covenant-meal the life of the community which celebrates it must move between the poles of promise and fulfillment. It follows that the church must exercise the role in society of "bearing the criteriological symbols" rather than those of social integration.[10] Nothing less than a complete

10. This suggestive phrase is taken from James E. Sellers, *Theological Ethics,* London and New York, 1966, p. 95. He continues: "Both Christian

disestablishment of the church vis-à-vis society, a genuine *kenosis*, can make it possible for her to fulfill this function.

What this involves positively and practically for the forms of ministry in this kind of church will emerge gradually and no doubt painfully. We can only say that the personal ministry must follow the lines of the ministry of the church as a whole: refusing the role of preserving emotional stability in society at any cost and of satisfying a given set of expectations. It is interesting to note that the troubled heroes of the three works of fiction mentioned earlier all make this refusal in different ways. All three, therefore, carry out a role which is as prophetic as it is priestly, if not more so.[11] The prophets all share the conviction that the contemporary social order is not in conformity with the fulfillment implicit in the promise. While they speak to that society of its future hope their function is disruptive rather than integrative. The word they address to it is a hammer that breaks up rocks.

It would seem natural to conclude from all this that the ministry must escape from class segregation. The tendency to assume a specific social class status affects all denominations, of course, but we are speaking primarily to the Roman Catholic situation. To make the point more clearly we might first consider a context other than that of the English-speaking countries. An odd fact about the Italian religious scene, often commented on but nonetheless striking, is that anti-clericalism is deeply rooted in working-class areas from which the Italian clergy is chiefly recruited. Anti-clericalism is a tradition which dies hard. An

---

and Jewish sectors have the broader responsibility of nourishing the ancient treasures of biblical symbols that go into the vision of man's hope. The vision may come to fruition elsewhere, outside this specifically religious sector, yet it is this sector that functions especially within the fuller community to preserve the living symbols of divine reality whence all promise and fulfillment come."

11. Even the Whisky Priest whose history we may, with some exegetical license, compare with that of Hosea.

Italian journalist told me of a village where the people still baptize their children in wine out of contempt for the church and have done so ever since the day, over two centuries ago, when a cardinal ordered the same village through which he had passed to be razed to the ground after his carriage had been stoned. This was in territory which once formed part of the Papal States and it is instructive to note that anti-clericalism is strongest today in those parts of Italy which were formerly papal territory.

A priest of working-class origin, especially but by no means exclusively in the milieu of Latin Catholicism, soon finds himself "out of his class," living at a considerably higher cultural and economic level than what he was accustomed to previously and perhaps eventually becoming estranged from those among whom he grew up. So far there have been only sporadic attempts to break through this class barrier. The worker-priest movement in France soon ran into official opposition. Father Borelli's courageous mission among the *sgugnizzi* of Naples provided proof, if it were needed, of the practical impossibility of exercising a Christian mission at the grass-roots in a working-class milieu while remaining within the structures of clerical Catholicism. In the English-speaking countries the problem of social and occupation segregation is sharpened by the practically total engagement of a great number of priests in teaching in private and sometimes rather exclusive schools and colleges. The point is not that this is illegitimate for a priest but it raises the question: if a priest can spend his life teaching chemistry or English literature to upper middle-class children why cannot he, for example, be a stevedore or a cab driver? In terms of the church's mission the answer must be that there is no reason at all why he should not. The real reason is, of course, that for historical and cultural reasons the clergy is regarded as a middle-class profession and that therefore certain occupations are compatible with it and others are not.

185

We saw in an earlier chapter how clerical celibacy can be a positive hindrance to pastoral mission especially in those areas where a pervasive incredulity exists with regard to this practice. The experience of worker-priests in France and Italy has shown how it greatly limits the opportunities for pastoral contact and tends to consolidate a residential chaplaincy type of mission. That the church in Latin countries administers chiefly to women and children, especially in rural and working-class urban areas, can hardly be denied by anyone who has, over a sufficient period of time, taken stock of the congregations which assemble for mass and devotions in these areas. We can hardly doubt that mandatory celibacy is a powerful factor in the class segregation of the priesthood especially in Latin countries. A last point which may be made before leaving this subject is that many leaders of local churches in the English-speaking countries have received most of their ecclesiastical education in national seminaries situated in Rome or elsewhere in Italy. Whatever advantages this may have are surely offset by the fact that the language barrier and other cultural factors make it practically impossible to prepare realistically for a pastoral mission. It is possible (and verifiable) that a student can live at the Venerable English College or the American College in Rome for upwards of seven years without effectively learning the language or having any genuine contacts apart from other clerics and seminarians. One can only admire those who come through this long period of seclusion with the will and ability to engage in genuinely pastoral work.

It would be generally true to say that with Vatican II the Catholic church took a decisive step out of its own private world into the public arena of our century. With this beginning of an exodus from ethnic particularism and cultic apartness the feeling of consistency, the sense of solidness and solidarity, has to some extent broken down, necessarily inducing a certain identity-crisis in all reflecting Catholics not least the clergy. The identity-crisis of the priesthood is very much bound up with this passage from a private world with its own private language into a wider sphere of communication. To put it in another way, the uncertainty as to the role and image of the priest is the result of the crisis in the self-understanding of the church. Since we cannot speak intelligently about Christian ministry without having some idea of the nature of the community to which the minister belongs and which he represents we shall therefore have to reverse the order implied by the title of this book in presenting the considerations on church and ministry which follow in the next two chapters.

8. A New Christian Presence?

I

The title of this chapter is taken, with some slight modification and the addition of a question mark, from the statement made by Charles Davis on leaving the Roman Catholic church two years ago. Part of his contention was that "the Church in its existing form seems to me to be a pseudo-political structure from the past. It is now breaking up, and some other form of Christian presence in the world is under formation."[1] I take this as my text for what I want to say in this chapter because I believe that his action has obliged those of us who remain within the institutional church to further clarify our position and the reasons we have for staying as he has clearly stated his reasons for leaving.

Insofar as a decision of this kind, brought to a head by different kinds of converging pressures, represents "an existential inability to do otherwise," hardly any kind of comment would be appropriate. All we could do would be to show sympathy and give assurance of continued friendship. In the last resort the decision to stay in or get out will depend on the understanding of one's own Christian vocation which is something unique and incommunicable.[2] But insofar as this kind of decision is no longer of rare occurrence, those of us who retain in however attenuated a way some form of denominational affiliation have a duty to re-

1. Charles Davis, *A Question of Conscience*, p. 16.
2. J. A. T. Robinson, "On Staying In or Getting Out," *The Christian Century*, May 22, 1968, makes this point clearly.

assess our position. Most people will have met committed Christians—Catholics, Anglicans (Episcopalians), Methodists, Church of Christ, Baptists—who have left their denomination to join another. Such a transference is often dictated by pragmatic (but nonetheless serious) reasons but there is generally an underlying concern about the nature and especially the future of the church. It is quite another thing when an equally committed Christian gives up any kind of denominational belonging, severing his ties with any of the existing institutional embodiments of the Christian reality. While making it quite clear that he believes in the church and considers himself within its fellowship, Davis has found it impossible to identify the church as he conceives of it with any of the denominations. It is clear that he is not thinking of an invisible church over against the highly visible institutional forms; this is implied in his expectation of some other form of Christian presence or embodiment in the future. Though he traces the process of corruption some way back through the history of Western Christianity he does not specify at what point it reached such dimensions as to invalidate the ecclesial claims of the church. It would, of course, be naïve to expect him or anyone else to do this, but the question remains as to the identity of the believing community in the past as well as the future, the source and center of witness, whence the Word has gone forth or, in other words, what is implied in the expectation of a "new" or "other" Christian presence.

It will be clear from the preceding chapters that I agree with many of the observations Davis makes on the present situation of the Roman Catholic church and its self-understanding as embodied in official pronouncements. What I would like to do in the present chapter is to take up his offer of dialogue by asking some questions about the dialectical situation of tension inherent in any kind of institutionalized community. Since this tension is endemic in institutional life of any kind it will also apply to future forms of Christian presence; hence the need to

189

appraise and criticize not just institutions but the process of institutionalization and to ask to what extent it is possible to write
off existing forms and make a new start. Closely bound up with
this is the need to speak of the future not just in the form of
prognostication—whether the Roman Catholic or any other denomination is likely to survive or to overcome the grave abuses
of the present—but in strictly theological terms, in terms of the
hope of this concrete community existing now in the midst of
corruptions, in terms of the future as determinative of the existence of the church in the present. Does the eschatological nature
of the church imply a radical discontinuity with the past at every
stage of its existence? This appears to be the argument of Rosemary Ruether in her recent book *The Church Against Itself.*
While not advocating the solution of Davis, she comes close to
it in her statement that "those most perceptive in understanding
and most active in exercising a witness to Christ are found on
the fringes of the institutional church, even outside its formal
boundaries."[3] Both think in terms of an ideal church over against
the present rather shabby reality; and it is the tension involved
in this way of thinking that I would like to examine more
closely in the present chapter.

The departure of Davis should at least make one thing quite
clear to Roman Catholics, namely, that denominational disaffiliation will, in the present circumstances, be not only legitimate but
existentially necessary for many perceptive members of their
church. In fact, it is difficult to see how this solution can fail
to be for Christians of any denomination a constantly present
option. In the words of a German theological student quoted by
Dr. Wilder: "We must try to be at one and the same time *for*
the Church and *against* the Church. They alone can serve her
faithfully whose consciences are continually exercised as to
whether they ought not, for Christ's sake, to leave her."[4] The

3. *The Church Against Itself,* London and New York, 1967, p. 65.
4. A. Vidler, *20th Century Defenders of the Faith,* London, 1965, p. 122.

time has long passed for using such words as "defection," "disloyalty," "apostasy" and the like. There is a growing need for dialogue between the disaffiliated and those who have preserved for their own good reasons some form of affiliation. As Albert van den Heuvel put it:

> Let those who are satisfied with the old structure live in it, but let them not hinder the others from working out their calling in today's world. Let them who worship happily on Sundays do so happily, but let them not hinder the others who live their *koinonia* in less traditional forms and on less traditional days. Let those who can still stand the heat of the day with their traditional confessions of faith do so, but let them rejoice in those who are for the total rethinking of all they know. Let not those who know laugh at those who do not know much any longer. The unity of the Church has to be kept between the traditionalists (in the best sense of that word) and the renewers. Both can claim legitimacy in the community of Jesus, but both should recognize that they exist by the grace of the other![5]

This implies, what Davis would readily admit, that disaffiliation is only one of several options open to the Christian today vis-à-vis the denominational situation. Davis borrows the term "creative disaffiliation" from Harvey Cox but in the passage in question, taken from *The Secular City*, this solution is proposed only for exceptional cases implying that the main force of criticism should be directed at the church-institution from within:

> But once again, this criticism cannot be rootless and detached. It should be uttered only when those uttering it are willing to take part in constructive formulations leading to a church which is more faithful to its purposes. The church is the church only when it is *semper reformanda*, when it is constantly being corrected and called back to its real task by the Word of God.[6]

5. Quoted in J. A. T. Robinson, *The New Reformation?*, London and Philadelphia, 1965, p. 15.
6. *The Secular City*, p. 230.

In his latest work, *On Not Leaving It to the Snake,* Harvey Cox thinks it is too early to give up hope for the reformation of present church structures but rather blurs his point by going on to state that the church of the future will emerge on the edges of the existing church. More recently still, in the television program *Frontiers of Faith,* he has put on record his conviction that denominational Christianity will be lucky to survive the century. Let us content ourselves with saying that in the present impasse more than one option is open to the serious but troubled Christian and that it will be difficult to avoid criticism whatever option one chooses.

Both in *A Question of Conscience* and elsewhere Charles Davis has challenged his critics to state the grounds on which they advocate staying in the Roman church as he has stated his for leaving it. Whoever takes up this challenge will of course come up against the basic difficulty of all dialogue between opposing points of view arising from the presuppositions from which each starts out and the terms of reference within which the parties are to speak. In this case one such questionable presupposition is the meaning which Davis gives to faith and the manner in which he associates Christian faith with its various objectivizations, especially statements issuing from official organs in the church. But since one has to start somewhere, even if one has to speak provisionally, the following observations could be made.

1. My first reason is pragmatic rather than theological in the strict sense of the term. For me a Christian denomination is a system of communications which enables one to listen and speak in a way which is not possible for the disaffiliated. Moreover, by leaving the Roman Catholic church I know I would be severing connections with a great number of those who wait, work and pray in the spirit of the biblical *anawim,* the "poor" of the beatitudes. This may not be the case in the future, even within, say, a decade, but it is true now and my decision has to be made

now. With Davis I believe that denomination-changing is pointless in the inter-church situation which exists today; but unlike him I believe I ought to wait for and work towards "the new presence" within what is still, when all is said and done, one of the mainstreams of Christian life and community today. Also I feel some responsibility arising out of my own past, perhaps I should say my complicity, with regard to the situation which has driven him and others to go elsewhere for an authentically Christian form of life. I feel no compulsion either psychologically or otherwise to stay in; it just seems the most practically Christian thing to do.

2. The entire denominational situation has changed radically in the last decade or two. It seems to me self-evident at the present time that every affiliated Christian who has reflected on this situation be committed to the eventual dissolution of denominationalism. Even on "official" terms this would appear to be the whole point of having an ecumenical movement. It is true that by "voting with one's feet" one can work towards this end free of certain hazards and unpleasantnesses which may lie in wait for the one who stays. It is also true that the crunch comes when one asks, as one must, whether Roman Catholicism can participate in this commitment. Davis did not think so and left. While fully respecting his decision I would want to ask whether he has not put too much emphasis on faith as conceptual and propositional and too little on faith in a promise which is capable of continually opening up a new future. Liturgies, confessional formulas and institutional forms (the sociological structure of the church) are objectivizations of Christian experience in a past age which have persevered into the present. Confessional formulas in particular can and must be relativized with reference to the kind of Christian experience which they embody. The difficulty with the Roman position is, of course, as Davis has pointed out, that it has absolutized and canonized its own self-understanding, embodying it in what appear to be un-

alterable statements hedged in with a battery of supernatural sanctions. If this were insuperable it would be difficult to offer any alternative to disaffiliation since it would be both idolatry and apostasy, a transferring of faith from the God of history and the promise to the human and fallible church. Unlike Davis, however, I believe there is evidence that this cult of the absolute has already begun slowly and painfully to dissolve. Despite its evident inadequacies, Vatican II did represent a positive reaction to creative thinking carried out in the previous decades. It was, moreover, specially significant at those points where it negated, though not of course explicitly, teachings formerly held officially and promulgated by the *magisterium,* in particular on the nature of the church, the relation between Scripture and tradition, scriptural inspiration and freedom of conscience.

The crucial question for Davis (as for the rest of us) is that of papal infallibility defined in 1870 and reiterated in Vatican II and in the so-called "Credo of the People of God" issued by Pope Paul on June 30, 1968. This, he believes, is not open to retractation or redefinition. It is on the record, is false and has contributed greatly to falsifying the Christian lives of those on whom it was imposed. What needs to be said here is that both the formulation of this doctrine and the concept of an infallible dogma of faith reflect the self-understanding of the Catholic church as a whole a century ago. The statement issued from an interrupted council convoked at a time when the vitality of the Catholic church was possibly at its lowest point in modern history. Theological reflection was barren, the papacy was deeply involved in the futile struggle to hold on to political power, clericalism and triumphalism were at their apogee. Today, a century later, the situation is very different and it is doubtful whether the formulation of 1870 would command consensus among reflecting Roman Catholics. This does not alter the fact that it has not been expunged from the minutes, but neither have

194

other statements which have been promulgated by pontiffs and councils and are now abandoned. Here as elsewhere it seems to me legitimate to work towards a fuller consensus among reflective Roman Catholics which will sooner or later make its impact where it is most needed and lead to a genuine and not just verbal ecumenical repentance.

3. The concept of *mission* is essential to the existence and definition of the church. This mission has to be accomplished by the church being a credible sign to the world of what it is to become in the future kingdom of freedom and love. Davis has pointed very clearly to the Roman church's lack of credibility as a sign and I suppose criticism could be directed at other denominations along the same lines. But if disaffiliation is the only answer to corruption in the churches the question arises whether this symbolic and criteriological function can be fulfilled by dissociated groups free of any overarching institutional framework. This is an open question to which no answer is presumed known; only the future will tell. Something similar may be said with regard to the church's involvement at the heart of the secular life of the world and her effort to bear on those structures which shape modern society. The suspicion cannot be dispelled that creative disaffiliation which breaks the tension inseparable from life in community may end up by surrendering to pietism and what Moltmann calls "the cult of the new subjectivity."[7] In other words, by breaking away from the structures and forming new unattached groups, generally groups of the like-minded, we may actually find ourselves in a worse situation for carrying out a Christian mission than we were previously, and, in any case, what guarantee do we have that corruption will not return as the "new presence" begins to take shape and consolidate?

7. Jürgen Moltmann, *Theology of Hope,* London and New York, 1967, pp. 311 ff. The reader's attention may also be drawn to the remarks on the institutional crisis of Christianity in Gibson Winter, *The New Creation as Metropolis,* London and New York, 1963, pp. 30 ff.

CELIBACY, MINISTRY, CHURCH

It is understandable that the Christian of today should suppose that he is in an entirely new situation in his choice of staying in the church-institution or leaving it. It is also a correct supposition since the Christian of every age is presented with a new situation, but this should not trap us in the adamistic heresy of supposing that we can write off the past and the tensions which the past brings with it into the present. Ecclesiology has given too little attention to the study of these tensions inseparable from life in the church. This is unfortunate since if we are going to live with them we would be well advised to try to understand them. In what follows I want to sketch out my approach to this task of understanding after a brief analysis of the present situation of ecclesiology in the Roman Catholic church.

II

Ecclesiology, like christology, is the child of polemics. For the first treatise on the church we have to wait until 1453 when John of Torquemada, uncle of the famous inquisitor, wrote his *Summa de Ecclesia*.[8] This treatise is really an anti-conciliarist tract and is therefore, as we would expect, top-heavily papalist, giving us a first outline of what was to be the classical, pyramidal model reproduced and perfected in later works. The polemical character of writing on the church is even more pronounced in the Counter-Reformation period as we see from the treatises of Bellarmine, Suarez and Melchior Cano. We may perhaps credit Cano with the discovery, or at least the elaboration, of the scriptural proof-text familiar to generations of Catholic seminarians. This involved both the subjugation of Scripture to the official organs of the church and its exploitation in the attempt

8. James of Viterbo's *De Regimine Christiano*, written almost a century and a half earlier, can hardly be called a treatise on the church.

196

to rationalize existing institutions. To understand the gravity of this abuse, we have to remember that the same approach to Scripture has obtained in Roman Catholic apologetics down to very recent times and is in fact still being practiced.

What was the situation which these apologists sought to legitimize with the help of scriptural proof-texts? The answer to this question cannot easily be given in a few sentences since it covers a large area of church history; besides, it is by now fairly well known. After the accession of Constantine Christianity became the state-religion and its liturgy the *cultus publicus* of the Roman Empire. The clergy were reorganized and meshed into the administrative machinery and civil service wherever possible: the pope became the *summus pontifex,* the patriarchs (including, of course, the pope) took over to some extent the function of the four *praefecti,* the bishops in many cases became important local administrators, the lower orders were lined up, as we saw earlier, with the *cursus honorum.* It was natural that much of the mystique of *Roma perennis* also rubbed off on the church and deeply influenced thinking and theologizing about the omnipresent institutional reality which it presented to the world. At the same time, now that the age of the martyrs was past, the primitive eschatological orientation of early Christianity, which had lasted in a diluted form into the fourth century, disappeared from mainstream ecclesiastical life.

This situation continued into the Middle Ages when the apotheosis of the institution was completed as a result of the victory of the papalists over the conciliarists. It was further reinforced by the polemicists of the Counter-Reformation. We may note in passing that of the three names from this period mentioned a moment ago two were Spanish and one Italian, pointing to the fact that the Counter-Reformation originated precisely in that part of the Christian world which had little contact with the reformers and also to a loss of catholicity which has afflicted us through Vatican II and beyond. We hardly need to prove any more that the modern world as we know it originated in a breakaway from this "sacred center." The more the church lost contact with a rapidly changing environment the more absolutist her claims became, reaching a climax in the political catholicism of the second half of the last century and the definition of papal infallibility in 1870 which was certainly linked with political catholicism. The epilogue, in the form of the ecclesiastical horror-story of the suppression of modernism, is already too well-known to justify repetition.[9]

All of this needs to be said, quite soberly and without exaggeration, in order to understand our present situation. What we are living through at the moment is the painful dissolution of "the cult of the absolute"[10] which underlay all this long development, together with the ecclesiastical and linguistic fundamentalism that went with it. That some progress has been made can be seen by comparing the constitution on the church of Vatican I, promulgated June 18, 1870, with that of Vatican II, promulgated November 21, 1964. Another crucial test is the answer to the two closely connected questions: Who belongs to the church? Can anyone be saved outside of the church? The latter has generally been formulated on the basis of Cyprian's dictum *extra ecclesiam nulla salus* though it appears that Cyprian enunciated it with reference to his (unorthodox) view that baptism administered outside the church, that is, by schismatics, was invalid. At any rate, the doctrine that full, juridical membership of the Roman Catholic church is necessary for salvation has been taught repeatedly by the magisterium. In 1442 the Council of Florence decreed that "neither pagans nor Jews, nor heretics nor schismatics can obtain eternal life but will be condemned to the everlasting fire which is prepared for the devil and his angels unless, before the end of their lives, they are received into the Catholic

9. For some colorful details see R. Adolfs, *The Church Is Different*, London and New York, 1966, pp. 22–33.

10. See J. Moltmann, *op. cit.*, p. 304.

Church."[11] I may be allowed to point out that, although this teaching has never been officially repudiated or expunged from the record, it is not now "officially" held, having become too incredible to be taken seriously. This may indicate that we should speak not only of the loss of credibility of the Catholic Church to the outsider, on which Charles Davis's *apologia* is chiefly based, but also and at the same time of a loss of credibility *within* the church vis-à-vis official organs and their pronouncements. This process of reduction, undoing, is also part of the purification of the church which seems to him to hold out such small prospect of success.

The rediscovered Pauline doctrine of the church as the body of Christ seemed to offer the curial theologians a convenient way of modifying a scandalous doctrine which had been promulgated since the time of Innocent III at the end of the twelfth century. It has been a commonplace of Catholic catechetics up to recent times that Catholics belong to the body of the church while non-Catholic Christians belong *only* to the soul. While it is true that this unintelligible statement is not found in the encyclical *Mystici Corporis,* and while what is found there is a distinct improvement on the medieval formulation, the restatement is still hardly satisfactory. Only Catholics belong to the body of Christ. All other Christians are related to it only by "some unconscious yearning and desire" and are urged to "extricate themselves from a state in which they cannot be secure of their own eternal salvation" (§102). This statement of the magisterium is not of course explicitly repudiated in the *Constitution on the Church* of Vatican II but the situation has, once again, shifted considerably, mostly as a result of incorporating the insights of Scripture scholars and theologians many of whom had been harassed and silenced during the previous decade. What we

11. Denzinger, §714. It may be that this statement was put in on the mistaken ground that it was written by Augustine; but it was put in nonetheless.

await at this stage is the miracle of a genuine ecumenical *metanoia* with regard to the Roman Catholic church's official self-understanding which could open the future to new possibilities.

The clearest indication of new thinking on the church in Vatican II is the title of the first chapter of the *Constitution on the Church* which speaks of "The Mystery of the Church." Here we find official recognition given to an insight which must be traced back to J. A. Möhler (1796–1838), who represents perhaps the first attempt to break out of the juridical and triumphalist thinking which had characterized Catholic ecclesiology from the Middle Ages on into modern times. Influenced by Schleiermacher and German romanticism Möhler spoke of the church's inner life in terms of organicity and immanent vitality. His own influence on writers such as Pilgram, Scheeben, Adam and Mersch paved the way for *Mystici Corporis*[12] while his return to the Fathers, paralleled by the much better known work of Newman in England, brought back into view the church as embodying the Christian mystery of salvation.

From the point of view of biblical and historical theology, there are two aspects of the use of this word "mystery" with regard to the church which are of particular significance for the impasse we are in today. In the first place, the biblical use of the word draws our attention at once to the future. One of its roots is the mythological image of the secret counsel of the gods in which the future destiny of mankind is decided. In exceptional cases some chosen individual is admitted to the counsel chamber and commissioned with the task of revealing some part of the deliberations to his fellow men. Something of this comes through in the account of the call of Isaiah (6, 1–13) and the revelation

---

12. The exaggerations and occasional woolliness found in some of these writers, especially Pilgram who wrote a book entitled *The Physiology of the Church,* were justly castigated by M. D. Koster, O.P., *Ekklesiologie im Werden,* Paderborn, 1940. See also Karl Adam's response in *Tübinger Theologische Quartalschrift,* 1941–1944, pp. 145–166.

of Micaiah the prophet to king Ahab (1 Kgs. 22, 19–23). This representation becomes a basic feature of Jewish apocalyptic writing and it is here rather than in the Greek "mystery-religions" that we have to look for a context of meaning. The "mystery" revealed to Daniel is concerned essentially with the future of his people then passing through the fires of the Seleucid persecution,[13] the "mystery" spoken of in the Qumran Habakkuk Scroll refers to God's providence for Israel, and for the community in particular, in the future. The "mystery" of which Paul speaks so often is concerned not primarily with the church but with the future destiny of mankind which is revealed in the kerygma.[14] I do not think it is merely a learned quibble to insist that in Paul the church itself is not the "mystery" and that he never speaks of the mystery *of* the church. The mystery is revealed wherever the gospel is proclaimed; it is therefore made known *through* the church: "he has made known to us the mystery of his will . . . as a plan for the fullness of time, to unite all things in him" (Eph. 1, 9–10); "this grace was given me to preach to the nations . . . to make all men see what is the plan of the mystery hidden for ages in God . . . that *through the church* the manifold wisdom of God might now be made known" (Eph. 3, 8–10). The mystery, therefore, is concerned essentially with the future of mankind and indeed of the cosmos, not primarily with the church. This mystery is revealed in the kerygma; and the kerygma has to do with the resurrection, that is, with the future of Christ in which is revealed the future of the world. The church is constituted by those who accept the

13. Daniel 2, 18. 19. 27. 28. 29. 30. 47. The word *"raz,"* translated as *"mysterion"* in the Greek Bible, is probably a Persian loan-word. See R. E. Brown, "The Pre-christian Semitic Concept of 'Mystery,' " in *Catholic Biblical Quarterly,* 20 (1958), pp. 417–443.

14. The most significant texts are Romans 11, 25; 16, 25; 1 Corinthians 2, 1 (here the reading is doubtful); 2, 7; 15, 51; Ephesians 1, 9; 3, 3–9; 5, 32; 6, 19; Colossians 1, 26–27; 2, 2; 4, 3; 2 Thessalonians 2, 7; 1 Timothy 3, 9. 16.

kerygma, and therefore the church's primary duty is to speak to the world of what it is to become.

The second aspect of the biblical use of this word presupposed by the first chapter of the *Constitution on the Church* starts out from the fact that Jerome translates the "great mysery" of Ephesians 5, 32 as "sacrament" (*sacramentum* also translates "*raz*" in the Vulgate version of Daniel). A sacrament is a sign and the church is the sign to the world of what it is meant to become. The miracles of Jesus, which are called "signs" in the Fourth Gospel, indicate the lines of force along which the new reality is breaking into the old world. When the disciples of the Baptist ask Jesus (in effect) whether he is the inaugurator of the new age he answers: "the blind receive their sight and the lame walk, lepers are cleansed and the deaf hear, the dead are raised up and the poor have good news preached to them" (Mt. 11, 5). What may escape us here is that this is simply a paraphrase of a prophetic saying in the Isaian collection about the eschatological age (Is. 35, 5–6). The same for the exorcisms (Mt. 12, 28). Christ, therefore, is the sign of a world in which there will be no more blind, deaf, lame, diseased or obsessed; where division will have given way to unity; where even death will have given way to life. But the answer also implies that the miracles of healing and the exorcisms point to the new transforming power as *already present* in history.

By speaking of the church first and foremost as "mystery" in the biblical sense Vatican II has certainly gone a long way towards closing a barren era of ecclesiastical fundamentalism, juridicism and triumphalism. The main weakness, as it seems to me, is that as yet the church has no language for speaking meaningfully of "the world," explained by the fact that language comes from experience and the Catholic church has for so long been, in Yves Congar's phrase, "a church without a world." Hence the pervasive fuzziness of the document dealing with "The Church in the Modern World." The church is meant to be a sign to the world of what it is destined to become; it is also meant to be the vehicle of a transforming power working through the historical process. As we approach the third millennium of its existence, however, there is still little sign of the destined end. The world is still full of division, poverty, disease, hatred and war. The church therefore can only be credible as a reconciling, healing, exorcising presence at the points where (in Moltmann's phrase) the negative has still to be negated. If it is not this it is not the church at all but only "a pseudo-political structure from the past" (Davis).

We would hardly do justice to the *Constitution on the Church* if we said nothing of the prominence which it gives to the concept of the church as the People of God (the title of the second chapter). At this point too it reflects an awareness of work done over the preceding couple of decades in the field of biblical theology, mostly by scholars outside the Roman communion.[15] To think of the church as the People of God has the decisive advantage of placing it in the context of concrete historical experience, and the chapter draws some fruitful consequences from this incontrovertible scriptural datum—as, for example, that the church must be the instrument of salvation for the world as Israel was in the understanding of the prophets. It also corrects what had become the traditional use of the Old Testament in the Western church by insisting that the church is the new Israel in the sense of the final or eschatological People of God and does this, to some extent at least, by adopting a typological approach: "All these things [election of Israel, covenant, and so forth], however, were done by way of preparation and as a figure of that new and perfect covenant which was to be ratified in

15. The most complete study in recent years is that of N. A. Dahl, *Das Volk Gottes,* Darmstadt, 1963, G. von Rad's publications on Deuteronomy have also been very influential. Roman Catholic treatment can be found in L. Cerfaux, *The Church in the Theology of St. Paul,* London and New York, and, most recently, in H. Küng, *The Church,* in which the treatment of the Old Testament material is not, however, very satisfactory.

Christ, and of that more luminous revelation which was to be given through God's very Word made flesh" (§9). One danger of this approach, which the constitution does not altogether avoid, is that speaking of the church as an eschatological community may be pure verbalism, a technique for differentiating the church and pointing up its uniqueness without drawing any of the necessary consequences, especially with regard to institutional forms, dogmatic affirmations and the like. In a somewhat similar way the council documents as a whole reflect here and there the unresolved tension between the standard juridical understanding of the church and the emphasis on *experience* as dictating and explaining any kind of religious objectivization, an emphasis which goes back historically to Schleiermacher and his disciples (further back still, to Kant) and was peremptorily banished from Roman Catholicism in the overkill of modernism. It seems to me that the treatment of the church as the People of God in the *Constitution on the Church* could be usefully supplemented by a consideration of the historical (political and religious) experience of Israel on the ground that the eschatological reality is already witnessed to in the Old Testament and that therefore the tensions inherent in eschatological existence are present there as they are, with a vital difference, in the Christian church. This may not only help us to understand the ambiguities through which we are living today but also, possibly, suggest a way forward.

III

The history of Israel is characterized throughout by dialectical tension. The name itself cannot be applied unequivocally to a racial unit; historically, Israelites never constituted a racially homogeneous group and, even more important, it was possible for peoples who were ethnically quite different to accept cove-

nant with Israelites and thus become part of Israel. In this respect "Israel" can be described as "an open concept."[16] and
Mendenhall is not far off the mark in speaking of early Israel
as "an ecumenical faith, a catholic religion in the best sense of
the term."[17] It is no longer possible to equate "Israel" unequivocally with any of the political forms which were adopted
throughout the history, especially the monarchy and the priestly
theocracy of the post-exilic period. In this respect "Israel" remains to some extent an ideal entity in tension with the empirical
Israel which is studied in the context of the changing social and
political patterns of ancient Near Eastern history. Insofar as
Israel remains conscious of drawing its existence from an absolutely antecedent act of God—just as the name itself is represented in the tradition as given by God (Gen. 32, 28)—the
existing institutional form is always under judgment and therefore can never be given absolute validity.

This tension can be considered under different forms: ideal
Israel over against the emperical reality, Israel as event over
against the institutional form, Israel in the world and apart from
the world, Israel living by the tradition and constantly moving
into the future. The significance of this characterization of
Israelite history was not lost on Christians of the apostolic age
as we can see from Paul's allegory in 1 Corinthians 10, 1–5;
after nearly two thousand years of Christian history it should
with less reason be lost on us. The hermeneutically crucial fact
is, of course, that the early Christian church identified itself with
the true or ideal Israel. According to Acts, the first question
which the original nucleus of a hundred and twenty ask the
risen Lord is whether he is about to restore the kingdom to
Israel (1, 6) and the first thing they do after the Ascension is
make up the number twelve as representative of the twelve-

16. Ludwig Köhler, *Theologie des Alten Testaments*, Tübingen, 1936,
p. 49; Dahl, *op. cit.*, pp. 3–4.
17. In *Biblical Archaeologist*, 25.3 (1962), p. 86.

tribal unity.[18] Jesus is represented in early preaching as the Saviour of Israel (Acts 13, 23) and Paul at one point claims that he is suffering "for the hope of Israel" (28, 20). Throughout the New Testament, and especially in Paul's letters, the Christian community is identified by means of terms such as "the people of the covenant" and "the Israel of God"; and the fact that Paul refers to the ethnic faith in which he grew up as "Israel according to the flesh" (1 Cor. 10, 18) implies that the Christian church embodies "Israel according to the spirit" even though this expression is not used. It is perhaps not superfluous to note that this usage does not flow from a purely typological approach. The discoveries at Qumran have made clearer what we knew already, that especially in sectarian Judaism of that time the most crucial theological question had to do with the identity of the true Israel. The Christian church regarded itself as the inheritor of that indefectible promise which brought Israel into existence in the first place. Early Christian eschatology is the successor of the eschatology of the prophets and he who raises Jesus from the dead is none other than "the God of Abraham, Isaac and Jacob" who spoke to Moses in the burning bush (Acts 3, 13).

Until recent decades the origins of Israel were bathed in a bright and foggy supernatural haze; in fact they still are for the fundamentalist. There is still much that we do not know, but what we *do* know points to the fact that from the beginning Israel was very much a part of the world at that time, the world of the ancient Near East towards the end of the second millennium. Her founding events are described in terms of tribal movements, the renunciation of political allegiance, land-tenure and the like. Even the covenant, the fundamental category in which she thought of her relations with God, is really a political cate-

18. Both in the Old Testament and at Qumran we find the people organized into groups or "cells" of ten, as we saw in an earlier chapter. This may explain the number 120 given parenthetically in the introduction to the account of the election of Matthias (Acts 1, 15).

gory modelled to some extent, as we now know, on international treaties of that time. We cannot even adequately understand what "the love of God" means in the Old Testament without taking into account the kind of language habitual in international treaties.[19] The founding-event has been well paraphrased by Harvey Cox as a massive act of civil disobedience. The prophets are concerned primarily with international politics rather than the enunciation of general religious truths. They inculcate moral conduct not in the abstract but with reference to a political goal or destiny which lies in the future. We do not find in their writings any extrapolation into a timeless or eternal world. Jeremiah buying a parcel of land in the beleaguered and doomed kingdom of Judah is a symbol of the prophets' declaration in favor of this devastated earth. When they speak we hear "the voice God has lent to the silent agony, a voice to the plundered poor, to the profaned riches of the earth."[20] Since Jesus and the community of those who believe in him must be seen at the same time as the continuation and summation of the prophetic mission this must be immediately relevant for the church's situation vis-à-vis the world.

Corresponding to the doctrine of the "marks" of the church (in the Catholic tradition: one, holy, catholic, apostolic) we may also speak of the "marks" of the Israelite community. In his attempt to characterize the Israel addressed in the homiletic sections of the Pentateuch, especially in Deuteronomy wherein is reflected the liturgy of covenant-renewal, Martin Noth enumerates them as follows: a common link with Yahweh, demarkation from the Canaanites, a common tradition about exodus and occupation of the land and the name "Israel."[21] We may note

19. W. J. Moran, "The Ancient Near Eastern Background of the Love of God in Deuteronomy," *Catholic Biblical Quarterly*, 25 (1963), pp. 77–87.

20. Abraham Heschel, *The Prophets*, New York, 1962, p. 8.

21. M. Noth, *The Laws in the Pentateuch and Other Essays*, Edinburgh, London and New York, 1966, p. 26.

in passing that it is theologically unsound (though it may be emotionally justifiable) to reject the church out of hand on the ground that these marks are not currently detectable without taking into account the kind of tension which must characterize any institutional embodiment of a religious idea or ideal. The prophets continually denounce "institutional" Israel for breaking the vital link with Yahweh, for adopting Canaanite religious ideas and practices and for perverting the tradition, without losing faith in Israel as the embodiment of an indefectible promise. That they do not thereby appeal to an ideal Israel entirely distinct from any current embodiment is seen in the fact that they denounce *from within* Israel and speak of its future—even when they do not detect the form Israel will take in the future—under the figure of the *remnant*.

To speak of "marks" implies individuation and separation and herein lies one of the main sources of tension and ambiguity in the historical existence of both Israel and the Christian church. The most basic of the four characteristics listed by Noth is clearly the common worship of Yahweh. It is this which provided the cement which bound the tribes together in a sacred federation. Though it is probable that this deity was worshiped by other groups before Israel came on the scene, the adoption of the Yahweh-cult by Israel became a mark which set her apart from "the nations round about." Yahweh chose Israel and called her out from the rest of mankind to be a people apart. It is at this point, the conviction of a divine election, that we have to begin in studying the ambiguity which runs throughout the whole of Old Testament history. It could and did lead, on the one hand, to an absolutization of Israel as the embodiment of the divine choice, the elect living in the midst of a godforsaken world. The peoples in possession in Canaan had to be exterminated (this was, of course, a theological postulate which was never put into effect), foreigners were to be excluded from the cultic assembly, marriage with the impure *goyim* was excluded. Israel was a sacred nation set apart from the profane reality of the world. Here we have one line of thinking which began with election and covenant and ended in the exclusivism of the post-exilic period when the priestly and scribal classes had achieved dominance. We have remarked already on the irony that this priestly-cultic-sacred theocracy from which Jesus and the first Christians broke away became, in more ways than one, the model for the Western church once it had become the establishment.

Side by side with this way of thinking, however, we find another much in evidence up to the time of the priestly theocracy. According to this view Israel's call is in virtue of God's concern for an alienated world; in fact, Israel is nothing else but the world beginning to respond in faith to God's summons. Whatever the actual facts may have been, the tradition represents Abraham obeying the call to set out on an unpredictable journey at a time when he "worshiped other gods" (Jos. 24, 2). The Yahwist writer prefaced the national (and often nationalistic) history of his people with a sketch of universal history concluding with the call of Abraham in order to identify Israel as the point at which the world begins to respond. In the vast panorama of ethnic and national groups in Genesis 10 it may seem strange that Israel is not mentioned until we recall that the point of vision is the divine purpose for the world which has begun to be realized in Israel.

This may help us to see that the church *is* the world insofar as it has become conscious of and has begun, however imperfectly, to respond to God's summons addressed to it through Christ. George Casalis puts it well by insisting that the church is "a segment of the world which confesses the universal Lordship of Christ; thus it is the place where the world becomes aware of its true destination, its true face."[22] This in its turn makes it difficult to speak of church and world as occupying two

22. Quoted in C. W. Williams, *Where in the World?*, New York, 1963, p. 48.

distinct spheres—sacred and secular, the city of God and the city of the world, or however else we choose to express it. In this case the question is bound to follow—and it is a serious one—why do we need a definite church-structure? One reason surely is that the church must be a sign *in* (rather than *to*) the world of what it is destined to become, of what kind of future is open to it, just as Israel, living in the midst of the nations, was to be a sign or light to them (Is. 49, 6). A sign has to be visible, a light has to be seen; hence the need for credibility. During its existence in Old Testament times Israel took on several institutional forms, in particular those of a monarchic state and priestly theocracy. Both came to be accepted though not without opposition and grave reservations. But when, as actually happened, they lost credibility as signs of what God was doing in the world they were rejected. No institutional form can claim finality.

The relation between Israel and the world in the Old Testament can be further illustrated with references to the relation between redemption and creation (providence). The standard approach in Christian thinking, both Catholic and Protestant, has linked the church with redemption and the world with creation. Quite apart from any implicit Manichaeism, of which quite a lot has gotten through into "official" Christian thinking, this has resulted in a tendency to polarize "worldly" and "churchly" concerns and thereby to minimize the redemptive value of "worldly" activities. A sound biblical theology does not support this dichotomy but unfortunately such a theology of the "worldly" still awaits elaboration. That creation is not a central and primitive element in the faith of Old Testament man is rather obscured, for many readers of the bible, by the fact that the whole collection begins with the creation story in the first chapter of Genesis. In view of this it must be insisted that the point of departure for Israelite faith is the creation of a new point of reference *within* the historical continuum which, so it was believed, gave sense and direction to the whole. This point of reference is *the creation of a people* out of an ethnically hybrid group of slaves who were serving time in Egypt. Moreover, the exodus from Egypt is, for the whole biblical tradition, the paradigmatic event of redemption. Redemption means aggregation to this new people, being franchised into the new community, escape from lostness, in a word, belonging. In the Old Testament creation is always, basically, soteriological and redemption is always creative. Psalm 136, for example, begins with praise of God in creation and goes on at once without interruption to exodus and the recital of what we usually call sacred history. We find in the Isaian collection from the exilic age a poem, or fragment of a poem, which uses the mythological motif of the cosmogonic victory of the god over the forces of chaos to make the same point:

> Was it not thou that didst cut Rahab in pieces,
>   That didst pierce the Dragon?
> Was it not thou that didst dry up the sea,
>   The waters of the great deep;
> That didst make the depths of the sea a way
>   For the redeemed to pass over? (Is. 51, 9–10)

Here the monsters familiar from Canaanite mythology (Rahab, the Dragon, Sea) are cryptogrammatic for Egypt and the Sea of Reeds through which Israel passed dryshod. This can only mean that exodus and creation (Israel and the world) are part of the one divine purpose which is first detected when Israel set out from bondage into a future unpredictable and dangerous but full of hope and promise.

A further point not unconnected with this ought to be made. One of the primary functions of the prophet in Israel's history is to direct the attention of the people to what God is doing in the world. Following Max Weber, we have already said that these men were interested above all in international politics and it is, at any rate, no coincidence that their preaching only began

211

to be recorded when Israel came under serious—and ultimately fatal—pressure from the great powers of that time, first Assyria, later Babylonia. In stating that Assyria is the rod of Yahweh's anger Isaiah of Jerusalem is evaluating Israel from the point of view of her place in God's final purpose for the world, a purpose which she was called to serve. Once this role is lost sight of, Israel ceases to have any significance *in herself* and is just one of "the nations round about." Amos, who clearly believed that Israel had defaulted, even says that hers was not the only God-directed exodus (9, 7). The anonymous prophet of the Exile, writing at a time when Israel had lost what little political significance she ever had, asserts that the God who called Israel into existence is now calling the Persian king Cyrus and making him his instrument. Looking out into the immeasurably greater political milieu into which his people had been thrust, he proclaims that "a new thing" is coming into existence which must bear radically on Israel's self-understanding.

In view of this we may, without undue moralizing, ask whether we as a church have been perceptive and humble enough to take stock of what is happening in the world and to understand our mission in terms of the world's needs, viewing ourselves "not as a separate sphere, but as the people of God in the world taking their form around the changing shapes of the world's needs."[23] What relevance, for example, has the Catholic church in America, with all the vast resources, manpower and influence of which it disposes, for the civil rights movement? To what extent are the present structures capable of enabling a mission to be carried out in terms of the present needs which are brought home to us every day in the papers and on the television screen? This mission cannot be exhausted in terms of the needs of individuals alone—this has been our mistake too long.

23. C. W. Williams, *What in the World?*, New York, 1964, p. 43. The whole section entitled "What is God Doing in the World?", pp. 29–47, bears on this subject.

It implies understanding and keeping pace with the changing political, sociological and economic dimensions of life in the world (which is, after all, our own life) and a readiness to modify even radically our own institutional forms in order to make this mission possible and credible. And if this kind of mission is an essential element in the life of the church we may even, with the Roman Catholic sociologist Greinacher, speak of getting rid of heretical structures in the church.[24] No matter how permanent it may seem, the present structuring of the Roman Catholic church has in itself neither more nor less validity, *in view of the divine purpose for the world,* than the monarchy and the priestly theocracy back in Old Testament times. And it is a sobering thought that both of these were ultimately rejected.

This brings us to a further aspect of the tension in the historical existence of Israel. Terms like "Israel," "the children of Israel," "the people of Israel," "all-Israel" refer primarily to the way the congregation was addressed in the cultic assembly of the tribes at the common sanctuary. Such terms are used throughout Deuteronomy which is pervasively homiletic and reflects the ancient ceremony of covenant-making and covenant-renewal. The *shema,* for example, begins with the words "Hear, O Israel!" (Deut. 6, 4). Now the odd thing is that, as we now know, Deuteronomy was promulgated in the kingdom of Judah some time in the seventh century B.C. By this time the kingdom of Israel, the northern kingdom which broke away under Jeroboam, had ceased to exist, and yet the community addressed in this book is never described as "Judah," always as Israel. This is all the more remarkable if we regard the book as containing what was, in effect, a state law. The only conclusion we can draw from this is that "Israel" cannot be identified with any particular institution, in this case a monarchic state which was all that was left of Israel after the deportation of 721 B.C. The

24. Quoted in C. W. Williams, *Where in the World?*, p. 82.

213

true identity of Israel can be established only by going back to the origins; and in fact the Deuteronomists aimed at doing just this—going back behind the corruptions and distortions introduced in the course of history to the aboriginal pattern. The purpose, however, was not simply to recreate this pattern but rather to re-actualize the event which brought Israel into existence and which was, ideally, constitutive of her existence in the world. Hence the emphasis in this book on Yahweh's search for a people among the nations of the world (4, 20. 34; 26, 6–7), his finding them in Egypt ("let my people go!"), his summons to them to come out from there (4, 32–37; 7, 7–8). This event is seen as constitutive of Israel at every moment of her history, a continuous *creatio e nihilo:* "not with our fathers did the Lord make this covenant, but with us, who are all of us here alive this day" (5, 3).

I suggest that we may find here something very relevant to the much-discussed need for renewal in the church. If it is to be in the truly theological sense a radical renewal rather than a more or less liberal tinkering with the institutions which we have it must return to the roots. The church must transfer its faith, love and adoration from itself back to God who alone gives it life. It must re-affirm its faith in the power of God which not only in the New Testament but also in the scriptures of Israel confronts us as love, a creative love, "love to the non-existent, love to the unlike, the unworthy, the worthless, to the lost, the transient and the dead."[25] The God whom we profess in our creeds is one "who gives life to the dead and calls into existence the things that do not exist" (Rom. 4, 17). Renewal within the church is only possible if we learn to see the signs of this creative activity around us, acknowledge it, rescue it from anonymity and fashion our own efforts around it.

A reading of Deuteronomy reveals how important it is to

25. Moltmann, *op. cit.,* p. 32.

214

distinguish between the constitutive event and the institutional embodiment of the event. The event must certainly be embodied in some way—there is no such thing as a spiritual church no more than there was ever a spiritual Israel, and a collection of dissociated believers cannot be a sign in the world. But if the church is not to fall into the sin of idolatry the institutional forms must not be absolutized. They come continually under judgment with reference to the antecedent event; outside of this reference they can hardly fail to be a positive hindrance to God's purpose in the world.

It has become quite popular of late to refer to the church as *event,* but what does this mean? And how in any case can an event in the past be re-actualized in the present? I would suggest one approach to an explanation starting out from this word "church." As is well known, early Christian writers use the word "*ekklesia*" of individual communities of the faithful.[26] Why they elected to use this term rather than any other (especially "*synagoge*") may be discussed; perhaps they simply wished to express thereby apartness from the religious and liturgical world of Judaism with which many would still have identified them (in Acts 24, 5 the lawyer Tertullus referred to them as a Jewish sect). In an earlier chapter, however, we mentioned another possibility, based on the use of "*ekklesia*" by the Greek translators of Deuteronomy corresponding to the Hebrew "*qahal.*"[27] In the phrase "the day of the assembly" (Deut. 9, 10; 10, 4; in Greek: "the day of the *ekklesia*") the substantive refers not just to those who are called together but also to the actual coming together, and it is interesting that behind both the

26. For example, 1 Thessalonians 1, 1; 2, 4; 2 Thessalonians 1, 1; Acts 8, 1; 1 Corinthians 15, 9. This last probably refers to the sum total of Christian communities.

27. See above p. 100, especially n. 8. The only occurrence outside Deuteronomy is Nehemiah 13, 1 which is an explicit reference to Deuteronomy 23. The *Constitution on the Church* adds Numbers 20, 4 but the Greek here is "*synagogē*" not "*ekklēsia.*"

215

Hebrew and Greek word there lies the idea of a summons or call. In Deuteronomy 23 we find a list of those who were disqualified on ethnic or ritual grounds from taking part in "the assembly of God" (in Greek: the "*ekklesia tou theou*") which shows, incidentally, how easily the doctrine of election could degenerate into exclusivism, as it has done in both Israelite and Christian history. Rather than concluding from this brief semantic study that the church is, in Newman's phrase, a community in the process of separation from the world, we should think of the summons as addressed to the world and of the congregation as the point at which the world responds.

It will at least be clear from this that "church" is essentially a dynamic concept. Several times throughout Deuteronomy we hear the divine summons: "gather the people to me" (for example, 4, 10; here the Greek verb is "*ekklēsiasomai*"), and this usage lies behind Paul's reference to the Corinthians coming together as an *ekklesia* (1 Cor. 11, 18). The new covenant has been established once for all in the Lord's death; by coming together we enter into this new relationship and take upon ourselves the burden and hope of the promise. Our gatherings are to be the foci of a new communalization, a passing from isolation to genuine community.

Having said this, however, we are still not appreciably nearer to an explanation of how we can speak meaningfully of the church as "event" rather than as institution. We might suppose, to begin with, that speaking of *event* implies thinking in terms of history and, in particular, of the future. When the Israelite congregation answers the summons to come together it does so in order to re-actualize the original redemptive event which was precisely a summons to go forward into the future, into a history which was not yet. Here, I think, we come close to the center of our dilemma. Abraham is called out to go on a journey and he went "not knowing where he was to go" (Heb. 11, 8). Israel is called out of the timeless present of bondage in Egypt into the

216

desert, in other words into an unpredictable future. The God who calls is a God "with future as his essential nature";[28] his refusal to give a name to himself or, in other words, to be pinned down to the present, is expressed in the answer to Moses from the burning bush—"I will be what I will be" (Ex. 3, 14). Israel cannot accommodate itself to the religion of the Canaanite baals which seeks to consecrate the eternal present and insert man into the security of the recurring processes of nature. The fundamental theological differentia in Old Testament religion is the abiding promise which is always incongruous with present reality and continually opens up to the people a new future—hence the intransigence of the prophets against any form of accommodation to the present political and religious reality. Insofar as it responded to the promise, Israel exhibited something genuinely unique in antiquity; not just, as is commonly said, a sense of history, but what Kierkegaard called the passion for what is possible. In their uncorrupted form, all of the institutions of Israel are charged with this sense of movement into the future: the calendar, mostly taken over from Canaan, is historicized and futurized, the old traditions about the fathers are written up around the theme of a promised future continually endangered and continually triumphing over danger,[29] the categories of curse and blessing are made to open up a new future for Israel and the world, the dynasty is taken out of the closed world of myth and made the vehicle of a future *shalom.*

If, in keeping with this, we wish to speak of the event-character of the church we will have to think of it as continually aware of and open to the creative possibilities of the future which means a new future for the world. The exodus-God is also the resurrection-God; and since we cannot separate cross and resur-

---

28. Moltmann, *op. cit.,* p. 16.
29. Read the different accounts of the endangering of the common ancestress (Genesis 12, 10–20; 20; 26, 6–11) and the story of the near-sacrifice of Isaac (Gen. 22).

rection we must think of the latter as the future of the crucified Christ and, at the same time, the future of the crucified and alienated world.

To speak in this way of the future at once introduces a tension between past and future. In both Israel and the Christian church great stress is laid on the tradition by which the community lives. This emerged very clearly in Vatican II's identification of tradition with the very life of the church—*omne quod ipsa est.* Studies carried out over the last few decades have emphasized the fact that much of Israel's tradition was preserved and passed on in liturgical form; in fact, it could be said that "the chief function of the cult was to actualize the tradition."[30] Now the overriding importance given to tradition could easily lead us to think of a religious community as living on and in the past and so tied to the beliefs and formulations of the past as no longer to be effectively open to the future. This is, in fact, what has so often happened in the history both of Israel and the church, but need it happen? The event commemorated in liturgical tradition is an act of the living God, a God, that is, who was not just active *there and then* but must also be active *here and now.* The voice from the burning bush identifies the speaker both as the God of the past (of Abraham, Isaac and Jacob) and of the future ("I will be what I will be"). He who called Israel out of Egypt calls her, some seven hundred years later, out of exile in Babylon. It is the same God who raises Jesus from the dead (Acts 3, 13) and in each age calls the church *e novo* to testify to what he is doing in the world.

Experience shows that more or less closed communities tend necessarily to be introvertive and self-regarding. The exclusivism which is already showing through in Deuteronomy was to become a determining factor of the post-exilic priestly and scribal theocracy. It was no accident that no prophets rose up during this period. A prophetic voice speaking within the community

30. B. S. Childs, *Memory and Tradition in Israel,* London, 1962, p. 75.

is always necessary to arrest the innate tendency towards the hypostasizing of institutions, religious institutions in particular, to interpret what is happening outside the community and point to the creative possibilities for the future. Perhaps the best example can be found in the anonymous prophet who spoke, and possibly also wrote, towards the end of the exilic period. Though not in itself an event of world-shaking importance, the exile must have been for many Israelites practically the end of the road. The God of battles had shown himself powerless to defend his people, the land was lost, the temple had gone up in flames, their liturgy had no more meaning. In this kind of situation—which might not unjustly be compared to that of denominational Christianity today—it was no longer possible simply to re-affirm faith in the old dogmas, to renew the old covenant and go on as if nothing had happened. The older among the exiles would still remember the great religious reform of Josiah and the rapid evaporation of reforming enthusiasm after his tragic death at Megiddo. Renewal could only come not by re-affirming traditional faith in traditional language but by looking outward at what was happening in the world. And so the prophet tells them not to recall the things of old but to look at "the new thing" which was taking place before their eyes if they could only see it (Is. 43, 18–19).

It would be pedantic to spell out the implications of this analogy for the situation of the Church today. In a certain sense, the inner history of Israel is one of disillusionment. The people continued to put their trust in their institutions and find security in them while the prophets relentlessly condemned this attitude. They had no difficulty in foreseeing that these institutions would be swept away while Israel would yet remain as the permanent sign and embodiment of the promise. What they condemned was essentially the heresy of institutionalism which consists in denying the freedom of God to adopt new ways and new forms in leading his people forward. The monarchic state, the temple, the

219

secure possession of the land may go, but Israel as the prophetic remnant will remain. To speak of a *remnant* is the prophetic way of passing judgment on existing institutions while leaving the future open. Thus Israel is continually under judgment in her existing forms of life and continually being called out into a future history by virtue of the promise.

IV

It might be worth while to draw some tentative conclusions from this rapid analysis of the dialectic tension at the center of Israel's historical existence. I say tentative because no one at this stage has the answers and certainly no Roman Catholic is in a position to compose a new ecclesiology as yet. Everyone, at least outside of the Vatican, knows that culture-Christianity and ethnic Catholicism are dead and some think that the Catholic Church is currently "a church out of balance and disintegrating."[31] What will come after the disintegration, what the "new presence" will be, we do not know. We can only pray, hope and think aloud among ourselves. What we need to avoid at all costs is cynicism of the kind which emerges with disturbing frequency in the letter column of the more or less enlightened Catholic press, since to be cynical implies that hope has already died. If it is true, as Heraclitus said, that "he who does not hope for the unexpected will not find it," it is precisely at such a juncture as this that we need to hope actively no matter how dim the prospects may seem to be.

Dialectical tension is a necessary characteristic not only of the individual but of any group of individuals; in fact, tension between opposite poles is characteristic of life at all levels, biological, psychological and social. As Moltmann puts it, "a thing is alive only when it contains contradiction in itself and is indeed

31. Robert Adolphs, in *New Christian*, 10 August 1967, p. 11.

the power of holding the contradiction within itself and enduring it."[32] It is only too clear that the Roman system has well nigh destroyed this vital tension by insistence on authority and jurisdiction and a theological rationalism pushed at times to almost lunatic conclusions. In working towards the dissolution of this system, however, we might easily fall into the temptation of dissolving the tension, so to speak, at the other end. It could therefore happen that those who follow Davis and go on witnessing and working from "outside" not only over-simplify and therefore misrepresent the nature of Christian community but find themselves ill-prepared when other forms of "presence" or embodiment begin to take shape. The authenticity of any kind of Christian *koinonia* is found at the holding point of different lines of tension and force some of which we looked at, with reference to Israel, in the preceding section: between past and future, between the community and the world, between the static and dynamic.

Disillusionment with the institution or system or what Rosemary Ruether calls the "it-structure" has reached the point where many are asking whether we need an institution or whether Christianity can properly be described as such. If we look closely at the primitive Christian tradition we would have to admit that the early Christians did not form an institution in the way this term is usually defined. If Jesus and his first followers had wished to set up an institution there were plenty of models around in the first century A.D., especially of course the Jewish state-church and the synagogue,[33] but there is no evidence that they intended to do so. The well-known gospel sayings on authority show clearly that no kind of political model was contemplated. One of the sources of the "official" self-understanding of the church

32. *Op. cit.,* p. 337.
33. This is not to say that the early Church did not borrow certain elements from the synagogue and even perhaps from sectarian Jewish groups; but this is something different from modelling itself on them.

surely derives from thinking in the first place of a kind of world-wide empire divided for convenience into provinces and sub-provinces (dioceses and parishes) rather than of the basic unit which is the sacramental community located wherever the eucharist is celebrated. Each local community has in itself all that the word "church" connotes.

This needs to be said but we should repeat that the problem of Christian community and institutionalization is fatally subject to over-simplification. As we have seen, history seems to teach that institutionalization is an endemic and inevitable process linked with the need for what Dilthey calls objectivization, and Max Weber, routinization. It also teaches how extremely difficult it is to maintain the tension. Take the case of a political revolution which begins by destroying the existing political and social institutions. Every successful revolution has a destructive and a constructive phase. The first provides no great problems apart from the application of force but with the second the revolutionary idea has to be objectivized and this inevitably starts off the process which we have called institutionalization. Consider once again the revolution of October 1917. The first or purgative stage was carried through by Lenin who completed the destruction of the autocracy and brought down the "bourgeois" revolutionary set-up of Kerensky. Marx had predicted that in a communist society the state would wither away; perhaps it will eventually, but within two decades of the inception of the revolution there arose on its foundations one of the most absolutist state-systems in history. Loisy's dictum that Jesus preached the kingdom and the church appeared points to a not entirely dissimilar process which began at an early stage in Christian history.

An important aspect of this process is the emergence of an élite which tends to identify itself with the institution and see its own survival as dependent on the maintenance of the institution at all costs. We may once again find an illustration of this in the history of Russia in the decades following the revolution of 1917. In the Christian context we have, of course, the fairly rapid emergence of a clericalist governing body which identified the church-institution with itself and its own interests. An apt illustration of the apparently unconscious nature of this association can be found in the remark allegedly addressed by a curialist cardinal to one of his critics in the early stages of the council: "we *are* the church; you belong to it." In general, we can say that the history of Christianity (and, let us add, that of Israel) demonstrates both the necessity and the dangers of institutionalization.

We must still insist, however, that "institution" is not necessarily a good descriptive label for Christianity. If we must find a suitable category we might suggest that of a movement. The difference between institution and movement is that the former is self-authenticating and self-perpetuating while the latter exists for a particular purpose, is defined, structured and activated with reference to that purpose, and ceases to exist once the purpose is realized. In practice, however, the distinction may get blurred: an institution may insist that it exists only for some specific purpose and a movement may easily get itself institutionalized. But if it is successful, an institution generally takes the process of self-authentication and self-perpetuation to its logical conclusion by giving it the force of law. The history of Christianity in the West is one of the clearest examples of this process. An example, seen already, is that of the celibate life which in the earliest period is freely undertaken in view of the "revolutionary" message and its propagation; then bit by bit it is drawn into the sacralized ministry (the élite); finally, in the twelfth century, it is fixed in legal enactment according to which the marriage of a cleric in major orders is, so to speak, ontologically impossible. The recent encyclical even spoke of it as "a gift corroborated by canon law." The emphasis here is clearly on the maintenance

223

of the institution rather than the mission of propagating a message.

The need for the Christian to live in tension emerges more clearly if we go on to ask whether, if we can speak of the church as a movement, we can go on to speak of it as a *revolutionary* movement. The historical record would suggest for most people that it most definitely is not. They will rightly point to the perpetuation of the feudal structure of society by the church during the Middle Ages, Luther and the Peasants' Revolt, the Anglican state-church, the Orthodox church and Tsarist Russia, the record of the papacy, the implicit alliance between the churches and capitalism during the most of the nineteenth and on into the twentieth century, the Catholic church in Germany during the Hitler regime. Yet at the same time we should bear in mind that the history of Christianity has almost always been characterized by tension and sometimes open conflict between "the establishment" and partially or wholly disestablished movements which favored revolution on behalf of the oppressed, such as the chiliastic movements of the Middle Ages. Similar lines of division run through most of the churches, not least the Roman church, today. The clericalization of the church which began on a large scale in the fourth century has made it difficult for us to take this wider view, but to think of the church as primarily clerical—as I think Davis does despite his disavowal—is necessarily to impoverish our vision.

The contrast between the record of the Christian establishment and the original message is startling and even dramatic. In its primitive form as found in Mark 1, 15 it runs: "change your life [do *metanoia*] and believe the message." Here is implied a radical change of the individual addressed which necessarily means changing society; the need for conviction (that is what *pistis* means etymologically); radical openness to the future since the message concerns the future. The two essential elements of

224

revolution—criticism of the present and openness to the future—
are bound together by a total conviction and commitment. The
individual is first seized by the message and then opens himself
to the future (that is, the will of God), in the light of which he
criticizes the present and commits himself to changing it. Christians of the first few centuries did not generally use the language
of revolution and it was only gradually that the incompatibility
between their message and the political status quo became apparent. When it did, at the beginning of the great persecutions,
we have what can claim to be one of the most sustained and
successful non-violent movements in history which issued in the
Edict of Milan and the beginning of an entirely new era with
entirely different problems.

We have often been told that the Constantinian era is finished.
If this means that, despite the persistence of archaic structures
not yet clinically dead, the church can no longer be considered
an "establishment," the statement is clearly true. Does this mean
that Christians can once again proclaim their own revolutionary
message or at least join forces with revolutionary movements
throughout the world? To take the second course *as Christians*
clearly involves being guided by criteria deriving from the
specifically Christian faith and hope. This faith and hope is in
the God who is the father of our Lord Jesus Christ and in his
coming kingdom which opens the limitless prospect of a future
when every rule, authority and power will be destroyed (1 Cor.
15, 24), the meek will inherit the earth (Mt. 5, 5) and the oppressed will be set free (Lk. 4, 18). This means that no social
or political revolution can by itself realize the kind of future
for the world which Christian faith demands. A Christian faith
true to its original formulation sees human misery arising not
simply from economic exploitation but also and principally from
enslavement to fear, guilt and selfishness or, in other words, the
domination of sin. A Christian church which did not present the
revolutionary of today with the challenge of transcendence would

225

no longer be genuinely Christian. In sharing in the efforts of those who are laboring and risking themselves on behalf of the poor and oppressed, those to whom the kingdom is promised, the Christian must therefore seek to clarify his own faith; his participation must be critical rather than total, unambiguous and unreflective. As Moltmann says in one of his more recent contributions to the subject, it would be false if Christians expended all their energy in political activity because of a bad social conscience.[34] Here again, therefore, the tension must be maintained, lived out, suffered, if we are to remain true to our calling.

What I have tried to do in this chapter is suggest an alternative to disaffiliation which is theologically justifiable and point to some ambiguities involved in disaffiliating. The alternative to disaffiliating is to do within the church what the Christian is in any case committed to do whatever choice he makes, namely, reshape the structures to enable people to live in openness to the future, in love and freedom. What is needed, and what in fact is emerging even within the Catholic church, is a new community no longer in the secure possession of answers to every problem which can arise in faith, morals or anything else, but based on asking questions together; *an asking and enquiring community.* This involves starting out at the opposite pole from the scholastic treatment of ecclesiology which Davis demolishes in *A Question of Conscience.* In practice, it means beginning with the micro-structure, the basic unity, the cell-church as a focus of concern and a rallying point for the new kind of communal living which gives body to the "new being." What precise forms this embodiment will take will emerge only from experiment, trial and error and especially from an active concern to

34. "Towards a Political Hermeneutics of the Gospel," in *Union Seminary Quarterly Review,* 23 (1968), p. 322. I would like to acknowledge here, what will be obvious from this chapter, how much I owe to Moltmann's constructive and imaginative thinking.

serve wherever there is a need. In the early days the cell-church met in homes, in a hired hall (Acts 19, 9), in prisons, the market-place or wherever circumstances dictated. The greater complexity of social infra-structures today implies that the options are more numerous and, at the same time, the inter-relatedness of these structures emphasizes the need for inter-relation between the individual "cells," reminding us that the church is a sacramental union in the body of Christ. We would therefore be led to think that only after a new and more relevant experience of the cell-church or local church will we be able to tackle the problem of inter-relation, still thought of in juridical, authoritarian and therefore archaic terms, in a realistic way.

And since the cell-church is essentially a form of service or ministry, since *koinonia* is inseparable from *diakonia,* it would be unrealistic to go any further without taking another look at what ministry means in our present situation. To this I would now like to turn.

9. A New Model of Ministry

I

It would be sociologically absurd to speak of "scrapping" the Roman Catholic institution and the priesthood with it or to begin speaking of much-needed reform in terms of something entirely different from the existing situation. While a radical biblical-theological understanding of church and ministry would lead, as we have seen, to something quite different from the present situation, the most practical strategy for translating this understanding into reality would seem to be by working *from within* towards the dissolution of those structures which impede the mission of the church in the world. This strategy has to be implemented not only from within but *from beneath* since history teaches that no effective, radical church reform has ever been effected from above. Recent papal pronouncements make it painfully clear that it is not, at any rate, to be expected from that quarter in the foreseeable future. The results of the opinion poll among American diocesan priests carried out by Joseph H. Fichter, S.J., point in the same direction: "The relative resistance to change on the part of men over fifty years of age becomes crucially significant when we realize that most bishops, chancellors and big-city pastors are in this age bracket."[1] Great as was the significance of Vatican II, we cannot really expect a council any longer to initiate the kind of reform which is needed. De-

1. *America's Forgotten Priests—What They Are Saying*, New York, 1968, p. 202.

228

spite appearances to the contrary, the contribution of the council was mainly verbal and conceptual; what it did was give official recognition to some part of what people had been thinking and doing, often in the face of official opposition, during the preceding decade or so. Council documents, moreover, have to be redacted in such a way as to represent the views of the participants, including the pope, all the way through the spectrum, even at the cost of the kind of confusion which emerges in the *Constitution on Divine Revelation.* They must also to a great extent limit themselves to general statements of principle. So, for example, the *Constitution on the Church in the Modern World* spoke enthusiastically in general terms of the need for a closer relationship, but we have noticed in several cases during the four years which have elapsed since the closing of the council that those who are responsible for translating principle into action have generally failed to do so.

Rather than merely presenting people with a blueprint for a new church we ought therefore to begin from the potentialities for reform and change within the existing situation and work outwards from this point of departure. This is what I would like very tentatively to do in the present chapter with respect to ministry in the church; to proceed from the actual to the possible, taking in first what is more immediately possible and practical, only then going on to speak of long-range possibilities, and ending with an attempt to gather up loose threads and sketch out a theological justification for a new model of ministry. I trust that this attempt will be taken not as an expression of presumption but of hope. If the hope appears to some naïve, I can only plead that it arises out of the imperative need not to despair in what seems a pretty desperate situation.

In the Catholic church ministry is, officially, practically synonymous with priesthood and the priesthood is probably the most

229

severely institutionalized group known to history, one which has shown practically no prospect or potentiality for change. The immutability derives from the fact, often illustrated in preceding chapters, that the priest represents and embodies the sacred. With the progressive decline in prestige (to the point of disappearance) of the sacred in modern life, however, the priesthood as traditionally conceptualized appears as an archaism, sometimes interesting but more often tiresome. The survival of this concept of a sacred office manifests itself in a variety of ways too familiar to require detailed comment: an authoritarian attitude in virtue of which an Irish bishop forbids dancing in his diocese after midnight, the requirement of wearing a black suit even when going to the theater or a ball game, the exhortation of an English archbishop to his clergy to play golf among themselves rather than with the laity.

Having said this, we have to add that we are talking about a survival from the past, that the process of dissolution is already well under way. The breakdown of the authority of the clergyman and the undermining of the traditional bases on which that authority was founded have affected the ministry in all churches, not just the Roman Catholic priesthood; and it could be argued that the sometimes rather frantic search for new roles to play stems from a basic uncertainty as to what the unique role of the clergyman in modern society is.[2] The loss of confidence in the current role and *persona* of the Catholic priest has been well documented of late, in the testimony of those not only in but on the way to the priesthood.[3] Many priests are already effectively desacralized and declericalized. The most intelligent and perceptive have ceased to take seriously the religious attitudes they

2. See J. M. Gustafson, "The Clergy in the United States," in *The Professions in America,* ed. by K. S. Lynn, Boston, 1963, p. 79; H. R. Niebuhr, *The Purpose of the Church and Its Ministry,* New York, 1956, pp. 48 ff.

3. See, for example, Charles Boxer, "The Priest in a Godless Society," in *Slant,* Winter 1965, and "Pre-Ordination Jitters" by an anonymous Jesuit scholastic in *Jubilee,* May 1968.

come up against so often in the confessional and in their more generalized contact with their parishioners, though not all are aware what a large share the popular conception of their own office has had in the formation of these attitudes and still fewer have done anything about it.

Perhaps the most significant of the conclusions drawn from the survey of diocesan priests in America referred to above was the need for "a new conceptualization of the clerical vocation, one that genuinely defines the diocesan priest as a professional career man."[4] There is, of course, a great deal of uncertainty and difference of opinion involved in defining what we mean by terms like "profession," "career" or "job," but we may at least begin by asking what the priest *does*. If asked this question, no priest would today simply reply that he says mass. He may, in addition, be a full- or part-time administrator, pastor or counsellor or be engaged in some specialized form of ministry like youthwork, university chaplaincy or education. By revealing a widespread dissatisfaction with the current role cast for them and a great waste of talent among the secular clergy the survey has emphasized the non-viability of the current conceptualization of the priesthood and the identity-crisis it has induced. What is needed is a genuinely professional ministry with adequate specialized training in place of the obsolete idea of the priest as a General Practitioner in religious matters. The author of the survey has more recently stated that "the priest who follows the book is closed to hope and involved in despair" and has argued that the only way out is to evolve what he calls "the hyphenated priest" (priest-teacher, priest-counsellor).[5]

It seems clear that this development towards specialization and multiple functioning is necessary and ought to be welcomed. It is necessary because demanded by the conditions under which one has to live usefully in modern society and welcome because

4. Fichter, *op. cit.*, pp. 208–209.
5. In *The National Catholic Reporter*, May 22, 1968.

it is bound to contribute to the dissolution of an inadequate and archaic conception of priesthood. It will also bring the Catholic ministry much more in line with the practice of the mainline Protestant churches and may even lead eventually to Catholic seminaries granting a professional degree in ministry as a necessary prerequisite for commissioning to pastoral work.

It must be added, however, that these advantages serve only to emphasize the need to correlate ministry with a correct understanding of the kind of society or community the church is meant to be. It would be no use and in fact impossible to have this kind of modernized and streamlined ministry operating within archaic structures and, besides, it is only a correct understanding of the role of the church in the world which will reveal the needs to which it must minister and the manner in which this ministry is to be articulated. Is the structural context to be thought of as a bureaucracy or a professional system or something that can be described as a familial-communal group?[6] It can hardly be doubted that the Catholic church has supplied, and continues to supply, plenty of evidence to those who see it primarily as bureaucratic. In a controversial article in *The Critic* Monsignor Ivan Illich argues that the church has always been overstaffed (it has about 1.8 million employees working full-time) and that clerical bureaucracy has increased rather than decreased after Vatican II.[7] His solution involves a radical reduction of the number of these employees dependent on the church for a livelihood and the ordination of self-supporting laymen to sacramental functions in the church. But admitting the need for bureaucracy and bureaucrats (which are not necessarily pejorative terms) in an overarching and interconnected world-wide society, the vital questions concern the local congregation. If we

6. J. H. Fichter, *Religion as an Occupation*, Notre Dame, 1961, pp. 219 ff., 232.

7. "The Vanishing Clergyman," June–July 1967, pp. 18–27.

are to take the New Testament model of ministry seriously we must conclude that ministry is not only open to but encumbent on all the members of a congregation on a reciprocal basis and that likewise all must minister to "the world" by the testimony of the Word of God and by responding to needs. In this context of understanding what is the function of the professional minister?

If we begin from the present understanding of this function we run up against some difficulties right away. There is, to begin with, something of a crisis of identity affecting the clergy of all denominations in those countries which are socially and technically more evolved. The kind of advice and counsel which was once invariably sought from the clergyman is now increasingly being sought from other specializations such as those of doctor, psychoanalyst and lawyer. There are, of course, roles which are specific to the religious minister in charge of a parish or congregation but there is some ambiguity as regards their priority. Samuel Blizzard has shown that among Protestant clergymen the role of administrator is considered the least relevant to their ministry and the least enjoyable and yet takes up more time and energy than any other.[8] The same may well be true of the Catholic bishop and pastor. The Fichter survey certainly shows that most bishops have little contact with pastors under their jurisdiction—no doubt due in part to the demands of their administrative role—and little contact with the parochial system is needed to show how much of the time and energies of the clerical staff go into purely administrative work which in many cases still includes counting the weekly income.

Traditionally, the priesthood has been thought of as a full-time and permanent vocation and this tradition is so deeply ingrained that to question it seems tantamount to heresy. Yet the

8. "The Minister's Dilemma," in *The Christian Century*, April 25, 1956, pp. 508–510.

New Testament shows that the normal pattern of ministry was carried on by people who were not full-time paid professionals but combined their ministry with a job or profession and no doubt often ministered to others through their work. The first Christian cell at Corinth was established by Paul setting up with a family in the same business (Acts 18, 3). Kenneth Scott Latourette writes that "the chief agents in the expansion of Christianity appear not to have been those who made it a profession or a major part of their occupation, but men and women who earned their livelihood in some purely secular manner and spoke of their faith to those whom they met in this natural fashion."[9] If today we press the need for "hyphenated priests" the question will sooner or later arise as to what the priest can be hyphenated with. As we have said, no one is likely to jibe at a priest-lecturer or priest-counsellor but what about a priest-stevedore or priest-cabby? On the basis of what criteria can we suppose that the priest simply cannot be hyphenated with certain jobs or professions?

It is only by asking such questions which, if asked a few years ago, would have appeared flippant if not downright mad, that we can really see the kind of dilemma the Catholic priesthood faces today. Now that the situation has changed we can only answer them by going behind the historical priesthood to a more fundamental understanding of Christian ministry and community and the intrinsic bond which unites them. We can call a ministry priestly only in so far as it represents the reconciling presence of Christ and at the same time is ordered to community, and reconciliation is community. Genuine priesthood happens wherever reconciliation takes place and community is formed, and this must be wherever people come together or are brought together within the changing shape of society. This involves freeing ministry from sociological servitude to the parish making it possible

9. *History of the Expansion of Christianity*, Vol. I, New York, 1937, p. 116.

to respond flexibly and creatively to needs and, in particular, concentrate at the points of disjunction and division in present-day society.

In practice, while there will probably always be a need for full-time coordinators of activities and full-time professional ministers, there seems no reason why the normal small community or church-cell should not be directed by a self-supporting adult layman who fulfills the criteria for the office of presbyter as laid down in the pastoral epistles, or something along those lines. This of course implies the dissolution of the present parish system though, here again, this will come about only after prolonged experimentation alongside the system, a process which has hardly yet begun.[10]

One of the main difficulties involved in thinking of Christian ministry as a profession emerges clearly when we ask whether it involves not only full-time activity but a permanent status. This is certainly true in principle of the major professions such as medicine and law and the same would apply *in principle* to those who have chosen to dedicate themselves in some specialized way to the Christian service of others. It would also clearly be appropriate, all other things being equal, for the president and coordinator of the local church, though neither he nor anyone else ought to be unduly burdened and if he wishes for any reason to resign no difficulty should be placed in his way. The most immediate difficulty is, of course, the mystique of character and indelibility which has surrounded the priesthood since the Middle Ages. That this mystique has, however, begun to lose some of its luster may be indicated by the Fichter survey which shows 64%

10. In *Ave Maria,* March 7, 1964, and *The New York Times,* March 9 of the same year, Bishop John Mussio of Steubenville, Ohio, has argued that the parish is obsolete and in need of radical restructuring. He suggests a central staff-ministry servicing local centers set up wherever convenient, in homes, public halls or the like. All routine administrative duties should be carried out by deacons or trained laymen, thus freeing the priest for a ministry which is genuinely pastoral.

of the respondents in favor of voluntary resignation and only 20% opposed to it.[11]

While it is clear from everything said so far and, in particular, from the form of ministry and community to which the future is calling us, that mandatory ministerial celibacy has to be superseded, it is far from clear what practical steps this involves. Illich has the interesting suggestion that the best course is to comply with the pope's position on celibacy to assure the speedy death of the clergy which he regards as "the one institution which has no future in the church."[12] Since it is unlikely that most Catholics who are still firmly anchored to the parochial system and the traditional image of the priest will accept a married clergy for the time being[13] some sort of gradual approach is obviously indicated. We shall, for example, have to go beyond the half-measure of Vatican II on the diaconate and laicize this office, leaving it open to married men whatever their age or men who are contemplating marriage (and, of course, women too). This will have the incidental advantage of decentralizing ministry in general and freeing it from its attachment to the "power" of orders and jurisdiction. As is well known, there are several bishops advocating this course of action especially in those areas where there is currently a shortage of priests. Since it is quite unrealistic to suppose that in the foreseeable future Rome is going to rescind the celibacy clause, change will probably be initiated by the ordination of married men or by an experimental married ministry apart from the existing parochial structure.

To choose this way, which amounts to a progressive subversion of the existing structures from within, is not without its dangers

11. *America's Forgotten Priests*, p. 167.
12. *Art. cit.*, p. 26.
13. However, a Harris poll the results of which were published in *Newsweek* on March 20, 1967, showed that 48% of the adult Catholic laity in America favored clerical marriage. This compares with 68% in Holland.

both for the one who undertakes it and for the church as a whole. Apart from the danger of unworthy motivation a movement of this kind is bound to attract many who are not deeply committed and look for change of any kind and at any cost out of boredom and restlessness. Moreover, one cannot discount the possibility that the tension involved in an uneasy co-existence of the old and the new side by side—which is surely inevitable for a long time to come—may even result in outright schism. It would not be the first time.

II

To look further into the future than this may well be presumptuous, but some things at least are beginning to emerge clearly: the need for a great simplification, pluriformity rather than uniformity, freedom to adapt to the needs of the moment, to experiment and make mistakes, revitalization of the small group mission. As long as the present structures remain, which is going to be for some time, experimentation will take place within the parish where this is possible but also outside of its structure. The revitalization of the house-church, which has already begun, should eventually lead to the scaling down of the present diocese to the dimensions of the parish, hence to a more pastoral concept of the bishop as a genuine "overseer" or coordinator in touch with what is going on. The Fichter survey has given some indication how much this is necessary by pointing to the inadequate vertical relationships within the present structures. Some part of this will be obviated by reviving the ancient practice of the people appointing a bishop to serve them, but it seems clear that the idea of territorial jurisdiction and geographical units must give way to something different. Illich has suggested that the basic cell should be a *diaconia* rather than a parish with the

237

deacons playing the same kind of role they did in the early centuries before this office was sacralized out of existence. What is clear at least is the need for basing any kind of new presence on a genuinely human foundation in the form of small, more or less informal groupings, the need, in other words, to break through the present anonymity into something which can be called a genuine community.

The principal objection to the parochial system is that it was devised—in its fixed form in the Middle Ages—to serve a local, static and residential community, and is now quite inadequate in a highly mobile society where men in particular are no longer primarily orientated towards the home but rather to their work. All of the denominations have been chasing or, in some cases, limping after people from the rural areas to the inner-city and now out to the suburbs and leaving behind them masses of masonry as monuments of their devotion. In the isolated life of the suburbs the truth has at last begun to dawn that the church's function is not, or not primarily, to provide what Gibson Winter calls "residential chaplaincies to family life." Hence the need, increasingly felt, to experiment outside of the parish structure in the hope of finding "shapes and styles of Christian living which will manifest the presence of Christ to men in those areas of life which are increasingly separated from the local community of residence and which for that reason are separated from the local congregations centered on the community of residence."[14]

Some of these "shapes and styles of Christian living" have already begun to emerge in such a variety of ways that it would be profitless to try to categorize them. In its most genuine form, the small group or cell goes back for its inspiration to the life of the earliest Christian communities which "devoted themselves to the apostles' teaching and fellowship, to the breaking of bread and the

14. Colin W. Williams, *Where in the World?*, p. 8.

prayers" (Acts 2, 42). These koinonia-groups or *ecclesiolae*[15] will avoid degenerating into small cliques of the like-minded only by a collective confrontation with the Word of God and the requirement of mission and will escape isolation and ultimate irrelevance only by coordinating with the life of the church as a whole. There can be no blueprint laid down in advance for the formation of such small-group witness and mission. The very anonymity and impersonality of industrial society positively favor the emergence of informal groupings which, however, must seek to bear on the structures of society rather than merely fulfilling the function of emotional release from these structures. Christian presence and witness is therefore most in need at what Colin Williams calls "the points of disjunction" in society—the struggle against poverty, the fight for racial equality, work within the alienated teenage culture, in industrial relations and so on.

Perhaps the most radical and reasoned approach to the kind of ministry appropriate to this new situation is that of Bishop Robinson, and though what he says is meant for his own communion much of it applies to any church situation and in particular to the Roman Catholic impasse. Instead of joining the lament for the decline in recruitment to the ministry he welcomes it as hastening the emergence of a "new Christian presence in the world." While all of what he has to say on this subject on both the theological and practical level is worthy of careful study,[16] I would like to draw attention here to the practical proposals which he makes for going beyond the current model

15. For the first term see Robert A. Raines, *New Life in the Church*, New York, 1961, and for the second Colin W. Williams, *op. cit.*, pp. 64 ff.
16. See *On Being the Church in the World*, London, 1960, pp. 72–82; *The New Reformation?*, London, 1965, pp. 55–104; *Meeting, Membership and Ministry*, Prism Pamphlet No. 31, London; "Ministry in the Melting," in *New Christian*, 10 February, 1966, pp. 11–12.

of ministry since they seem to be even more relevant for the
Roman Catholic than for the Anglican situation.

Beginning from the fundamental New Testament position
that ministry belongs of right to all baptized Christians, he suggests that this can only be actualized in the present situation
by breaching the clergy line. We have seen in an earlier chapter
that this distinction into *ordo* or *clerus* and *plebs* derives not
from apostolic Christianity but from the pervasive influence of
the Roman political system especially after the Constantinian
peace. With this distinction there will also disappear the whole
superstructure built upon it, the idea of ecclesiastical and juris-
dictional *potestas* and the indelibile character of orders in particular. It will *not* involve ecclesiastical anarchy; the injunction
of Paul to "do all things in order" will still involve distinction
of functions and office. Instead of speaking of lay apostolate
(which Pius XII characterized as a form of humble cooperation
with the hierarchy), we shall be able to think in terms simply of
Chrisitan ministry, witness and apostolate and undo the concentration of ministry and charism in the priesthood.

The predictable decline and fall of clericalism in the church
will lead us to see that the emphasis must be put, in practice
not just in theological theory, on a ministering laity and that it
was wrong from the beginning to arrogate ministry to a professional class. Such a change of emphasis is, in any case, being
forced upon us by the conditions under which the church can be
effectively present to society today. The training prescribed for
candidates for the priesthood provides them with a certain minimum of theological expertise and some pastoral skills. This enables them either to enter academic life at some level or minister
to the personal needs of those with whom they come in contact.
But we cannot any longer conceive of the church's mission
exclusively or even primarily in terms of ministering to the individual. If ministry has to do with the exercise of responsibility

in the world or, as Gibson Winter defines it, "discerning the promise of the saving history in the historical decisions of public responsibility,"[17] then the principal burden of ministry must be borne by the convinced Christian in his "secular" occupation. This would oblige us radically to alter the emphasis in our thinking on this subject. The religious professionals, especially the theological specialist and the coordinator of activities in the local church, would serve as auxiliaries to the main thrust of church ministry especially by helping the layman clarify the issues met with in his daily work and witness in theological terms.[18] This would suggest that "the problem of vocations" is in need of drastic reformulation and that we need less seminaries and more training centers for the development of an active lay ministry.

This leads on to Bishop Robinson's second point, namely, that the dissolution of the clergy demarcation line will greatly facilitate and be facilitated by the breach of the professional line. While the emphasis in Catholic circles has been on hyphenating the priesthood, Robinson prefers to think of laymen ordained in their regular employment. But from whichever end one begins, the result will be a much more open and comprehensive deployment of talents and gifts in the service of the local community and in its mission outwards into the environment in which the community lives. We have already seen that a first important step in this direction would be the laicization of the diaconate.

Finally, the sex line must be breached by the ordaining or commissioning of women to those functions which hitherto have been restricted to men. There are clearly many church functions which women can fulfill as well as if not better than men. On the purely practical and even banal level, a woman would generally make a better job of baptizing a baby than a man, but of

17. *The New Creation as Metropolis*, New York, 1963, p. 59.
18. The necessity of this *volte face* has been argued most persuasively by Gibson Winter in the above work and in *The Suburban Captivity of the Churches*, New York, 1961, pp. 76 ff.

241

course the issues extend far beyond the purely practical and banal. The sex line has already been breached in several communions—principally in the Presbyterian and Methodist—and there is a small but significant number of women students in the theological colleges. The complete exclusion of women from any meaningful ministry in the Roman church is only one example of many which reveal to what extent we belie the title of a catholic or universal communion.

The need to associate the familial-communal and professional aspects of church life may well be met, to some extent at least, by further experiments in group- or staff-ministry which would replace the unsatisfactory state of affairs in current parish ministry revealed by the Fichter report (assistant pastors subject to one man and waiting for anything up to twenty-five or thirty years for promotion). A relationship of superior and subject would thus be replaced by that between professional associates, all trained for some form of specialized ministry, all working together towards the same end. Something of the kind has been suggested by Bishop Mussio as we saw earlier. Bishop Robinson has extended the idea further to take in what he calls a "team episcopacy." Roman Catholics would certainly do well to keep their eye on developments in this direction which are currently under way in other communions.[19]

What we may, finally, hope for is that experiments in new or, better, renewed ways of Christian witness and ministry carried on outside the parish structure may some day unite and coalesce with experiments within the existing structures giving us eventually a model of ministry and a presence more conformed to apostolic Christianity, one which no committed Christian will feel called upon to leave behind in disgust. While it would be wrong and naïve to be over-optimistic of success it would be even worse not to hope at all.

19. See K. R. Mitchell, *Psychological and Theological Relationships in the Multiple Staff Ministry*, Westminster, 1966.

III

In his *Church Order in the New Testament* Eduard Schweizer has pointed out the difficulty if not impossibility of reconciling any historical form of ministry with that found in the New Testament.[20] The new honesty which is beginning to make headway in the Church is at last making it possible for theologians to admit "that a frightening gulf separates the Church of today from the original constitution of the Church"[21] and to do this without feeling obliged to go elsewhere. A further consequence is that we cannot regard what the New Testament tells us about ministry as a blueprint or law which has to be implemented; to do this would be a perversion of the freedom which the gospel brings, a reduction of gospel to law of the kind castigated so often by Paul. Moreover, the gospel itself presupposes ministry and came into existence as the result of "ministerial" activity in the early church. As Barth points out, the categories of ministry found throughout the New Testament are already variations of basic forms and a basic pattern which is never spelled out explicitly.[22] This imposes on us some methodological limitations in speaking about reform of church ministry and the prospects for the future. We must continually go back to the New Testament not with the purpose of identifying the precise forms and variations of ministry in order to reimpose them but to discover behind the forms a spirit, a meaning and a pattern.

One conclusion which should be reached at an early stage of our enquiry is that ministry is unintelligible without community, that *diakonia* and *koinonia* belong inseparably together. Until

20. London, 1961, *passim*.
21. H. Küng, *The Church*, p. 413. An examination of Davis's arguments on the historical claims of the Roman Catholic church (*A Question of Conscience*, pp. 118–162) is outside the scope of the present work, but it may be suggested that a comparison with Küng, *op. cit.*, pp. 388–480, would prove interesting and instructive.
22. *Church Dogmatics*, Vol. IV.3.2, p. 860.

we know what kind of community the church is meant to be we are going to be in the dark as to the kind of ministry we are meant to fulfill. It may well be, as hinted earlier, that this is the fundamental reason for the current uncertainty about ministry prevalent in almost all of the churches today; and it may be taken as certain that the current crisis of self-understanding in the Catholic church is the main reason for the crisis in her ministry.

In New Testament terms, the association between ministry (*diakonia*) and community (*koinonia*) derives from the conviction that both are the creation of the Spirit of God now manifest and operative through Christ. Perhaps the most explicit statement of this can be found in Paul's defense of his own ministry in 2 Corinthians. He and his colleagues are ministers of a new covenant realized in the Spirit (3, 6) and as such their work is to announce and thereby realize anew the reconciliation between God and the world brought about by God's act in Christ (5, 18–19). Their ministry is therefore in the first place one of reconciliation to be realized in a new covenant-people. The self-authenticating experience of the Spirit in the early communities is a guarantee (5, 5) that they are within the new convenant, the nucleus of a new humanity. Paul's treatment of the charismatic gifts points in the same direction. The *charismata* are all expressions or articulations of the one *charis* with which the community is endowed. The manifestation of the Spirit is given to each for the common good (1 Cor. 12, 7). From the point of view of Spirit-endowment, there is no distinction between rulers and ruled. Not only tongues and prophecy but also administration flow from the risen Lord present through the Spirit in the community. Jesus is not raised and glorified for himself. The spelling out of resurrection, ascension and the giving of the Spirit, as in Luke-Acts, may at first obscure the essential simultaneity (in the Fourth Gospel all take place on the same day) and the issue of the one saving event in the giving of the Spirit promised for the eschatological time. It is this which makes

244

possible the mission and commission of the church, and ministry within the church is essentially ordered to the mission of the church to the world. This comes through quite clearly in the Pentecost story in Acts 2.

It has been one of my main contentions throughout this book that the problem of ministry in the Roman Catholic church will not be resolved without a radical rethinking of the meaning of priesthood. Historically, the priesthood has separated itself from the community as it gradually developed into a class or caste apart. It is very difficult to suggest, against the weight of more than a millennium and a half of history, that here too progress is possible only by taking seriously the basic New Testament pattern. In the work referred to earlier, Küng spells out in detail the reasons why the early communities had no priestly office, why priesthood is predicated only of Christ and of the community as a whole and is not found among the "gifts" of the Spirit. He criticizes the process of sacralization which resulted in the emergence of a priestly order and goes on to speak of a pastorate and pastors (not of a priesthood and priests)—but at this point leaves the question in the air.[23] Similarly, Gregory Baum shows how the convergence of new insights has resulted in our viewing the priesthood as ministerial rather than cultic but does not answer the question how this new concept of "priesthood" differs essentially from Protestant concepts of ministry.[24] Despite the attempts of Vatican II to re-appropriate what has for long been considered a Protestant doctrine, namely, the priesthood of all the faithful, it is doubtful whether it will be really meaningful as long as the clerical priesthood remains as it is.

Perhaps the most pressing temptation in our present difficulties is to reduce ministry to the alleviation of human needs and thereby to reduce the church, in Niebuhr's phrase, to a social and

23. *The Church*, pp. 364 ff.
24. "The Ministerial Priesthood," in *The Ecumenist*, November–December 1965, pp. 4–7.

counselling agency. Support for this view is usually found by appealing to the ministry of Jesus himself—the healings, exorcisms and the rest—and we are often reminded that in the New Testament *diakonia* is used for the collection in support of the indigent Christians of the mother-church in Jerusalem. While no one woud deny that this is part of what Christian ministry means, to define it purely in these terms condemns the church to the secondary task of caring for the dropouts of society and filling in the gaps left by the failure to arrive at what is essentially a political solution to social problems. According to the New Testament the primary ministry is that of the Word and therefore the primary categories are those of speech, sign and language. Jesus' miracles of healing are signs of a new age, a new possibility for man struggling with the questionableness of his existence. The great commissioning at the end of Matthew's gospel speaks of convincing, making disciples, teaching. Paul is above all "a minister of Christ Jesus in the priestly service of the gospel of God" (Rom. 15, 16) The Twelve very soon began to delegate the administration of social welfare in the early church to others to leave themselves free to preach the Word of God (Acts 6, 2).

In view of the low esteem in which preaching is held in the Catholic community and the generally low level of performance of this aspect of the ministry among Catholic priests it may be a little hard to accept what is in fact obvious, that preaching is an essential and irreducible part of the church's task according to the New Testament. The generally pejorative sense which this word now has is no doubt to be explained on the ground that it is thought of as an art form and that, as Aldous Huxley remarked, in this as other arts the bad practitioners far outnumber the good. The primitive Christian understanding of preaching is, however, something quite different and Paul's gravamen against Apollos seems to be that he was making preaching of this kind precisely into an art form. Paul, at any rate, states unequivocally that he is first and foremost a preacher (1 Cor. 1, 17). The crucial role in the whole process he is trying to initiate is given to *the word:* "How are men to call upon him in whom they have not believed? And how are they to believe in him of whom they have never heard? And how are they to hear without a preacher?" (Rom. 10, 14). As in the missionary preaching of the Old Testament prophets, the word is the concrete expression of God's action in history, a conviction stated compendiously in the phrase "the word of the cross." This word is defined as *power* (1 Cor. 1, 18), the power to save, to effect a real change in the human condition. Hence ministry, if it is to preserve a specifically Christian character, must be first of all a service of the word, a witness to the purpose of God in the world.

A necessary and obvious corollary of this, obscured by the routine usage of the words "minister" and "ministry," is the primacy of the Christian community's relationship to the world over the reciprocal relationships within the community. These last have to be understood in function of the relationship of the community to the society of which it is a part since the purpose of preaching understood as communicating the Christian message is to build up a community which will serve the world. But even within the community the word has primacy since there can be no community without communication; hence the number and importance of the "gifts" which deal with speech and communication: prophecy, teaching, exhortation, tongues and the interpretation of tongues. This would imply that ministry must have something to do with creating channels of communication; in the broadest sense, with building community.

Anyone who has stayed with me this far will be just as aware as I am—if not more so—that the suggestions made do not amount to anything like a blueprint for the future. Those who

247

have more insight and more experience than I are welcome to criticize them and put something else in their place since what I have said has no value or significance apart from the dialogue currently in progress. I would, however, like to emphasize once again that my chief concern has been to make a biblical and theological contribution to the self-understanding of the church and to suggest that structural changes must be linked at every step with a growing awareness of what the church is meant to be and what it is not yet. Hence the need for experiment and the impossibility of blueprints at this stage.

Someone's dying, Lord!

The plaintive words, often on the lips of the marching generation, could well be true of us trying to live as Christians in a new world yet still tied to forms and structures of church life inherited from the past. We have always understood that the basic pattern for the individual Christian is new life through death, resurrection beyond crucifixion; maybe what we are now called upon to learn is that what is true of the individual is also true of the church. If it is to be true to the pattern of Christ's ministry it must make a positive choice of humble service ("the Servant of the Lord") and even anonymity ("the Man"); and like him it cannot take on the form of a servant without first emptying itself. If it is to have a future it cannot be other than the future revealed by the risen Lord whose body still bears the print of the nails.

Index

249